Work, Wisdom, Legacy

Work, Wisdom, Legacy

31 Essays from India

COMPILED BY

Y. V. Reddy

WITH

Ravi Menon,
Shaji Vikraman, and Kavi Yaga

Orient BlackSwan

WORK, WISDOM, LEGACY: 31 ESSAYS FROM INDIA

ORIENT BLACKSWAN PRIVATE LIMITED

Registered Office
3-6-752 Himayatnagar, Hyderabad 500 029, Telangana, India
e-mail: centraloffice@orientblackswan.com

Other Offices
Bengaluru, Chennai, Guwahati, Hyderabad,
Kolkata, Mumbai, New Delhi, Noida, Patna

First published by Orient Blackswan Private Limited 2025
Reprinted 2025

ISBN 978-93-5442-886-9

041148

Typeset in
Goudy Old Style 11/13
by Le Studio Graphique, Gurgaon 122 007

Printed in India at
Rathna Offset, Chennai 600 014

Published by
Orient Blackswan Private Limited
3-6-752 Himayatnagar, Hyderabad 500 029, Telangana, India
e-mail: info@orientblackswan.com

To my father, Yaga Pitchi Reddy,
who set the example I strive to follow

Contents

PART IV

Banking

PART V

Media

PART VI

Academia

Abbreviations

ADB	Asian Development Bank
ADRs	American Depository Receipts
AI	artificial intelligence
AIIMS	All India Institute of Medical Sciences
APTS	Andhra Pradesh Technology Services Limited
ATM	automated teller machine
BDO	Block Development Officer
BHPV	Bharat Heavy Plates and Vessels Ltd.
BIS	Bank for International Settlements
BJP	Bharatiya Janata Party
BSEB	Bihar State Electricity Board
CAR	capital adequacy ratio
CEA	chief economic adviser
CMD	Chairman and Managing Director
DCMS	District Cooperative Marketing Society
EEC	European Economic Community
EPW	*Economic and Political Weekly*
ESG	environmental, social, and governance
FCNRA	Foreign Currency Non-Resident Account
GATS	General Agreement on Trade in Services
GATT	General Agreement on Tariffs and Trade
GIS	Geographical Information System
GST	goods and services tax
HUF	Hindu undivided family
IAS	Indian Administrative Service
IASC	International Accounting Standards Committee
ICRIER	Indian Council for Research on International Economic Relations

ICS	Indian Civil Services
ICU	Intensive Care Unit
IDRBT	Institute for Development and Research in Banking Technology
IFS	Indian Foreign Service
IIM	Indian Institute of Management
IIMA	Indian Institute of Management Ahmedabad
IMF	International Monetary Fund
IIT	Indian Institute of Technology
IPS	Indian Police Service
ISCON	Indian Steelworks Construction Co. Ltd.
IT	information technology
ITDA	Integrated Tribal Development Agency
ITEC	Indian Technical Economic Cooperation
ITI	Industrial Training Institute
LIC	Life Insurance Corporation
LTTE	Liberation Tigers of Tamil Eelam
MIT	Massachusetts Institute of Technology
MLA	Member of the Legislative Assembly
MNCs	multinational corporations
MODVAT	modified value-added tax
MP	Member of Parliament
NACO	National AIDS Control Organisation
NASSCOM	National Association of Software and Service Companies
NDA	National Democratic Alliance
NEFT	national electronic funds transfer
NIC	National Informatics Corporation
NIE	National Institute of Engineering
NPCI	National Payments Corporation of India
NSDL	National Securities Depository Ltd
ONDC	Open Network for Digital Commerce
PMO	Prime Minister's Office
PSU	Public Sector Undertakings

RBI	Reserve Bank of India
RRA	Regulation Review Authority
RTGS	Real Time Gross Settlement
SBI	State Bank of India
SC/ST	Scheduled Caste/Scheduled Tribe
SEBI	Securities and Exchange Board of India
SIES	South Indian Education Society
SSLC	Secondary School Leaving Certificate
STD	subscriber trunk dialling
STEM	science, technology, engineering, and mathematics
TECS	Tata Economic Consultancy Service
UDCT	University Department of Chemical Technology
UNCTAD	UN Conference on Trade and Development
UPA	United Progressive Alliance
UPI	unified payment interface
WCED	World Conference on Environment and Development
WHO	World Health Organization
WTO	World Trade Organization

Preface

A few years ago, I was at a low point physically. I had to take a crucial decision about my health. Should I opt for a difficult surgery, or not? The doctors bluntly laid out the chances. While they said the likelihood of recovery was fair, they warned that improvement could be minimal. My children and my wife convinced me to opt for the surgery. They said they wanted to see me do the things I love to do.

One of the things I love most is my work. It is next to impossible for me to imagine a life without work. It was so for many in my generation. Yet, I look around now and see people retiring at the age of forty. I ask myself what I would say if one of my grandchildren asked me why I worked all my life. Why didn't I retire at forty?

I wondered how people in my generation would convey our thoughts on work to our grandchildren's generation. Would the younger generation even be interested? The second question was idle speculation. The first, I could do something about. This is the reason I started thinking about this book.

Since collective wisdom is usually better than an individual's account, I requested various people to contribute their essays on work in a way that their grandchildren could relate to. I am grateful to the contributors, people for whom I have respect and regard. They have risen to the challenge and have generously shared their personal experiences of work, the process of working, and the meaning of the workplace in simple and interesting ways. Taken in aggregate, the essays will, I hope, provide our grandchildren a glimpse into our values, our working lives, and our vision of the nation we were trying to build for them.

Older generations might find this an interesting retrospective. After all, one forgets that we built a nation not only during periods of peace and growth, but also through four wars, two assassinations, several economic crises, seismic societal transformations, and more. Sometimes, we know how far we've come only when we look in the rear-view mirror.

This, in all probability, will be my last book. In my working life, and even in my personal life, what I have learned is this—one does not have all the answers, but ask the right questions, and you may arrive at something meaningful. This book will, I hope, help readers ask the right questions.

Acknowledgements

It is with great gratitude and satisfaction that I acknowledge those who contributed to the development and publication of this book. Frankly, unlike my earlier works, this project faced unique challenges and frustrating moments due to my ill health. I often doubted the book would see the light of day. Yet, thanks to the many people who worked with me, it has been completed. While it is difficult to name everyone due to space constraints and readers' attention, I would like to acknowledge some individuals whose efforts were crucial in bringing the book to fruition.

First, I would like to thank Nandini Rao of Orient BlackSwan for stepping in at a crucial time during our search for a publisher. Her intervention made the entire process exceptionally smooth. I also want to express my gratitude to C. Rammanohar Reddy, who has supported us from the beginning and whose wise guidance has been invaluable. Editing a book with multiple contributors is never easy, but Nilanjana Majumdar at Orient BlackSwan, who has edited some of my earlier work, steered this one with her usual assured hand. My thanks to her and her team for their work and for fast-tracking the project.

Proteeti Banerjee at Orient BlackSwan has been a wonderful editor, and I thank her for her support and for expediting the process. Anil Menon vetted the manuscript with a deft touch, serving as both copyeditor and intelligent reader. His swift work was very important. Many thanks to him.

My able assistant, Audrey Angela Rose, played a critical role, especially in the final stages. She followed up with contributors on various issues, collated the essays, and implemented many changes.

This book was completed over sixteen months when I was often weighed down because of my health. But if I still managed to overcome that and pursue what was my passion project, it was thanks to my family's immense support and motivation. My wife Geetha was supportive as ever. My daughter Kavitha stepped in at the right time and took ownership of the project with her customary efficiency. A writer herself, Kavitha's creative contribution is also reflected in the essay which she has co-authored with me. My son Adithya and my son-in-law Hari offered valuable suggestions and often jogged my memory on many issues and incidents.

At the core of this book is the belief that collective wisdom works better in dealing with complex issues than an individual's understanding. This is reflected in the diverse perspectives of the writers, all of whom, as I have mentioned before, I have had the privilege of working with. Each contributor responded to my request spontaneously, despite their busy schedules and, in some cases, their own health issues. The book greatly benefits from their insights, wit, and guidance; I am deeply grateful to each and every one of them.

There were others who generously contributed their essays which were good, but unfortunately, could not be included for various reasons. My special thanks to these contributors for responding to my request.

As mentioned in the Introduction, this book is for my grandchildren and for all grandchildren. I hope they enjoy reading the book. I hope the wisdom in these pages helps them navigate the challenges of a new workplace environment driven by technology and shifting values. And I hope that my grandchildren will carry with them throughout their lives, the enduring values which shaped and guided the contributors in this book.

Introduction

All through history, human beings have struggled to define our ever-evolving relationships with nature, with other humans, and with ourselves. In an essential sense, all of public policy seeks to constantly redefine and renegotiate these foundational relationships. The essays in this volume shed some light on how we, in our generation and social context, negotiated these relationships in our working lives.

Throughout my professional life, I have enjoyed interacting with every one of the essayists in this compilation. Each essayist has unique strengths, and each has reached the pinnacle of their respective professions with these different strengths. The depth and breadth of perspective provided by these distinguished people will, I expect, provide some insights to readers as they navigate the joys and challenges of their working lives.

The essays in this work do not form a comprehensive, exhaustive, or representative compilation. The contributors were chosen at random, mostly from my professional circles, and are mainly from the fields of banking, public policy, journalism, the private sector, and academia. Unfortunately, this means that the contributors are from a tiny, privileged section, which might be as low as 10 per cent of the population. Privilege brings with it the luxury of contemplation—the remaining 90 per cent of people must dedicate their mind space to worrying about livelihoods and other basic concerns.

Some of the essays are anecdotal, others more analytical, some contemplative, even philosophical. Each essay is unique. However, they share some commonalities.

In all the essays is a sense that the writer belonged to a unique time in history. The contributors were aware that they were not just working for a living, but were helping an infant nation, born against all odds out of the heady victory of independence and the aftermath of Partition, to find its feet and grow wings. Many felt a great debt to the leaders who struggled and sacrificed for independence. They understood that the work they were doing would lay the societal, economic, and political foundations for the future of India.

A recurring theme in all the essays is work as a deeply social endeavour. The essayists have explored the question of having a workplace. Post-pandemic, people are redefining workspaces. Work from home, work from office, and hybrid versions of the two are being discussed. However, for many contributors in this book, the daily act of leaving home to commute to the office and the interactions, lifelong friendships, mentors, and professional connections they made at the office were vital and indispensable aspects of their working lives. Work without an office was unimaginable.

On the other hand, one should note that, historically, almost half the population has always worked from home. For example, caregivers, homemakers, weavers, artisans, and others continue to work from their homes or very close to their homes. In some ways, the current trend of office workers telecommuting may help remove the stigma of working from home. It may encourage vulnerable people with social or safety/harassment concerns and domestic or caregiving responsibilities (which fall overwhelmingly on women) to enter and stay in the workforce.

All the essayists were guided by values. They were dedicated to a purpose in life rather than solely working for a career. Underlying the essays is a sense of the collective, rather than the individual. People thrived on feeling like they were part of a greater whole. The essayists' concern for people is evident.

Most of the contributors spent much of their lifetimes in their careers. They were part of institutional history and were drawn into institutional attachment and loyalties. These qualities are apparent in all the essays.

Many contributors in this book were in government service. Most felt they were in their jobs (and perhaps in the world as well) to serve people. There was a feeling that too much had to be done and that there was not enough time to accomplish everything.

It went without saying that the people they served wanted to be served—too much of India was mired in poverty and illiteracy and were desperately looking for someone to lead them on the way to a better life. (These days, the emphasis is more on empowering people than on service.)

As noted, many contributors came from educated, privileged backgrounds. Just a generation or two earlier, their families had been living within rigid, near medieval social structures. Mingling freely with people outside their social circles would have been unthinkable. For the contributors, their workplaces enabled them to engage with people of various backgrounds, castes, geographies, and genders in a way that would have been impossible for their grandparents.

When reading the essays, it becomes apparent that nothing is clear-cut and defined about work. Why do we work? What do we like about it? What makes us happy at work and what deflates us? How do we define success and failure? What values do we bring to work and what values do we imbibe from it? The questions we started with are far from answered and vary from one essay to the other.

The final essay, 'Rear View', explores the unique time and context covered in this book. The essayists shaped, and were shaped by, our nation's tumultuous journey from independence to our current position as the fifth largest global economy. The essay sheds light on India's efforts to grapple with its own paradoxes and complexities while demonstrating its resilience as a nation. 'Rear View' aims to provide a time and context for the reader by exploring the constantly evolving relationships between State, market, and citizen, all of which defined our working lives.

One lesson that I have learnt in all the years of my working life is the eternal truth that change is inevitable. Things are always starting, changing, and ending. We know this truth, but we are blinded by the moment. Hopefully, these essays will remind us that whether we are old or young or in-between, we need to understand how to embrace change, to cope with it, and to contribute to it.

Y. V. REDDY

God Laughs and Other Reflections

Y. V. REDDY AND KAVI YAGA

My father's ancestral house is in a small village in Rayalaseema, Andhra Pradesh. The house still stands, although it is no longer ours. It was sold by an uncle to a man who had once worked in our fields, but then went to the Gulf and made money. He had bought our house with his hard work and savings. The fact that he now lives in the ancestral home of his former landlords is a great point of pride for his family. Yet, just a generation earlier, it would have been economically and socially unimaginable for him and his landlords to contemplate that a man who was once a farm worker would buy his landlord's house. This is an illustration of progress. Urban migration and upward mobility were only some of the sweeping societal transformations of those times. The adage that 'all things change' has always been true. However, the pace of change is now dramatic in every sphere, including in the workplace.

I started working sixty years ago. My working life was not so different from my father's. My son's working life is not entirely different from what mine had been. But my grandchildren's working lives are likely to be unrecognisable to me. Such profound changes bring about profound opportunities and challenges, and raise questions about values, self, and society. One can never be sure how the next generations will cope with these changes when their evolutionary impulses engage with modern realities.

Despite changes, some things will, presumably, remain much the same. *First*, at work (and at home) younger generations will still need to interact with other people and these interactions will still require judgements and skills. *Second*, the younger generations' belief systems and values will be in constant negotiation with the belief systems and values of their workplaces and society. People of my generation have spent many decades facing these same issues and opportunities. Our learnings might perhaps be relevant to others, even in this dramatically altered modern world.

I have, consciously or unconsciously, developed governing principles, values, and approaches in my working life, and they have served me very well. They will, I hope, be of some use to younger generations.

Assess, Don't Judge

As a young officer in the Andhra Pradesh government in the 1970s, I had a posting that I loved and a boss for whom I had enormous respect. During this time, the Government of India requested me to work in Tanzania for three months as a part of the Indian Technical Economic Cooperation (ITEC) programme. This was not unusual. Government officers considered experts in their fields were offered short overseas assignments ranging from a few days to a few months. These coveted, prestigious assignments were good for the officer's career, and the officer's exposure and learnings were good for their department. Tanzania was my second foreign assignment in the same year. As in the past, I expected my boss, with whom I had a great relationship, to approve the deputation wholeheartedly.

I was mistaken. My boss said he could not keep my post vacant during my longish absence. Informally, he had already told the ITEC team leader that releasing me from my post would be difficult. The implicit message was clear–if I took the Tanzania assignment, I would lose my current position.

I was taken aback, even indignant. He knew the assignment was good for my career and for our department. Why had he refused it? On reflection, I suspected it was a personal issue. My boss had not yet received a foreign assignment. The question now was: What was my reaction to be?

Convinced of the superiority of our own worldview, we tend to bring in our ideas of morality and judge others. But in organisational interactions (and in personal interactions as well), assessing the situation by looking at the context, the alternative options, the big picture, and the other person's family and social circumstances helps to suspend, or at least delay, judgement. Also, assessing one's own limitations can temper one's views on the limitations of others.

That day, instead of being accusatory or confrontational with my boss, my response was cordial. I told him I understood his predicament. I said I held him in great respect and was keen to continue working with him on my return. The conversation ended there. When the time came, my boss changed his mind and approved my Tanzania deputation.

Just before my departure, my boss came to my house for a drink. The conversation was pleasant, as usual. Over the course of the evening, he fell into a contemplative mood.

'I say, Venu,' he told me, 'I must confess that I was a little jealous. That's why I did not enthusiastically clear your proposal to go to Tanzania.'

As human beings, we all suffer from shortcomings. We have thoughts and emotions that are far from noble. What is truly admirable is mustering the strength to admit to them. At that moment, my respect for my boss doubled.

I said, 'No problem, Sir.' I reiterated my respect for him and my keenness to work with him after the Tanzania stint.

Sure enough, when I returned, my boss welcomed me back to my post. Over the years, our relationship only grew stronger.

When one assesses without judging, it does not mean that one is endorsing every kind of behaviour or that one is turning a blind eye to other people's limitations, ambitions, or actions. 'Assess, don't judge' means taking a broader view of the larger context, enabling one to work with the strengths in people, to work with all kinds of people, and to find unexpected synergies. Indeed, 'assess, don't judge' has been one of the most useful guiding principles in my entire career.

Integrity, Intellect, Industry

While evaluating who to assign for which role, I calibrate the person on three I's—Integrity, Intellect, and Industry. Many people have none of these. If someone has one of the I's, I know they will perform tolerably. If a person has two, they will be in good shape, and I will be happy. Someone who possesses all three is a gold mine. I will grab the person to come and work with me.

As Governor of the Reserve Bank of India (RBI), I needed a new Deputy Governor. The Chairman of Union Bank, V. Leeladhar, was an excellent candidate. He possessed all three I's in plenty, which was not easy to find. When I offered him the post of Deputy Governor, Leeladhar did not commit to it. He said he would get back to me in a few days.

As promised, he visited me. The moment he entered my room, I greeted him with a hearty welcome. I said I was delighted that he had agreed to honour my request and had come all the way to my office to let me know. He would, I pronounced, make an excellent Deputy Governor. We shook hands on it.

I learnt later that neither he nor his wife had been keen on the Deputy Governor posting since at Union Bank, Leeladhar had stature, perks, a long tenure of service, and independence as the head of an institution. He was visiting my office to decline my offer, not accept it. Why, then, did Leeladhar accept the Deputy Governor post? Perhaps he had been nonplussed by my enthusiasm and was won over by it. Perhaps he did not have the heart to refuse me in that moment. The happy outcome was that the RBI and the country gained the services of an excellent Deputy Governor with all the three I's.

As a matter of fact, all the RBI's Deputy Governors, such as Shyamala Gopinath, Usha Thorat, and Rakesh Mohan, had the three I's and the RBI benefitted greatly from their service.

Naturally, I do not expect all people to have all three I's. While assigning functions, I evaluate which of the three I's the person possesses. If, for example, someone has Intellect and Industry without Integrity, I will not let them near exchange rate management, which is critical and requires access to sensitive information. But I might consider them for the publication station, where they cannot do much harm.

In reality, everyone has the three I's in different proportions. Of the three, I give the most weightage to Integrity.

Style Matters

As an officer in the Government of Andhra Pradesh, I was in an official meeting where my boss made a derogatory remark about certain castes.

Outraged, I snapped at him. 'You should not talk like that!'

My boss was furious. A junior had reprimanded him, and that too in front of everyone at the meeting.

He snapped back, 'How dare you talk to me like that!'

Immediately, I put on a smile. Toning down my voice, I said, 'Sir, my humble submission is ... you should not talk like that.'

He laughed, and the tension eased. We proceeded with the meeting. But my point was made, and well taken.

There are two takeaways from this.

The *first* is—substance is important, but style also matters. When I conveyed the same rebuke to the boss in a different style, he accepted it. The *second* is—humour is your best friend.

Humour Is Everyone's Best Friend

I cannot resist a good joke. After all these years, delivering a quick quip has become second nature. Because of the formality of my job in the RBI, the public often expected me to be serious. They were constantly surprised that I could be humorous.

In my first year as RBI Governor, I was at a press conference when a journalist asked whether I was comfortable with the prevailing exchange rate.

I said I didn't know.

He asked how I could intervene in the market if I did not know the desirable exchange rate.

I said, 'I can't define God, but I can recognise the devil. And whenever I see the devil, I fight it.'

The journalists at the press conference were delighted with this reply. The quip and the analogy conveyed my thinking better than any serious explanation.

In another interview, I spent a lot of time explaining the circumstances under which no major policy action was taken. In monetary policy, there are competing considerations for action or non-action, and in some instances, you reach a stage where they cancel each other out.

When I finished speaking, a journalist put his hand up and said he was more confused at the end of my talk than he was at the beginning.

I had all the points of view, but going into the details of my decision-making process would not bring any more clarity. The question was: How could I frame my reply without sounding evasive?

I said to the reporter, 'Good. I'm glad that I could successfully communicate my confusion.'

Everyone burst out laughing. There wasn't much more to add to the discussion and the press conference ended amicably.

Soon after I joined as RBI Governor, a journalist asked why I didn't raise policy interest rates although all the statistical indicators pointed to the need to do so.

The answer was complicated. In India, the statistical system has provisional estimates and preliminary estimates, and these are revised till the actuals are finalised and released. At the time, I knew the reliability of those changing statistics and knew I would have to supplement my numbers with intelligent evaluations. Also, in any situation in India, we could not blindly take important decisions purely on the basis of immediately available relevant data. Therefore, the statistical indicators that the journalist pointed to were not the ones I was relying on entirely. I could not reveal this–it might have seemed like I was undermining our own data.

In response to his question about why I was not changing the policy interest rates, I said, 'Everywhere around the world, the future is uncertain. In India, even the past is uncertain.'

The journalist was from the United States. He had a Western faith in all things data-related. The line resonated with him and he quoted me in his piece. I have found that the basis for the best jokes is the truth.

One day, I went into a press interview knowing it was going to be tense. I entered the room, and, as usual, people greeted me with a 'Good Morning, Sir'. Uncharacteristically, I did not reply and began my speech.

The speech ended. I looked around the room. I said that I deliberately had not responded to the good morning greetings. If I had, I pointed out, the press would have started wondering why. Was I saying good morning because the previous morning had been bad? Or did it mean the evening before was bad?

A moment later, laughter filled the room. The press interview was not so tense any more. Humour helps to effectively drive a difficult point across without the other person taking offence. It is hard to take offence when you're laughing.

Second Chances

When someone makes a mistake, the incident and the intentions warrant examination. Was it a genuine mistake, a display of callousness, or a deliberate move? I decide on the course of action after placing myself in the other person's position. For callous mistakes, there should be little scope. If it seems to be a deliberate move or sabotage, I act instantly, and with a heavy hand.

If it appears to be a genuine mistake, I try to overlook it. If overlooking is not possible, given institutional dynamics, I keep my action to a minimum. Mistakes happen to the best of us, but people should get a second chance to move on.

In Delhi, I took over as Deputy Secretary in the Department of Economic Affairs, Ministry of Finance. I learnt that just before I joined, there had been a mix-up. A section officer in my division was to send demi-official letters from the finance minister to all chief ministers of the states on the use of external-aided project funds. The officer was to also send similar letters from the finance secretary to the states' chief secretaries on the same subject.

The section officer got the letters mixed up. He sent the letters intended for the chief secretaries to the finance minister for his signature, and he sent the letters intended for the chief ministers to the finance secretary for his signature. The finance minister and finance secretary signed without noticing the letters were not for their intended audience. The mixed-up letters went out. Needless to say, this created great embarrassment for the ministry.

I was asked to take disciplinary action against the section officer, whom I knew. He was a decent and sincere fellow. In this case, he was not as meticulous as he should have been. It was, I felt, a careless mistake. Perhaps it was even a genuine mistake as the finance minister and finance secretary had not spotted the problem with the letters either.

I chided the section officer. Rather than punishing him, I transferred him to a desk with less responsibility. He was grateful that his career had not been ruined. I expect he was much more careful going forward.

I try to think about the purpose of the punishment before meting it out. Punishment is usually, in different degrees, a deterrent for the person, a deterrent for others, and an example. I am of the view that punishment should have some purpose and should not be a vehicle for vengeance or anger.

Work versus Working

As Deputy Secretary in the finance ministry, my boss was Manmohan Singh, then Secretary, Economic Affairs. After I had transferred the section officer who had mixed up the letters in the finance ministry, a young man was assigned to replace him.

When the young man reported to work, he let me know in no uncertain terms that he was not happy about the posting. I assured him that there was no compulsion to join a position he did not want. But might I know the reason? The young man pointed out that he belonged to the Indian Economic Service. He felt he should not have to do the work of a mere section officer and 'spend the whole day pushing files'.

I told him that he should not join the post if he did not want to. I could get someone else. But I encouraged him to pursue his studies in economics wherever he decided to work.

Before he left, I gently informed him, 'By the way, do you know that Manmohan Singh spends most of his time pushing files?'

The next day, the young man returned and requested me to post him as a section officer.

Exciting and significant work can often require a lot of routine day-to-day working.

One Extra Option at No Extra Cost

While making work decisions, I always like to keep an extra option open at no extra cost. After my term as RBI Deputy Governor, there was a good chance that I would have to leave government service. Yet, I wanted to continue working. I then joined the arbitration council. This came with little extra cost to me, and with my background, I was also well-qualified.

As it turned out, I did not need the arbitration option. But if I had needed it, it would have been ready at hand. The point of having an extra option is not that you will certainly use it, but that you will have it if needed.

In reality, there will be trade-offs. But generally, having an extra option in one's career often strengthens one's existing position.

Second and Third-Order Effects

When a political party sweeps to power, they sometimes abandon the unfinished projects started by the previous regime in order to start their own new projects, which are in alignment with their particular agendas. But abandoning projects close to completion, especially those that were 80 per cent or more complete, had been proving to be highly wasteful.

As Secretary, Planning, Government of Andhra Pradesh, I went to Chief Minister N. T. Rama Rao with a proposal to earmark Rs 1 crore per district (it was a substantial amount in those days), purely on grounds of efficiency, for projects that were 80 per cent completed (last mile projects). This Rs 1 crore would be spent only to complete these last mile projects. These projects were to be identified by a technical committee headed by the district collector and would be outside the normal budgetary allocations to the department concerned. The district collector's office was not subject to short-term political changes and would, I reasoned, ensure a longer-term perspective. I argued that the funds should be sanctioned straightaway as 'crucial balancing investment'. It would, I argued, greatly improve efficiencies.

The then Secretary to the Chief Minister and my dear friend, U. B. Raghavendra Rao, was not convinced. He warned me that it would undermine both the process of expenditure authorisation by the government and the parliamentary system. I disagreed and persisted. NTR approved the crucial balancing investment scheme for each district. For a while, it was a success.

After about five years, a weak Collector gave in to pressure from local politicians. The Rs 1 crore was distributed equally among Members of the Legislative Assembly (MLAs) without the need to follow the 80 per cent completion guideline. Over time, this malpractice spread to other districts. Later, even the guideline of 80 per cent completion was officially diluted. Exactly the opposite of what was intended had taken place, and the original problem had worsened. Raghavendra Rao was proved right. Later, a similar scheme called the Members of Parliament (MP) Local Area Development Scheme was adopted by the Government of India with an even greater dilution of guidelines.

What seemed at first an obvious solution using a pragmatic, dynamic plan to improve efficiency had had unintended consequences. This happened because I did not pay attention to possible second-order and third-order effects. A costly mistake, indeed.

Although it is impossible to accurately envision all possible second and third-order effects, I have found that it is important to at least contemplate them. Over time, one's skill and judgement pertaining to next-order effects get honed, providing a very useful framework.

Agree to Disagree

Before any formal negotiation in the World Bank, I would informally, over a cup of tea, meet my counterpart in the negotiations. We would divide the issues under negotiation into three rough categories–what we could agree on; what we disagreed on; and everything in between. Later, in the formal meeting, we would quickly agree on the common points, and then proceed to the in-betweens. We left what we disagreed on till the end. Usually, once we had got so far, it was hard to go back.

Importantly, in all negotiations, I never questioned the professional competence or intentions of the other party. Though we can disagree, we can still have conversations and friendly relations.

Who Are They Teaching?

In the late 1970s, I was posted to the World Bank. Curious about the education system in the US, I enrolled for one semester in a management class at George Washington University's night college. The instructor described the characteristics of employee goals in organisations. He stated that the boss determined employee goals.

I asked what would happen if a conflict arose between institutional loyalties and the boss's goals. The instructor responded that independent institutional loyalties did not apply. I pushed back, citing my experience in government. The instructor informed me that my experience was not relevant to the class. The class was geared towards white American males in the private sector.

I had gone in thinking I would be taught overarching management principles that had universal applicability. But this class was implicitly addressing a different demographic and culture.

In textbooks and courses, teachings are presented as universal truths or principles. But they are often addressed to specific audiences—in the case of my teacher, the white American corporate male. Social science research papers are based on work done on specific (often Western) people and contexts, but are presented as being applicable to all societies. I have great regard for teaching and research, but I try to be evaluative while consuming them.

Theory versus Commonsense

Even sound theoretical frameworks should make sense in the real world. Professor Jan Tinbergen, who won the first Nobel Memorial Prize in Economic Sciences (along with Ragnar Frisch), was the fountainhead of econometrics and developed some of the first macro-econometric models. In 1968, he was my professor during a one-year stint at the Institute of Social Studies in The Netherlands. At the end of one of his classes on building sound econometric models, Tinbergen gave us some advice. If the model violates commonsense, verify, he told us. If it still violates commonsense, throw it out, and start working on a model once again.

I am not a prisoner to any theory or model, but try to view them in the time and context of their application.

Samayam, Sandarbham

The Telugu phrase '*samayam, sandarbham*' translates to time and context. Samayam, sandarbham are always predominant in my decision-making. Nearly all actions and situations are meaningless when stripped of their time and context.

What are considered pillars of virtue in one society (for example, the quality of harmony and collectivism in certain Asian cultures) might be less important in another, or might even be considered inferior (for example, in certain Western cultures, disruption and individualism are valued over harmony and the collective good). Also, developed markets with robust legal systems can support certain policies. These same measures will not work in less developed markets that lack strong and swift legal systems to which citizens can turn in the case of fraud or failure.

Formulaic prescriptions should be viewed in context. There is a standard formula for measuring the optimum level of foreign exchange reserves of a country. In India (and elsewhere), forex reserves are the reserves of foreign convertible currencies (mainly US dollars) and gold held by the monetary authority for various reasons, including to provide stability to the system. (The International Monetary Fund's [IMF] Special Drawing Rights form much smaller components of the forex reserves.) The optimal level of forex reserves is calculated in economic terms and exposures.

But what of geo-political factors? I maintained that we needed to also take geo-political risks and security into account. President Bill Clinton was once quoted as saying that the US should help bail out Mexico in a time of need, but not some other country such as India. (He specifically mentioned India as a country that the US would not help bail out.) In such a situation, Mexico can afford to have fewer reserves than India, which must have more because it does not belong to any block and cannot expect a bailout from anyone. India has to take care of at least three potential shocks from the external sector–food, fuel, and finance (external finance).

I have also learnt from the sound counsel of Bimal Jalan. The RBI manages the public debt of the Government of India through the public debt office. In 1997, as Deputy Governor, I argued for creating an independent debt office, separate from the RBI. This separation of powers seemed logical, efficient, and consistent with international practice. I made a presentation to Governor Jalan. He listened attentively and complimented me. Then, to my surprise, he asked me to write a note opposing my own recommendation (I later realised this was to help me think through the opposing view).

On reflection, I understood his viewpoint. Our context was unique. When the RBI is the public debt manager for the government, it keeps in mind the government's interests. Once that function is taken out of the RBI's purview, the government is exposed to market risk and possible vested interests. Jalan felt we should hold off till our markets were sufficiently well-developed and the government was able to raise money without the RBI's help as a public debt manager. My initial view, while attractive at first, did not give sufficient weightage to these realities. The experience of Greece (and several other countries) during the financial crisis of 2008 supported Jalan's wisdom.

In summary, it is wise to look at formulae, theory, standard practice, and the experience of others while crafting policy or making decisions. To then evaluate their relevance in the particular samayam and sandarbham of the practitioner's system is even wiser.

Right Timing

The RBI viewed certain financial innovations as healthy, but only in small quantities. A proliferation of these innovations often presented systemic risks that could be difficult to undo. Also, unlike Food and Drug Regulation authorities, which can first carry out controlled experiments with a drug before releasing it into the larger population, financial systems do not first test the safety of financial innovations before injecting them into markets.

Timing can be crucial. In the 2004 elections, the Bharatiya Janata Party (BJP)-led coalition government, the National Democratic Alliance (NDA), was defeated and the United Progressive Alliance (UPA) coalition government, under the Congress' Sonia Gandhi, was elected. Although eventually Manmohan Singh was declared the prime minister, there was, for one day, great uncertainty about who would lead the country.

During this time, there was an attack on the stock exchange. This resulted in a huge dollar outflow due to demand for the currency. The rupee began falling dramatically. The market sentiment was totally against us and acting in such an environment posed risks and costs. In addition, as RBI Governor, I had to keep the political leadership informed of my actions in a situation where we were politically rudderless.

I called the outgoing finance minister, Jaswant Singh. I explained that I was not intervening immediately, but would act at the appropriate time. Jaswant Singh was puzzled. He pointed out that he was not the finance minister anymore. I told him that, legally, until the next Cabinet was formed, he still was. Therefore, I reported to him. I assured him that he could convey this information to anyone he wanted if he felt it was appropriate.

The rupee continued to fall, but we at the RBI did not act. By late morning, several people were asking the RBI to intervene. The clamour grew louder, as did the support for intervention. A little after lunchtime, we acted. The RBI intervened in a massive way—spending huge amounts to buy dollars, showing our strong determination, and stemming the slide. The markets stabilised.

If the timing was wrong, the costs of intervention would have proved prohibitive in an environment of adverse market sentiment. We waited till such time as there was a critical minimum level at which at least some people in the markets started thinking that enough was enough and demanded that the RBI intervene. That was when we considered it appropriate to hit hard and decisively—we turned the anti-rupee sentiment into a pro-rupee sentiment.

In all this, timing was absolutely key.

Biodiversity

As RBI Governor, I had the reputation of running a tight ship. People said I was something of a tyrant. To the outside world, it appeared that everyone at the RBI had no choice but to appear united behind official decisions. It was rumoured that the RBI left no scope for internal dissent. But the reality was very different.

Behind the scenes, intense consultations and meetings where diverging views were exchanged were common. (This has been recognised in a compilation of RBI's history.)[1] The word I used was 'biodiversity'. Biodiversity is important in the world of ideas.

When a file from a junior colleague came to my desk and I did not agree with it, I would call the colleague to my room. I would discuss the file with them, and either they would convince me or I would convince them. That way, I had access to their thinking and they had the satisfaction of being heard.

Finally, if I could not convince my junior colleague and they were unable to convince me, I overruled them. I was very cognisant that my decision was final not because I knew more than my junior colleague, but only because the organisational workflow necessitated that one person have the final say. I made this clear to the colleague whenever I overruled them.

I encouraged RBI Deputy Governors to bring their junior technical people to meetings. I encouraged the most junior of them to talk first so that they could speak uninhibitedly. I felt this encouraged and enabled everyone to air their honest views to the institutional head. It also built an institutional commitment to debate and a respect for good ideas across hierarchies and levels.

Yes, Sir. No, Sir.

I was working at the World Bank in the late 1970s when Mary, my colleague, heard me addressing my boss, Gopi Arora. After Arora left, Mary said, 'Venu, you always say, "Yes, Sir, Yes, Sir". I can call my boss by his first name, Ernie. I can say, "Yes, Ernie, Yes, Ernie".'

I replied, 'Mary, you can only say "Yes, Ernie, Yes Ernie" to survive. But I can say "No, Sir, No, Sir" and still survive.'

She laughed and understood the point. What is important is the freedom to disagree.

One Job, Many Pursuits

I finished my Ph.D. in 1976 while in the Indian Administrative Service (IAS). Throughout my career, I published books and attended conferences. (At one time, people thought there were two Y. V. Reddys—one an academic and the other a public service man.)

I also never gave up on my urge to start organisations whenever I felt they were needed. In 1977, at the beginning of my career, my friend Anjaneya Reddy and I started a non-profit organisation, the Hyderabad Study Circle. A coaching centre to help underprivileged people from the districts crack the civil services examinations, the Hyderabad Study Circle was the first and only one of its kind in Hyderabad. (In those days, there were only one or two study circles in India—one in Delhi and one in Madras. Both were for profit and catered to a more elite audience.) The Hyderabad Study Circle produced hundreds of young people who went on to have long careers in the IAS, Indian Police Service (IPS), Indian Foreign Service (IFS), and other civil services. (It also had a multiplier effect, and many other study circles cropped up.)

Sometime after my RBI tenure, I became involved in the University of Hyderabad, bringing eminent economists to lecture at the then Department of Economics. Many youngsters were inspired by these interactions. I also spent a couple of years helping to found the School of Economics at the University of Hyderabad, which was formally established in 2012.

Of course, in between, there were efforts in my career that did not take off or did not live up to expectations. However, almost all my professional pursuits outside of work complemented and enhanced what I did in my primary job.

For example, my research work strengthened the theoretical foundations of my public policy work (and helped me defend my approach on the basis of research), while my job in public policy enabled an understanding of the real-world implications, applications, and limitations of the theory. These diverse pursuits helped to bridge the distance between theory and practice, international and national, and rural and urban.

Helping versus Nepotism

In the late 1960s, when I was posted as the Sub-Collector in Gudur, I toured remote villages. There were no restaurants to eat at, and one option was to eat in the homes of local families. Some of those families were connected or distantly related to me. In those days, the Sub-Collector's post was quite powerful and people vied to host the local official because it would raise their status in the community. It would also give the impression to the Sub-Collector's subordinates that they shared a special relationship, and that their work with the government should be treated favourably.

To avoid complications, I carried my own food. When I left my quarters very early in the morning, I carried slices of bread in one pocket and hard-boiled eggs in the other. This would be my breakfast and lunch as I toured villages.

This desire to be (and to be seen as) impartial has perhaps cost me the goodwill of some friends and relatives. It was the norm in those days for friends and family to expect favours from government servants. These expectations contrasted with my guiding principle of being very impartial and professional–the government and its officials should be seen to favour no one. Such favours, in my mind, constituted nepotism.

This was at odds with the prevailing culture where dispensing favours was considered as being 'helpful' to one's near and dear. Perhaps this favouring is rooted in history and culture. Given that we had been governed by outside forces for centuries, one had to make up for the sin of joining the ruling authority by dispensing favours to one's circle. By not obliging this cultural expectation, I was being 'unhelpful'.

Although my approach may have cost me socially, I believe it was the right one. It helped me obtain the best talent, maintain high standards, and avoid trade-offs. My reputation as a 'strict' officer also meant that people hesitated to approach me for favours.

Lots of Questions

I have learned from many people, including politicians. I had the pleasure of working in several capacities with Manmohan Singh and gained from his wisdom. He would ask a lot of questions. Initially, I was often perturbed and defensive. Was he questioning my hypothesis? Did he suspect me of ineptitude? Later, I realised that he was most often just inquiring. Sometimes, he was asking for more information to arm himself against those who might dissent. At other times, he wanted greater clarity before taking a final view.

I learnt that questioning properly and thoroughly before acting is very important. Questioning does not immediately imply disagreement or doubt.

Haddu-Paddu

In Telugu, *haddu-paddu* denotes limits and a monitoring or keeping of an account. It is the process of defining a limit for an activity and of monitoring the activity, thereby encouraging some level of restraint.

At work, haddu-paddu was very useful in monitoring large sets of data. Financial markets tend to have a huge number of transactions. It was not feasible for me as a senior RBI officer to monitor all transactions. But I defined certain limits for transactions and made a system whereby anything above the norm was to be reported to me. Therefore, any substantial material deviations from the normal pattern were brought to my attention. In the daily financial markets committee briefings, I was given a one-page summary of events of an extraordinary nature or magnitude. These, I examined closely.

I made sure the regulated knew about my scrutiny—I felt they should know they were being monitored. This helped them to stay within their haddu-paddu as well. Also, it reduced the need for punitive action later on. Any act can be a precedent and may be capable of replication, but acts kept within certain boundaries leave some scope for correction. Therefore, limits are important, especially in policy.

Limits go both ways—up and down. As a regulator, I was watchful not only when things were going too badly, but also when things were going too well. For example, if an enterprise was growing too quickly, I would note that there might be cancer growing and it would have to be investigated. (As a regulator, what was important was not just regulatory compliance, but regulatory comfort as well.)

Even in our personal life, too much of a good thing can be harmful. While eating or exercising or sleeping or working or having fun, it is wise to act with some restraint. I used to joke that I maintain a delicate balance—between good health and bad habits!

Have Some Model

When I joined the IAS, we were sent for training to the Lal Bahadur Shastri National Academy of Administration in Dehra Dun. We were assigned hostel rooms to stay. Some rooms were good and close to the main buildings, while other rooms were neither. The criterion for allocating the rooms was the first name, in alphabetical order, although there was no good reason for this.

The management could just as easily have used some other metric, such as the reverse alphabetical order of the last name or the date of birth. What was important was not the particular metric (as long as it was justifiable), but rather the act of selecting it and ensuring its enforcement. Without any criteria or metric or model, there could have been some scope for management to show favouritism or behave in an irregular manner, and scope for students to harbour suspicions of favouritism or irregularities.

In systems where there is no basis for choosing any particular criteria, it would be better to pick some model or criteria and enforce it, rather than have no model at all. Later, depending on the situation, the model could be changed.

Gratitude is a Bonus

Gratitude is a difficult emotion. Usually, a person hates being put in the position of being obliged to someone else. Roman historian Tacitus observed, 'Men are more ready to repay an injury than a benefit, because gratitude is a burden and revenge a pleasure.' Therefore, a favour to someone should be given without expecting its return or even without expecting an expression of gratitude.

Economist and civil servant Abid Hussain (my one-time boss) was very popular and helpful. Many people benefitted from his assistance. During Abid sahib's tenure, a well-known public figure in a senior government position lost his job. Till today, no one knows why he lost his job (officially, he voluntarily handed in his resignation, but in reality, he was pressured to leave as a *persona non grata* to the authorities). No one would have risked giving this person a job, given the murky circumstances of his removal.

Hussain stepped up. He convinced the authorities to give the public figure a job, but in another capacity. This proved essential in reviving that person's fortunes. Later, this public figure rose to even greater prominence.

Years later, Abid sahib passed away. His family and some others planned a book in his honour. I requested the public figure to contribute an essay in Abid sahib's memory. The response was lukewarm, at best. In the end, the person did not contribute even a short essay or tribute to Abid sahib's volume.

Although such behaviour is, thankfully, not common, it is not unusual either. The point is that when I encounter gratitude and acknowledgement, I treat it as a bonus rather than an expectation.

Housekeeping

Regulations, reporting requirements, and communications are introduced for a particular purpose at a particular time. Over the years, they may become outdated. As RBI Deputy Governor, when Bimal Jalan was Governor, I had instituted the first Regulation Review Authority (RRA) in 1999 (the second review was done in 2021 by Governor Shaktikanta Das).

The job of the first RRA was to review all existing regulations on the assumption that any regulation could be questioned. The burden of defending it fell on the regulator (the RBI), not the regulated. After much debate and a thorough review, a consolidated circular with an updated set of regulations was sent out every year.

Unnecessary regulations or rules that need removal or outdated regulations or rules that need revision tend to accumulate and stagnate. This increases inefficiency, compliance costs, and complexity. Therefore, I made it a point to review and vet regulations periodically.

Observations, Inquiries

I try to be sensitive to people's moods. When we see someone in the office, we tend to forget that the person comes from some personal and social situation. Who knows what their troubles are? Whether it is a peon or a president, I try to observe what the person's expression and body language convey and inquire about their health or their day. Sometimes, when a person is looking sad, a joke livens things up.

One day, I got into a lift in the North Block in Delhi. The lift operator usually greeted me with a smile. That day, I noticed he did not look very cheerful. As the elevator doors closed, I turned to him and asked, '*Kya bhai*? Why the bad mood? Quarrelled with your wife today?' He burst into laughter.

Of course, I would try to keep cultural contexts in mind. For example, if this was in the US, the same interaction would be construed as an intrusion on privacy. In that case, a neutral joke or observation could lighten the mood. To observe people and inquire about their lives makes us aware of and sensitive to all those around us. Even small gestures, like an acknowledgement or a pleasant expression, can make people feel good, build connections, and remind us of our common humanity.

Goal and Path

People often confuse and conflate the goal and the path. While the goal may be inflexible, the path may be flexible, and *vice versa*.

Regulatory capital is required for the capital adequacy ratio (CAR) of regulated bodies (such as banks and non-banking financial companies). Simply put, this ensures that the regulated do not take too much risk or leverage. But the regulated might feel a financial pinch when complying with the ratio. During my tenure as RBI Governor, the bank fixed the capital adequacy ratio. The ratio was the goal and it was non-negotiable. But I was willing to discuss the timing, the path, and the means to achieve the milestones leading towards the goal.

One advantage of this approach was that the regulated did not feel that they were only at the receiving end of policy. They felt a sense of involvement in the process of developing the policy, and importantly, in implementing it.

This approach of goal and path was not just confined to my handling of regulatory capital, but was ingrained in my style of functioning.

Not My Job to be Liked

As a regulator, I found that some of my goals and regulations were not always popular with the regulated. I told the regulated that just as their freedom was my constraint, my instrument was their constraint.

Some of the policies I enacted were unpopular, at least with vocal and influential players. For example, when the RBI saw that some foreign banks were using off-balance sheet vehicles (these could be used to conceal debt), we prohibited them in India. This caused an uproar (including pressure applied through global political channels). In this and other instances, people spoke out against my policies, sometimes even publicly and in harsh terms. But I was clear—a regulator should be respected or even feared, rather than liked.

Also, a measure popular with some may be equally unpopular with others. Some financial market *wallahs* criticised the RBI during my tenure for its curbs on capital flows. They accused the RBI of attempting a bureaucratic power grab and of trying to bring back the licence control raj. Others criticised the RBI for not having been stringent enough on capital flows.

In another instance, as RBI Deputy Governor, I gave a speech on exchange rate management in Goa in 1997. RBI Governor C. Rangarajan had carefully edited the speech. The Goa speech was an unusual approach to induce a correction in the exchange rate of the rupee through an oral communication (the so-called 'open mouth operation', but unusual because central bankers do not like to talk down their own currencies). We at the RBI were deeply concerned that the rupee had been overvalued up to a persistent and discomforting level. We did not want to wait for the markets to bring down the rupee and wanted the Goa speech to bring it down at the timing of our choice. The speech had the intended effect. The rupee began to depreciate, and the markets were unsure of what to do.

Although the government was at first on board with the strategy, it was, for some reason, taken aback by the depreciation, which, in its opinion, was too rapid. The finance minister suggested we backtrack. Some in the government warned that I would never be forgiven for what I had done.

On discussion, the RBI decided later to intervene in the markets, but lightly, to retard the pace of depreciation. In retrospect, we certainly avoided the fate of the East Asian countries, which incurred the steep cost of depreciation of their currencies brought about by market forces during the Asian crisis of 1997.

S. S. Tarapore, my predecessor in the RBI, later wrote in an article, 'Dr. Reddy will come out as saviour of Indian exchange rate policy'. Others vehemently disagreed. To this day, there is a debate on whether I was a sinner or a saviour. (I feel I was neither; I like to think of myself as a messenger.)

In short, rarely can you please everyone. Although it goes against most people's inclination to not be disliked, sometimes the job demands it. This applies not only to regulators, but also to other jobs and situations where rules must be set and enforced.

Extracting the Good

Encounters with people and media–books, essays, videos, papers, and the like–of excellent quality leave me delighted. They have been invaluable in my career and personal life.

However, sometimes I end up with interactions and readings that are not of the highest quality. An awareness of quality is important. But focussing on the substandard portion takes away from what can be gained or learnt from the good portion. Even if a paper or a meeting is 99 per cent useless, I appreciate the 1 per cent that is useful and move on. In other words, I try to extract the good from a situation and put the rest aside.

Of course, in the future, one can use this prior knowledge to assess whether to consume more material from the same source. Yet, there is nothing to be gained from focussing on what has not been gained.

Communication in the Wrong Hands

With any important communication, I always assume it will fall into the hands of not only the intended recipient, but also the person at the receiving end of my policy dispensation, or even my opponent. Therefore, I craft the language of every communication keeping both the intended and the unintended recipients in mind.

A Conceptual Rogue

When I was Deputy Governor RBI, Governor Jalan once complimented my ability to sniff out potential scams in the markets. He asked me how I did it.

I responded that I knew the goal of the market was to make money. I put myself on the other side of the fence and imagined all the ways in which I could make money through a change in the policy or law under discussion.

'Conceptually I'm a rogue, but not a practising one,' I joked.

The question to ask is: What are the interests of the other party? When in doubt, do not suspect their integrity, suspect their interests. Underlying this is an understanding of incentives. Incentives are paramount because they drive people. Understanding incentive structures can help us understand the behaviours of market players (individuals or institutions). The behaviours of these players can be nudged with carefully designed incentives. The goal of good policy design is to ensure that individual incentives are compatible with the collective interest. This is self-evident to many in public policy; in my case, it has governed all my actions.

Career Turns, Lifetime Work

Although I dedicated myself to whatever role I was in, I was open to opportunities. When things did not go as expected, I found other paths and opportunities to learn from, to move on. In some ways, I was on a continuous job improvement mission. I always made an effort to be prepared and work in ways that made others keen to help me.

Every IAS officer is entitled to a study leave of two years on full pay. In the late 1980s, although I had reached a senior level in the government, I took advantage of this study leave. I went as a visiting professor to Osmania University for six months; as an honorary faculty of the Administrative Staff College of India, Hyderabad, for one year; and later, as a Visiting Fellow, London School of Economics, for four months (all on a full-time basis).

I worked in different capacities with the IAS, the World Bank, the IMF, and the RBI, all of which were vastly different in culture, scope, and functionality. Yet, every one of them added to my skill set and honed my thinking and judgement.

One may have no choice but to yield to the twists and turns and uncertainties in life. However, having a broad purpose is essential to staying focused. Throughout my life, despite career turns, my lifetime goal—to serve the Indian people, particularly the common person—has stayed steady.

No Need to be Anti-Rich to be Pro-Poor

As a government officer, my father would visit the villages in his jurisdiction. Despite his stature, he would sit with farmers and talk about their problems in local gathering places. He showed his deep empathy for the poor. During my vacations, I would accompany him. My father's concern for the common man influenced me greatly. As a student in Anantapur, I had shared a hostel with young men from poor families, and this close experience also had a deep influence on me.

As RBI Governor, while crafting monetary policy, we understood how sensitive the poor were to risk. We understood the importance of extending formal financial services to their households because the poor relied greatly on social and non-formal systems.

The RBI kept in mind the interests of depositors (the vast majority of whom are usually poor or middle class and retirees). In my five years, we increased the policy interest rates, and one effect of this was that depositors could get more money for their bank deposits. Increased policy interest rates also put pressure on financial institutions and markets to reduce their margins and increase their efficiencies. Obviously, this was carefully balanced to ensure growth with equity.

The RBI also made financial inclusion a big thrust during my tenure. We introduced the banking correspondent system to bring banking to the people. The ATM is where the rich and the poor stand in the same queue. ATMs were important to the RBI and we worked on reducing or abolishing fees for using them, benefitting both rich and poor.

Pro-poor does not mean anti-rich. There is no need to be anti-rich to be pro-poor. I wanted to be seen as not unfriendly to the rich, while being concerned about vulnerable people.

In 2008, the housing market bubble in the US burst, triggering a major global financial crisis. The prevailing view of the US central bank was that since asset bubbles could not be accurately defined, it was best to manage them and clear them up after they burst.

In India, we took a different approach. At the RBI, where I was Governor in the years leading up to the crisis, we were unwilling to risk the bubble that we sensed was ballooning in the real-estate sector. We felt that the gains from the bubble went disproportionately to the financial sector, while the pains of a burst bubble would be borne disproportionately by the middle class and, eventually, the poor. (This proved to be the experience of the US.)

Keeping this in mind, the RBI strengthened the stability of our financial systems and ensured liquidity. For example, we restrained our banks from giving loans and from investing in equity markets and real estate. We increased the risk weightings on commercial real-estate construction, thereby requiring the banks to keep aside almost double the amount of capital in reserve. We increased interest rates, anticipating inflationary pressures, and one of the consequences was that house loans became more expensive, thereby reducing the demand to buy houses. For every loan, we made banks put aside extra capital. We used these and several other direct and indirect measures to balance between many factors to ensure growth while constraining undue risk, especially to the vulnerable. (In general, I believe the financial sector can only follow or facilitate, but should not lead growth in the real economy without disproportionate risk. When in doubt, I looked to international experience.)

Needless to say, the 'stringent' measures by the RBI were deeply unpopular with many in the financial sector at the time of their implementation. Financial market *wallahs* felt they were being unnecessarily restrained, or even penalised.

Then, in 2008, the financial crisis hit. Of course, India did not escape unscathed, but the Indian financial sector was affected far less severely than many other countries. Our banks had liquidity and we could avoid much of the financial instability. This not only cushioned the vulnerable from shock, but also benefitted the financial sector greatly, as well as the rich. Importantly, the years leading up to the crisis were a period of record high growth rates with price stability, and forex reserves had increased to ensure external sector stability.

Although many factors went into policymaking and decision-making at the time, a concern for the vulnerable was a principle that was always at the back of my mind. I believe that this principle can be applied or acted on in different ways, depending on the nature of the job or institution.

For example, a civil services officer is bound by strict rules and procedures. Yet, the officer can exercise discretion within the structure of the rules. In general, any law says that something is prohibited or that something should be done. Between the two, there is a vast area. I used my initiative to tap into this area while I was in the IAS. (This is an important principle that can be used almost universally by public servants.)

For those not in public service, similar areas can be found between institutional rules and guidelines. Capitalism is a system in favour of the few, although it is not necessarily against the many. Often, the balance is tilted towards the rich, but there is no rule that says it has to be so. It is left to the practitioner to decide how to interpret and augment these systems.

Presenting Problems, Presenting Solutions

While working with N. T. Rama Rao in the Andhra Pradesh government in the 1980s, my colleague T. L. Sankar and I felt that the government should not have to rely solely on the efforts of the National Informatics Corporation (NIC) to provide free computers to our state. We needed our own computers and we needed to enable our workers to use them competently. Sankar and I mapped out an organisation for providing computers and technology services to our state government departments–Andhra Pradesh Technology Services Limited (APTS).

We first presented the problem to NTR: we pointed out that relying solely on the NIC would limit the state's independence. We then presented our solution: a proposal for APTS, which could provide computers for the planning department's district offices, in the commercial tax department, and in the government printing press to reduce exorbitant overtime payments. We could also eventually connect the various decentralised computers in different departments.

NTR was a man who had an almost childlike fascination for technology. He readily agreed. (The opposition felt it was a wasteful expenditure, but NTR pushed it through.) This was one of the reasons for the early and deep penetration of e-governance in Andhra Pradesh.

If we had presented only the problem to NTR, he might not have agreed so readily, and would not have felt he had the necessary information to later defend the policy against criticism from opposing forces. No boss wants to hear only about problems. When bringing a problem to my boss, I also bring one or two possible solutions, and their implications. Going to the boss with a well thought-out answer and a list of pros and cons makes them feel supported. It makes the boss feel like you are a part of the solution, rather than the problem. This is true regardless of whether your solution is the one that is eventually implemented.

God Laughs

At heart, I am an economist. I started my career as a research scholar and lecturer. I greatly enjoyed academia and engaged enthusiastically in discussions, conferences, and deliberations. I loved new ideas, analysis, conceptualisation, and synthesis. As a young man, I was sure I had found my calling. I expected to spend a lifetime in academia and hoped to eventually retire as a professor at a university.

They say that man plans and God laughs. At the age of twenty-three, for family reasons, I joined the IAS batch of 1964. Although disappointed to leave the world of academia, I learnt to enjoy my work as an IAS officer and quickly made the transition from the analytical to the operational. Next to politicians, IAS officers had the best opportunity and capacity to understand the dynamics of Indian society, and be closest to the people and their political systems. My time in the IAS strengthened my sensitivity to the real problems of the common person–a rooting that stayed with me throughout my career. In my IAS career, the handling of the balance of payment crisis in 1991 was a particularly exciting time. So was the Asian crisis of 1997. It was also lively throughout the 1990s and early 2000s, with reforms and liberalisation when I handled the financial sector.

At a professional level, my life in the IAS had worked out splendidly. At a personal level also, my batchmates had become like family and I was certain I would retire, quite contentedly, along with them. Again, God laughed.

In 1997, my dear friend S. S. Tarapore was retiring as RBI Deputy Governor and persuaded me to consider succeeding him. For professional reasons, I agreed. I made the unexpected move to the RBI to work as a Deputy Governor under Governor Rangarajan, my guru.

For the first time, I found an identity at the national level. As Deputy Governor, I got a chance to be an independent public face, especially since Rangarajan, and later Jalan, gave me full freedom to express myself on policy matters. The highlights of my time as a Deputy Governor were my monthly trips to the Bank for International Settlements in Basel, Switzerland. There, I would represent my boss, the RBI Governor, in confidential meetings and engage in discussions with central bankers from the world over. This fascinating experience helped me understand the inner workings of the minds of central bankers from all over the world.

After seven years as a Deputy Governor (my five-year term was followed by a two-year extension), I was set to join the Indian School of Business in my hometown of Hyderabad. I also joined the arbitration council as a back-up retirement plan. I thought I had come full circle and that my retirement would be mostly spent in academia.

God was still laughing. In 2002, I was posted to the IMF as an Executive Director. I was on the IMF board and closely saw the events and decision-making during the Argentina crisis (after their economy collapsed in 2001) and the economic upheaval in Turkey (after an unprecedented financial crisis in 2000–2001). With this ringside view from the IMF, I was convinced of the need for autonomy in policymaking and understood that it was possible only through stability in the macroeconomic environment. At the IMF, I had global exposure, gained friends, and made a name in international circles.

The IMF posting also came at the right time in my personal life. My wife, Geetha, was happy. She was living closer to both our children and their families, who were settled in the US. Also, the IMF paid very well and had generous retirement benefits that increased the longer I worked there. It seemed a fitting end to my professional career—I would retire comfortably after my stint at the IMF.

On a late summer morning in 2003, the phone rang in my Washington, DC apartment. The caller was RBI Governor Jalan. He said I might have to return soon to India to succeed him as RBI Governor. I protested. I had already informed him and the government that I wanted to stay at the IMF. A move to India would imply significant familial disruption and material loss. Jalan persisted. He pointed out that both the prime minister and the finance minister wanted me. Just days later, the Government of India appointed me as Governor, RBI.

Of course, it was a great honour to serve my country, and I joined as Governor in September 2003.

Central banks are governor-centric. I had the autonomy to shape and strengthen the already professional and well-respected Reserve Bank. I had the privilege of mentoring excellent professionals such as Usha Thorat, Shyamala Gopinath, Rakesh Mohan, Leeladhar, and many others who served with distinction and dedication. Statutorily, the RBI is one of the weakest in terms of independence. In practice, due to the good traditions built, particularly by Rangarajan and Jalan, I was lucky enough to negotiate the RBI's independence with the government. (I once quipped, 'The RBI is independent. I am independent. I've taken the permission of the finance minister to say so.')

At the RBI, one of the highlights was the chance to meet and interact with distinguished people. I served under Manmohan Singh and worked with P. Chidambaram, Yashwant Sinha, and Jaswant Singh. The RBI board meetings were a delight. The Board of Directors included many eminent people–scientists such as A. P. J. Abdul Kalam and U. R. Rao; industrialists such as Ashok Ganguly, Ratan Tata, and Narayana Murthy; economists such as A. Vaidyanathan and Mihir Rakshit; and social workers such as Amrita Patel and Sashi Rajagopalan. The insights and perspectives gained during our regular meetings, as well as relationships formed during those sessions, still stay with me. I hosted many central bankers from other countries and a G20 summit (which at that time came and went without much fanfare). I also greatly enjoyed my interactions with journalists and looked forward to the friendly banter and repartee I shared with them. My job as RBI Governor was the ultimate in satisfaction, and in many respects, the highlight of my entire working life.

My tenure as RBI Governor ended in 2008, and I returned to Hyderabad. The University of Hyderabad appointed me as a visiting professor and there I published and edited several books. In 2013, however, I was appointed Chairman of the 14th Finance Commission and we moved to Delhi once again. In two years, the Finance Commission visited every state capital and interacted with a cross-section of political parties. We also oversaw the division of funds between Andhra Pradesh and the newly formed Telangana state. I gained enormous insights into Centre-state relations.

Professionally, I had had a dream run and my working life had been intense, eventful, and consequential. In addition, I was immensely fortunate to be recognised for my work internationally and nationally, including with a Padma Vibhushan.

The point of the above summary is that throughout the incredible journey of my life, I was certain about one thing– God was laughing at all my plans. Looking back, I realise that I too spent all those years laughing along.

Note

1. Tirthankar Roy, *The Reserve Bank of India: Volume 5, 1997–2008*, Cambridge University Press, 2022.

Part I

Public Life

1

Never Give Up, Fight to the End

Lessons from Changing Professions, Losing Jobs, and the Ups and Downs of Life

ARUN SHOURIE

Dr Y. V. Reddy has been one of the saviours of our country. But for him, we would have landed in a ditch during the 2008 crisis. More than that, he has been a beacon. It is not just that he has been one of the most outstanding professionals of our times. He has been an example—a professional who has lived and worked by the highest values. He has asked me to list lessons from life and work. He says he wants these to be set out for our grandchildren. When Dr Reddy asks me to do something, his wish is my command.

I have changed professions four times. I was dismissed from a job twice. Because of the blows that have struck Adit, our son, and my wife, Anita, I have seen much suffering first-hand. So, I will list lessons from these.

Professions

The first thing to remember when you choose your job or your profession is the counsel of the Buddha—'right livelihood'. That is, we must earn our livelihood in ways that bring happiness to others, that heal our society, our earth. Becoming rich selling cigarettes and then giving something in charity to a cancer hospital is not the right way to organise our lives. It is to put lipstick on our leprous lips.

Of course, we must put into the job or the profession that we have chosen all the effort that it requires. But if, after putting in all the effort, your heart tells you that this is not what you want to be doing, don't just let things drag on—*change*. Among the best things I did in my life was to give up my job at the World Bank—all my interests were in India and those days the convention there was that one cannot work on one's home country. Had I not given up that job, I would be quite a rich fellow today, but I would have wasted my life in routine and boredom. Another excellent thing I did was to give up my job—quite a senior one—in one of our principal newspapers as I realised *ki yeh akhbaar naheen, sarkaar hai*. So, don't let years drag on—*switch*.

Everyone will tell you that you will be going into a world of limitless opportunities. That it is a world full of opportunities is true. But it is also a heartless world. There is no place for the second-rate.

So, pursue excellence. Not fame, certainly not money. When you have excelled, fame will come—or, if it does not come, it will no longer matter. Similarly, once you excel, you will always have enough money to live well. One of the first lessons that Anita taught me when we got married was, 'We must be satisfied with enough. And at any moment, "enough" is what we have at that moment.' But if you set out to pursue fame or money, you will be easily led astray. So much of fame in today's world is an artifice, it is fake, it is the result not of intrinsic worth but of publicity, of self-projection. Pursuing it, you will become the captive of marketeers. And if you pursue money, you will never have enough of it. Someone else will always have more. One of the attractive things about excellence is that there is much less competition in the field.

There is a sharper reason also for not pursuing money. So many of our professions have been ruined, indeed, they have become a menace because, for the professionals in them, money has become all—law, medicine, to take just two examples. This pursuit of money has consequences beyond ruining those professions. Freedom, democracy, and the like have been fought for and kept alive by the middle class. And professionals are the bulk of the middle class, they are the backbone of the middle class. But when professionals are preoccupied pursuing money, who will guard discourse, institutions, values—the very foundations of democracy and freedom and good governance? So, the next time you are awed by some rich man, remind yourself of what a diplomat-philosopher once said. A person in the gathering referred to some very prominent man, 'such a rich man,' he said.

'What did you say?' asked the diplomat-philosopher. 'A rich man? No, no. Not a rich man. He is a poor man with money.'

So, pursue excellence. But a word of caution—the world is changing so fast that what is excellent in the morning may become obsolete by the evening. So, even as you attain excellence in one field, learn others. Have another job, another profession handy. Learn not just a subject, learn how to learn—how to keep learning all your life.

Even that will not be enough. Howsoever good the embroidery we do, if the whole cloth burns, our handiwork will also be reduced to ashes. So, even as you strive to excel in your profession, devote some time and the skills you have acquired to public issues—to issues that concern you no more than they concern the average citizen.

In spite of doing all these things, and more, there will be setbacks—often for no fault of yours. I am probably the only Editor who has been dismissed from his job, not once but twice. So, I am in a position to report from personal experience—there is life after dismissal. In any case, work in such a way that when you are dismissed it becomes a mark of honour, a distinction. Similarly, I lost the job, in fact jobs that I had in Atal Bihari Vajpayee's government for no fault of mine—I lost them because the government lost the elections. At such times, remember two words—*defy fate.*

Life

Enough about our jobs and professions. Three-four things about life itself.

Among the truest things I have read is 9:11 in *Ecclesiastes*:

> I returned, and saw under the sun, that the race is not to the swift, nor the battle to the strong, neither yet bread to the wise, nor yet riches to men of understanding, nor yet favour to men of skill; but time and chance happeneth to them all.

So, setbacks will happen to each of us also. We too will lose jobs, we too will lose loved ones, often we too will not get what we want, what we think we deserve.

There is a Russian proverb– 'When difficulties come your way, put them to work'. Often we are stuck in a rut. But we have been in it so long that we have become accustomed to it, we are comfortable in it. That setback is a boon–it jolts us out of those comfortable routines. Actually, it gives us the opportunity, it forces upon us the opportunity to step out of those deadening routines.

Look at the Dalai Lama–revered beyond comprehension, his country captured, the monasteries destroyed, monks tortured and killed, his religion almost erased in his homeland, the Dalai Lama himself forced into exile. He did not sit down, his heart broken, and begin wailing. He has put the calamity to work. He has used that unimaginable reversal in fortunes to save Tibet's great traditions, indeed to spread the light of those traditions and of Buddhism throughout the world. Learning from the Dalai Lama's example, confronted with a reversal we are not to sit down, moaning. We have to actively seize the opportunity. We have to think, to think deeply about the new thing that we should do. And we have to do it–however difficult or pointless it may seem at first.

Think of the new ways that you can adopt, think of the new direction that you should take. Do not give in. I will tell you how this was driven into me once again last year. Anita, my wife–who along with our son, Adit, is my life–was dangerously ill. She had been in the intensive care unit (ICU) for weeks. She was unconscious, she had become so weak that she could not expel or swallow even the secretions that were accumulating in her throat. As a result, breathing was becoming more and more difficult. The doctors and nurses would extract the secretions through suction tubes. But even this became very difficult.

One afternoon, they told me that she could choke to death that night, that the only alternative was to put her on a ventilator. In those Covid days, we had heard all sorts of frightening accounts about persons who had been put on ventilators, that it was excruciating; worse that once you were on a ventilator, you just did not survive. Because they are very close to each other, because they love each other dearly, I rang up Anita's sisters and brother. Each of them said, 'No, no ventilator under any circumstances. She has suffered so much in her life. We must not put her through more agony.'

The doctor in the ICU asked me what we had decided. I said that I would first like to hear the opinion of four doctors whose judgement I had come to trust in those dreadful weeks. So, the four doctors gathered in the corridor outside the ICU. Among them was Samiran Nundy, one of our dearest friends, a renowned surgeon and the Dean of the hospital. When I said that I would first like to hear their opinion, he said, 'No, you tell us what you people have decided.' I told them that I had consulted Anita's sisters and brother and everyone was of the view that we should not put her through the trauma of a ventilator. So, no ventilator.

Samiran shot back, 'Arun is talking nonsense. He does not know anything about the subject. He is going by the opinion of his family, who also know nothing about the matter. We put patients on ventilators every day, and they come out of the procedure. So, put Anita on a ventilator immediately.' He was the Big Boss at the hospital. So for a deathly moment, everyone was silent. Then a junior doctor spoke up. Addressing me, he said, 'But it is my duty, Sir, to inform you that, with Mrs. Shourie having had Parkinson's for thirty years, if we put her on a ventilator, there is only a 10 per cent chance that we will be able to take her off it.'

'YES,' said Samiran, his voice raised. 'There IS a 10 per cent chance. I never give up. I always fight to the end. Put her on the ventilator. Immediately.' She was put on the ventilator. On the third day, they were able to take her off it. She survived. In two weeks after that, we were able to bring her home.

So, never give up. Fight to the end.

At such times, when blows strike, remember first of all what the Bible said in the lines I quoted, that 'time and chance happeneth *to them all*'—you are not being singled out. So, no reason to sit down, pitying yourself, feeling persecuted. Second, bring to mind the calumny, the enormous hardships, the physical and mental agony that were hurled on the very greatest and noblest persons who have ever lived. The Buddha had to face false allegations of the worst kind—including the calumny that he had made a young girl pregnant, and then had her killed. Not one but three attempts were made to assassinate him; Jesus was nailed to the cross; Gandhiji was assassinated; Sri Ramakrishna and Ramana Maharshi suffered all sorts of ailments and in the end, both died painfully of cancer.

And not just these saints of the spirit. Think of Nelson Mandela, a nobler person, and a more regal person can scarcely be imagined; and yet, twenty-seven years in prison. Think of Aleksandr Solzhenitsyn—the years in deathly slave labour camps, the starvation, the beatings in Siberia. But they persevered. What are our difficulties compared to what they had to bear?

When you have suffered a blow, when you are feeling sorry for yourself, look around, and notice—notice deeply—the thousands and thousands who are at that very moment having to cope with even greater hardship and suffering than the one that has fallen on you. That looking around does not just put our difficulties in perspective, it also gives us the opportunity to deal with it.

The sentence to remember is one of the Dalai Lama's pearls of wisdom—'If you want to be truly selfish, help someone.' When we set out to help someone, our mind throws up a hundred reasons why we need not do so, indeed, why we *should* not do so—'Why does he not help himself? Why are his brothers not doing more for him? He is the one who has brought this upon himself—why has he been wasting his time? He never helps anyone, why should anyone help him?' Whether true or not as far as that person is concerned, as far as we are concerned, these are just excuses, excuses for not getting out of our comfortable chairs and helping.

So when we set out to help another person, we get to see our mind. And seeing the mind is the first step to controlling it. And controlling the mind is the first step to happiness.

But if we help someone who is a big fellow—a prime minister, a rich man—the counsel does not work. Time goes by and we begin to feel, 'I did so much for him, I got him out of such deep trouble; three years have gone by and he has not raised even a little finger to help me with my problem.' No therapeutic effect.

So, I have been impertinent enough to add a few words to the Dalai Lama's counsel 'If you want to be truly selfish, help someone who cannot do anything for you in return'—the poorest of poor persons, a handicapped child. The help you render will help you no end, it will transform you.

That is the lesson I have learnt by serving Anita and our son, Adit, the lesson that has given meaning to my life.

In the end, here is a Sufi story to remember—I read it perhaps in one of Idris Shah's books. Two prisoners are locked in a cell. It is their last night. At dawn, as the first rays of the sun hit the prison walls, each is to be executed with one slash of the executioner's sword. They are downcast, silent. Their uneaten food is lying before them. Suddenly, from the street below come shouts of the town-crier:

> His Majesty, the Emperor is looking for someone who in a week can train his horse to fly. He will give half his kingdom to the one who does so. But if someone comes forth, takes the precious time of His Royal Highness, raises his hopes, and then fails to make the horse fly, that person will be put to death in the most painful way—his skin will be peeled off, molten lead will be poured down his throat, flames will be put to his limbs....

People in the street turn away. Who can make a horse fly?

But one of the prisoners jumps up, scurries to the barred window, and shouts that he will make the horse fly.

There is commotion in the street. The town-crier takes down his particulars and leaves. 'You will hear from the court about the time and date,' he shouts to the prisoner as he leaves.

'You damned fool,' shouts the second prisoner. 'Why did you accept the challenge? Who can make a horse fly? Tomorrow, we would have died painlessly—one swish of the sword, and gone. Now you will be put to the most horrible death.'

'You are right, my friend,' said the prisoner. 'But a week is a long time: The King may change his mind; the King may die; or, the horse *may* fly.'

So, when in difficulties, don't lose heart, never give up, fight to the end. Always remember: *the horse may fly!*

2

Three Workplaces and Lessons Learned

P. CHIDAMBARAM

I must confess that I have never held a 'job' in the sense that I was in a 'master and servant' relationship. Unless, of course, I count the summer job in New York between the first and second year of a graduate course at university.

I qualified as a lawyer, acquired an MBA degree abroad, and promptly returned to India with the intent to join the family business in Tamil Nadu. Four was a crowd, and things did not work out. Five months later and married, I joined as a 'junior' in the chambers of a distinguished senior advocate, and his son, both of whom had a substantial and flourishing practice. Consistent with the practice in Chennai, there was no 'job' and no 'salary'. It was work round the clock, work on Saturday, and work on half of Sunday. One accepted whatever the senior gave you every month, and in austere Chennai, the sum I was given was quite generous. Our expenses were limited; for example, it cost Rs 100–150 to drive our Ambassador car for a whole month.

At work, I learned my first lesson—in an inversion of Parkinson's Law, 'time expands to do the work that had to be done'. I also learned that human capacity is elastic, expandable, and can breach assumed limits. I have lived by these lessons all my working life, which I believe is not over yet. I have tried to pass on the lessons to others who worked with me. Many absorbed the lessons and were pleasantly surprised by the discovery. Some did not or would not. In my notebook, the former were the winners. The winners went far and accomplished much. The names—I shall withhold them—are easily recognisable. Many of them were recognised by the government of the day and were conferred the highest civilian honours of the country. Those who did not learn the lessons were, in my book, the shirkers.

If I count my 'workplaces', there are three—courts of law, political party, and government. The environment and the rules of each workplace are different. In a single day, I found myself moving from one workplace to another. I was reminded of N. R. Narayana Murthy's pithy observation a few years after he co-founded Infosys in Pune/Bengaluru, 'Every morning, I travel from the third world to the first world and travel back in the evening to the third world.' Very true. He was referring to his home in Pune/Bengaluru in 1981–1983 that was in a third world town and the commute to his office in which the founders had created a first-world work environment.

Courts of Law

I learned several lessons in a court of law. I learned good advocacy. I learned the merit of simple and clear speech. I learned the value of extensive research (with only books and law reports at that time). I learned to draft petitions. I learned court craft. I learned the value of perseverance. All these I learned from fellow lawyers and the titans of the profession by observing them closely as they argued their cases.

Courts of law in 1969 had primitive infrastructure, a leisurely pace of work, and high ethical standards. There were formal rules for everything. Legal contest was according to rules. Decisions invariably followed the letter of the law and precedent. I learned the need for, and value of, patience and abiding by the law, even if the letter of the law seemed, at times, unjust. The people I worked with were normal men (and a few women) with normal strengths and weaknesses. I learned that losing one's patience or temper—which I did quite often in the early years—did not yield results in the short or long run.

The concept of 'law firm' was mostly absent in Chennai. It was an individual-centred profession, and I believe it largely remains so today. One either succeeded or failed. As one grew in the profession, one took in 'juniors'. A capable junior would grow into a competent and successful lawyer. I took few juniors because I liked to work personally on every brief that I accepted. I declined to take more work than I could personally handle—a principle that I follow until this day.

Over time, the infrastructure of courts of law as workplaces has vastly improved. Technology has made access easier. Young lawyers are intrepid. The quality of advocacy, especially of those graduating from the premier law schools, is exceptional. I find that lawyers are versatile in different branches of law. Women lawyers have proved they are equal to men. Yet, there is something lacking, and that is a sense of complete justice. I have been in cases where my advocacy failed and my client lost the case, but I left with the satisfaction that complete justice had been done between the parties. Even at that time, there were, unfortunately, some exceptions but, in the present time, the exceptions have multiplied. There are too many cases where justice has not been delivered (especially in criminal cases) and appeals and further appeals have increased manifold.

If a young law graduate wishes to be a good lawyer, he or she must be willing to be patient, put in long hours of study and research, hone one's speaking and writing skills, and accept success or defeat in a case with equanimity. I recall a colourful lawyer explain an adverse judgment to his client—the honourable judge has passed an order permitting you to file an appeal!

One's accomplishments as a lawyer can be summed up by reading the law reports. N. A. Palkhivala, M. K. Nambiar, F. S. Nariman, S. Sorabjee, and many others may not have left behind huge wealth but what they left behind—the reported cases in the law reports, the lectures, and the books—was far greater wealth than assets or money.

Political Party

My second workplace—politics and a political party—is a unique place. Politics is not kind to everyone; or kind to anyone all the time. I have experienced kindness and unkindness. There is no gainsaying that politics, political parties, and political behaviour have changed for the worse over the last five decades.

Some conclusions can be unhesitatingly drawn—1. Ideology is dead; 2. Loyalty to a party or to a leader is practically dead; and 3. The sole goal of politics is to win and retain power. If politics and your work as a politician result in good outcomes for the country and the people, count yourself lucky.

Currently, there is no ideology or principle that distinguishes one political party from another. That is why politicians find it easy to defect from party A to party B and re-defect from party B to party A. That is also why a political party is able to easily welcome defectors and reward them. There are many constituencies in which there is a 're-match' between two individuals who contested against each other in the previous election and are contesting against each other again—after switching political parties and exchanging election symbols. Party workers also do not seem averse to crossing the fence along with their leader. Voters also vote for a defecting candidate despite the fact that the candidate had changed parties. There is no 'embarrassment' or 'shame' in politics. I am afraid we have plumbed the depths of political immorality.

The driving forces behind politics at the individual level and at the organisational level are power and money. A politician denied power will happily settle for money. Politics has become a lucrative business if one knows how to operate the levers. It is not individuals alone; political parties also crave to become rich. Those are the reasons why there is corruption. Those are also the reasons why politicians and political parties befriend rich people and rich companies. The politician's justification is that fighting elections, running a party, and nursing a constituency require money. That is very true. There are solutions but no political party is willing to explore them. The so-called solution—electoral bonds—turned out to be the most corrupt solution to the problem, besides creating a treacherous, unlevel playing field for the opposition political parties.

If there is one word that characterises most political activities, it is betrayal. Betrayal is common among colleagues and friends. Betrayal of ideology is now commonplace. Betrayal of one's conscience is the road to corruption. If one wishes to be active in politics, one must be prepared to encounter betrayal and deal with it.

I hope that as India grows into a developed country and there is more equitable distribution of wealth, and the people are more educated, politics will return to the days when honourable men and women steered the politics of the country. I can pass on two lessons that I have learnt:

1. Find an innovative solution to the issue of funding of political parties and funding elections.
2. Impose, by law, term limits for every political office, starting with the prime minister and chief ministers. A limit of two terms is reasonable.

Government

As far as I am concerned, the most interesting place of work was the government. Starting as a junior minister, I held various portfolios, including finance and home. I have interacted with hundreds of officers. I admired many of them and I enjoyed working with them. On the other hand, many officers flew into and flew out of my professional life as minister and left no impression on me.

The relationship between a minister and a civil servant is complex. Both enjoy different degrees of power and hence the relationship is largely influenced by how the power is exercised by the minister and the civil servant. Knowledge of the subject or lack of knowledge adds to, or detracts from, the power. The best and most productive pair will respect each other's knowledge and capability, and work to accomplish some pre-determined objectives or goals. Unfortunately, government is not as organised as a well-functioning company—in many ministries/departments, there are no clear objectives, no plan of action, no progress chart, and little is accomplished by the end of the tenure. Political uncertainty surrounding a minister, or the government as a whole, dampens the spirit and darkens the path—as a result, little is accomplished.

The best teams of minister and civil servants, working in an environment of mutual trust and respect, can deliver outstanding results. Examples are the prime minister's office, the ministry of finance, and the ministry of commerce in 1991–1992. The government had great teams in some ministries in 2004–2009. It is not necessary that personal loyalties should be cultivated or that personal friendships should be forged; it is sufficient if there is mutual trust and respect.

Talent is available at every level. It is well to remember that the later batch of officers, occupying the lower rungs of the bureaucracy, is as educated and competent as the senior batches, and is generally more capable technologically. I found that it was more productive if the junior civil servants were involved in the decision-making process. I did not hesitate to consult them individually or include them in the discussions. The lesson that I would commend is that hierarchies must be disrupted wherever it is possible. While the hierarchy may be respected for keeping in-house law and order, if you want to do anything substantial, break the hierarchy.

Other difficulties may be encountered. The Director General of Foreign Trade may think that liberalisation of exports and imports is wrong, and licensing and controls are necessary. The Disinvestment Secretary may not support disinvestment. The Banking Secretary may think he knows better how to run a bank than the Chairman and Managing Director (CMD) of the bank. The tax-collecting authorities may think that the taxpayer is an enemy who has to be confronted while taxes are extracted from him. These are occupational hazards. The solution is to transfer the official concerned. The process is painful, but the option of retaining the officer and changing his mindset will seriously jeopardise the government's objectives and erode its credibility.

The relationship between a minister and investigating agencies and a minister and independent/autonomous bodies is more complex. The investigating agencies are supposed to be answerable only to the law, but they will grow into unruly horses if the minister or the secretary does not keep a close watch over them. What people tend to forget is that in the Indian parliamentary system it is the minister who is accountable to parliament and the minister who has to answer questions in parliament. If courts pass adverse orders or judgments, it is the government as a whole that will be on the mat. Besides, whether the law is administered fairly, impartially, and in accordance with the fundamental principles of constitutional and criminal law, is a matter that should be of the highest concern to the minister as an elected representative of the people. Look at the gross violations of law as a result of the weaponisation of laws and the pretence that the investigating agencies are independent and do not take their orders from the government. When a minister says that, you can be absolutely certain that the minister is using the investigating agency to transgress the law and harass his political opponents.

In the case of regulatory bodies like the Reserve Bank of India (RBI) and the Securities and Exchange Board of India (SEBI), the relationship is always fraught because the perspectives and objectives are apparently different. Nothing illustrates this better than the fraught relationship between the central bank (RBI, in India) and the ministry of finance in all countries. I have not come across a finance minister or a governor of a central bank anywhere in the world who agreed all the time. The trick is to manage the differences without affecting personal or institutional cordiality. Some ministers and central bank governors succeeded in this difficult task; some others failed, leading to bitterness or resignations. No one has yet found a perfect solution to the fraught relationship between a finance minister and a central bank governor.

Technology is invading every workplace and changing things at a pace that is frenetic. Legal research and access to cases decided in other jurisdictions have become tools in the hands of every lawyer and empowered her—even in small towns—and the competition among lawyers has increased. Political parties are more technologically driven, election battles are fought more on the social media than on the roads of India, and rallies and roadshows have become glitzier. Availability of data and technology has led to micromanagement of elections at the booth level. In government, the technologically abled have gained an advantage over the pure generalist. The lesson is to keep pace with science and technology or perish.

Since I continue to be active in politics and in the practice of law, but no longer in government, I continue to learn new lessons.

3

Teaching, Service, Politics, Governance

A Journey

YASHWANT SINHA

I grew up in Patna in the 1940s and 1950s. Although Patna was the capital of the province of Bihar, it was still considered a mofussil town compared to the metros and other bigger cities. In those days, like today, one had to start looking for a job immediately after finishing one's education, if not before, depending on one's financial circumstances.

This was the era before the IITs and IIMs (the Indian Institutes of Technology and Indian Institutes of Management). The only jobs on offer were the coveted civil services, central and state services, teaching, or a position in Tatas or in a 'box wallah' company (an elite firm). My case was no different. I was very lucky. Soon after my postgraduation in political science, I got my first formal job as a lecturer at Patna University. For a year-and-a-half, I taught my immediate juniors and other students, many of whom were good friends.

I enjoyed it thoroughly, even though, in the beginning, my 'students' had a lot of fun at my expense. Although our career options were limited at the time, my short teaching stint proved to be useful. While teaching, I was able to prepare for the civil service examinations. One lesson from this is to make the most of whatever opportunities, big or small, that come one's way to grow.

I managed to clear the civil service examination in my very first attempt and was placed twelfth in the all-India list. I immediately became a hero in Patna. I was euphoric. I embarked on my new career believing more than ever before that I was really brilliant. The first reality check came at the IAS Academy in Mussoorie. I realised that many of my fellow probationers were far more brilliant and smarter than me. This was an excellent first lesson in humility.

Our salaries were modest then, but adequate to run a home. Our working conditions were quite different from those of today. In that era—the 1960s and early 1970s—we did not have the luxury of air-conditioners or staff cars. The office infrastructure was limited to a typewriter, a telephone, and a litho machine or copier.

The first few years of my civil service career were transformational. I was posted in Arrah in the Shahabad district of my home state of Bihar (then undivided, with present-day Jharkhand being part of the state) as assistant magistrate under training. A few months later, I was posted for survey and settlement work in the same district. Indian Administrative Service officers at that level worked closely with the local people. That gave us, as a friend in the IAS put it, a 'worm's eye view' of life.

This 'worm's eye view' allowed me to gain a deep understanding of the details of how government worked at the grassroots level, so that while framing policies at state or national levels, I could relate them to the real world and its challenges. For example, when the government was acquiring land for the Heavy Engineering Corporation in Ranchi, as a young IAS officer, I walked with the Amin to measure the land, the details of the tenants, and prepared updated land records. It seemed like drudgery then, but this survey and settlement work in the early years would give me a solid grounding in revenue work.

My early work in the civil service was a key learning experience, as I realised years later when I joined politics. Unlike many new lawmakers, I knew how the policy would actually be implemented on the ground. I understood the role and limits of power of a Block Development Officer (BDO), a Sub-Divisional Officer, and others in the bureaucratic chain. This deepened my understanding of the process and the people and enabled me to tap the right people for the right work. What may at first seem to be drudgery or inconsequential may turn out to be useful later—the trick is to keep learning.

My first exposure to finance was as a deputy secretary in the state finance department in Patna. I learnt a great deal, not only about finance at the state level, but also about people and decision-making. One case I recall was when my junior IAS colleague rejected a proposal for setting up a chicken dressing plant. When the file came to me, I was a little intrigued by the description 'chicken dressing plant'. So, I asked my junior colleague if he knew what a chicken dressing plant was all about.

To my great surprise, he confessed that he too did not know anything about the working of such a plant, but had rejected it anyway. For any officer in the finance department, the first instinct is to say 'no' and reject the proposal for some reason or the other. Later, I called the director of the animal husbandry department to explain the proposal. The proposal was a sound one and we approved it. The lesson was that it is important to keep an open mind and get all the information before taking a decision, even in jobs where one is often encouraged to say no to proposals.

In the next two decades, I had several life-altering experiences. In one instance, I was working as deputy commissioner in the Santhal Parganas district (at that time in unified Bihar state, now in Jharkhand). It was 1967 and we were faced with a severe drought. All of us in the administration were struggling to provide relief to the affected people. The Congress party had lost the state assembly elections and Samyukta Vidhayak Dal had formed one of the first coalition governments in the country. The chief minister of the state was Mahamaya Prasad Sinha, a freedom fighter. He visited Dumka, my district headquarters, for official work.

As usual, a crowd had gathered at the circuit house to welcome the chief minister and the accompanying minister. Then began my interrogation. The chief minister waded into me, speaking harshly in front of everyone. I was upset. Unlike other officers, I did not accept the public humiliation quietly; instead, I publicly protested the treatment. My unexpected response surprised and upset him. The meeting ended in chaos.

Soon after, the chief minister and I met in a separate room for tea. He told me that my behaviour was unbecoming: I should not have behaved with him like I did. I replied that he should not have acted the way he did as such a public castigation would undermine the sanctity of the post that I held. That sanctity was important for me to do my job effectively. He angrily retorted that I should look for another job.

I told him, 'That is my option. I can become a chief minister one day, but you cannot become an IAS officer.' My reply was instinctive and immediate. Of course, the consequences were also swift as I was transferred and, predictably, remained in the doghouse for quite a while. But I was convinced that I should stand my ground and refuse to undermine my self-respect. (It was this belief that, many years later in 1990, prompted me to walk out of the Rashtrapati Bhavan. I was General Secretary of the Janata Dal and Prime Minister V. P. Singh had consulted me on the formation of his Cabinet. He had named some of my party colleagues as Cabinet ministers. Yet, he chose to appoint me as only a Minister of State. I walked out of Rashtrapati Bhavan instead of taking the oath.)

I often tell people of the younger generation not to allow anyone, even people in positions of power, to intimidate or insult them. Another piece of advice I offer to young officers is not to compromise on rules of procedure when political bosses seek to cross lines. Throughout my career, in civil service and politics, I have remained firm in my belief that what counts in life is values and self-respect.

A working career can be accident-prone and those accidents in life can be good or bad. Some may call it destiny. In my case, I encountered more of the good. In one instance, I decided to visit my boss at the time–Commerce Secretary K. B. Lall, a famous ICS officer and former Ambassador to the European Economic Community (EEC), whom we affectionately called 'Khuda' or God–to tell him that I was underworked. My friends had warned me against it; they were sure I would be fired. But instead of firing me, 'Khuda' ensured that I was assigned more work. My advice to young people, therefore, would be not to hesitate to approach the boss if you are underworked. That is something people seldom do, but it works.

After K. B. Lall's intervention, my stint in the commerce ministry became more fruitful and I learnt a great deal about international trade and trade negotiations. It soon became the springboard for my next assignment as First Secretary (Commercial) at the Indian Embassy in Bonn, which was then the capital of West Germany, from 1971–1973. This experience influenced some of my subsequent decisions when I was a minister in both the finance ministry and later the foreign office.

During my stay in Germany, I travelled on the high-speed autobahns that connected various parts of the country and parts of Europe. I saw how important infrastructure was to the efficient functioning of the country. Also, I understood the importance of reducing the transaction costs of the economy to make it more competitive. I have always kept myself open to learning from my experiences and after my stint in Germany, those two things stayed with me—the importance of building world-class infrastructure and connectivity and the need to reduce transaction costs or the overall costs of producing and delivering goods and services for the economy. I am proud to have contributed to those goals when the Vajpayee government launched the National Highways Programme and the Golden Quadrilateral, which links the country from north to south and east to west.

In our lives, there are often powerful people who influence us. One such leader in my life was Jayaprakash Narayan, or JP as he was popularly known. In addition to his extraordinary leadership and integrity (for which he was recognised with many awards, including a posthumous Bharat Ratna award), he was also compassionate and observant. Midway through my career, in 1968, I was considering leaving the civil services to join politics. I met JP along with my wife at a friend's place to tell him about my career plans. JP suggested that it would be better to join politics only after my wife was fully on board. He had noticed a tear in the corner of her eye. Of course, I heeded that advice. I signed up for politics many years later, in 1984.

My next *karma bhoomi* was the political arena. I had nothing going for me—neither money nor caste, nor muscle power, nor a political background or legacy. But I was determined to prove that merit also has a place in politics and that I could succeed on merit. By this time, in 1984, JP had passed away. But I always felt that I owed it to him to do more good for the country, and politics is, I always tell young people, one of the most direct ways of working in national interests. I joined the Janata Party and in 1986, I was the party's All-India General Secretary. In 1988, I was elected as a Rajya Sabha member.

Compared to the bureaucracy, in politics and political parties, things were highly disorganised. That did not shock me. I had earlier worked as a secretary to the famous Bihar Chief Minister Karpoori Thakur, who was quite disorganised himself. He was also one of the sharpest men I have ever met in my life—both in civil service and in politics—and had unmatched integrity (known as Jan Nayak, he was recently awarded the Bharat Ratna posthumously). Integrity and simplicity were considered values of great importance in those days.

I recall that as late as the mid-1990s, almost all politicians used to travel by train. Three decades later, it is special or charter planes, the status symbol of security cover, and top-of-the-line SUVs that distinguish many netas. After forty years, I must say that the political climate has deteriorated, and everything is designed with an eye on the polls and winning.

In November 1990, I became finance minister in the short-lived Chandra Shekhar government. It was a tough initiation into the world of economic management as the economy was on the brink of bankruptcy.

In 1990 and the early months of 1991, India's foreign exchange reserves were dangerously low and we were faced with a severe economic crisis due to a balance of payments deficit. We had two choices. As the minority government, we could have bought time and kicked the can down the road for another government to take some difficult decisions. Or we could take some difficult decisions ourselves and act immediately to ensure that there were enough reserves for the next government to subsequently take the next steps.

I felt it would have been irresponsible on my part to take the easy option or to abdicate at such a crucial juncture. I did not want to leave the country's foreign exchange reserves empty. I decided to act. In that short period in office as India's Finance Minister, I was clear that we could not allow the country to default on its international repayment commitments, nor did I want to dent India's prestige in the global economic community. We made the critical decision to pledge a substantial portion of our gold as collateral to secure foreign exchange. This move enabled us to fulfil our financial obligations and bring some much-needed stability to the economy.

The decision to pledge our gold during that critical period was controversial and troubled me for a long time. But I do not regret it one bit. What many people do not recognise is that the first tranche of gold that was mortgaged to the Bank of England was gold confiscated from smugglers and held by the State Bank of India. (A decision to pledge gold from the Reserve Bank of India's [RBI] reserves had also been taken on file, but it was executed later when Manmohan Singh was the finance minister.)

One of the most important lessons in government is that if you have to repair the mess created by others (including previous governments), do what you are convinced is right and move on. It is important to deal with these decisions or issues philosophically, adopting a more pragmatic approach to avoid repeating the mistakes of the past.

The trust and faith of the prime minister are also critical. No finance minister can be effective without the full backing of the prime minister, as the finance minister must deal with political conflicts with colleagues, which can wear you down. I joined the Bharatiya Janata Party (BJP) and was elected to the Lok Sabha from Hazaribagh, Jharkhand. In 1998, I was appointed Finance Minister in Prime Minister Atal Bihari Vajpayee's government. When discussing the Union budgets with me, Prime Minister Vajpayee would never ask about the political impact of a proposal on the party. Instead, he would just ask how good it was for the country. He was a fantastic boss.

Again, this was a critical time. To further our global security goals, India conducted nuclear tests in May 1998. In response, the US and several other countries imposed economic sanctions on India. We knew there would be severe challenges on the economic front, yet I was proud that we were now a nuclear weapons State and was convinced that it was a sacrifice worth making and was ready to face the consequences. We coped with the crisis with several measures, including by boosting domestic production and industry, and implementing fiscal reforms. Our response was steely, and this later led to the sanctions being withdrawn.

Being successful in politics means managing relationships with people. During the balance of payments crisis in 1990 and 1991, it is important to note that the finance ministry and the RBI worked in tandem. This teamwork made all the difference. In our long history, there have been many instances of conflict between finance ministers and RBI Governors. Yet, I enjoyed a harmonious relationship with Governor Bimal Jalan and his deputy, Y. V. Reddy. Jalan had rich experience, and Reddy was respected for his expertise. The key to strengthening institutional ties is, I believe, to build on personal relationships too. The fact that I used to consult Jalan on many issues outside the RBI's remit is a measure of the excellent working relationship that we had.

As a minister, I had IAS officials in my team who had been my seniors in the IAS, yet I was now their minister and they reported to me. I was in a unique position, and I made an effort to show respect to my IAS colleagues. They, in turn, reciprocated and we got along well. At work, although I believed in hierarchy to the extent it was needed, I did not hesitate to adopt the concept of level jumping—to seek the views of mid-level or junior officers. My advice to them was to express their opinions freely, and if I disagreed, I would write a note explaining why. What I looked for among officers was the integrity of advice and hard work.

The role as Minister of External Affairs (2002–2004) was thoroughly enjoyable as I dealt with the wider world. I encouraged officers to prioritise economic work in tune with a growing economy.

It was a learning experience in gaining a better understanding of global issues.

These days, more young people from the civil service are leaving the civil service to enter politics. I am not sure what motivates them to do this. My only advice to them is to first work and gain professional experience and be financially independent.

After over five decades of work in public service and public life, I would say that if anyone gets an opportunity or is given some responsibility in public life, accept it, always keeping national interests in mind. That is what matters. Not gaining positions nor winning or losing elections.

Part II

Private Sector

4

Product of Values

NARAYANA MURTHY

My values in working life have been influenced by my parents, my early teachers, and my bosses. Almost all the values I practised at Infosys came from these people.

The earliest memory of this was in 1960 when I was in my 10th grade in Sharada Vilas High School in Mysore. When the results of the mid-term examinations were released, I took it to my father who was wedded to discipline in everything he did. He was a high school teacher who taught Physics, Mathematics, and English. While I had done well in mathematics and science subjects, I was not the first in the class in history, geography, and civics.

My father generally did not show affection to his children, nor did he openly appreciate any of our achievements. But he did express much pride about us in private to our mother. He came from the old school that believed any such appreciation of children from parents was likely to swell the heads of the children. So, with a deep sense of trepidation, I talked about my top performance in science and mathematics. Then, in a low voice, I told him that I was not the top student in history, civics, and geography.

He thought for a moment and asked me to show him my timetable for studying at home. I was completely lost and sheepishly admitted that I had no timetable for home studies. He visibly showed his disappointment in me. He said that every student had to practise the discipline of preparing a timetable for home studies since it would force the student to devote adequate time even to subjects that he or she did not like. He went on to say that a diligent student would allot more time in his timetable to subjects that he did not like much and was therefore weak in.

He further said that my mother had told him about my improvement in studies, and that the only way I could aim higher was by creating a suitable timetable and having the discipline to follow it without fail. Having said these few words, he went away for his siesta.

Preparing a timetable for home studies was very valuable advice. It helped me overcome my weakness in arts subjects and perform better in the Secondary School Leaving Certificate (SSLC) examination. Following a timetable for studies translates to strict discipline. I would recommend this timetable regimen to every student who aims high. Such a focus on discipline helped me devote time to every one of my functions at Infosys, right from the beginning—leadership and foundation level training, employee issues, sales, finance, human resource development, software development, quality, productivity, excellence, planning, physical, technological infrastructure, and visitor management.

My father taught me another important value. That was to aim higher and higher no matter how well you did. Those days, the 11th grade public examinations, or SSLC examinations, were conducted during the third week of March and the results were announced in May. Those days, the top 10 ranks in the state would be announced in newspapers the next morning. We did not subscribe to any newspaper at home. My neighbour came rushing to our home, showed me my name in the newspaper and congratulated me for obtaining the fourth rank in the SSLC exam.

My father had already left for the office. My mother, brothers, sisters, and my paternal grandmother were happy. My father returned home that night around 8 PM. I was quite excited to go and tell him about my success in the SSLC examination. His reaction was not what I expected. With a serious look, he asked me, 'What happened to the other three ranks?', and went away to wash his face.

I ran to my mother, told her what had happened, and asked her why my father did not show any happiness. My mother told me that it was his way of encouraging me to aim higher in my next examination. She also told me that my father believed in continuous improvement and that he wanted to encourage me to get the first rank not just in Karnataka but in the entire country. This value that I learnt from my father is what led me to strive for excellence in everything we did at Infosys.

It is fair to say that K. V. Narayan (KVN), the headmaster of Sharada Vilas High School during the 1950s and 1960s, taught me the most important value necessary for good governance in a corporation. KVN taught chemistry in my SSLC class. Three of my friends and I sat on the front bench. KVN would conduct chemistry experiments on his table in the class.

One day, he was conducting an experiment that required putting some sodium chloride (common salt) into a test tube. KVN took quite some time to carefully pour a minimum amount of salt into a test tube. He appeared very stingy with the salt. That made my friend Anantha Srinivasa Prasad burst out laughing. KVN stopped the experiment, came to our bench, and sternly asked my friend why he laughed. Generally, children tend to be more honest than elders. So, Prasad answered that KVN's care in pouring the inexpensive common salt into the test tube had made him laugh.

KVN said,

> Young man, this common salt is the property of this school. This community property belongs to you, to me, the sixty students in this class, every teacher, every student and every one of this school. This is the property of this community. Therefore, I must treat it more carefully than I treat my personal property. Please come with me to my house after the class. I will give you a free jar of common salt. I can be generous with it because it is my property.

What KVN said that day has had a deep influence on me. It showed me that in a civilised society, people will treat their community property better than their personal property. This important lesson from my high school days led to my focus on the fundamental principles of corporate governance at Infosys. I took much more care in spending Infosys money than I took in spending my own money. This is a very important principle for developing countries such as India where public resources are treated with scant respect, often leading to corruption. The result is that little attention is paid to the quality of community infrastructure projects.

Another important value that I learnt from my father and my teachers at the National Institute of Engineering (NIE) in Mysore was that we, the educated citizens, should discuss contentious issues in a civilised manner with the authorities rather than wasting our precious time and our parents' hard-earned money by resorting to strikes and violence. An incident that brought this value is etched indelibly in my memory. It was a student strike in 1964 against a fee hike. I spoke to my father and some of my teachers. They advised me that the right method for students was to hold a dialogue with the authorities, find out what the reasons were, and then come to a civilised and peaceful solution to the problem.

My father also told me that being a National Scholarship holder, I had to set an example by attending college classes. I told my classmates that I believed in this and that I would not participate in the student strike. It so happened that I was the only student in my 'Strength of Materials' class that day. My parents were worried that I would become the victim of violence by rival students. But I had the resolve to do what my teachers and parents felt were right. Many of my classmates were very upset with me. But none of them could answer me about how their method of not attending classes and going and watching movies would reduce the fee.

I was also disappointed with the attitude of some of my classmates who would show disrespect to teachers and create havoc in the classroom with their pranks. These were the worst performers in the examinations. They rarely attended classes. None of them rose to be good engineers. Today, most of them repent their misbehaviour as students and advise their children to be disciplined. I feel that students should focus only on studies during their student days. They may spend time on sports and cultural activities during their free time. I do not believe that they should align themselves with any political party. Their parents spend their hard-earned money on the education of their children. The least the children can do is to do their best in studies and make their parents happy.

My mother taught me the importance of generosity. My mother would often tell us stories about characters from the Mahabharata. I remember one incident. That day, she took us to watch a night-long play called *Daanashoora Karna* (the warrior of philanthropy). There were tears in our eyes during scenes depicting the meeting of Kunti, the mother, with Karna, the abandoned son. The drama highlighted the generosity of Karna.

Pretty soon, I was confronted with a dilemma. After my second year of engineering, my mother had given me about Rs 50 from my scholarship amount of Rs 900 to get a Terylene pair of trousers and a Terylene bush shirt. I got them stitched, had not used them, and saved them for wearing on a special occasion. A couple of months later, my brother, Vasu, obtained a job as a lecturer in Economics at Poorna Prajna College in Udupi. But he did not have proper clothes to wear. My mother got him a pair of trousers and a white shirt. In addition, she requested me to give my new clothes to Vasu so that he could take them to Udupi.

I began thinking and did not take any action till the evening. Vasu had to leave for Udupi the next morning. My mother sat down with me that night and asked me what I had learnt from the drama, *Daanashoora Karna*, and how I was going to translate that lesson into action. She was very gentle and told me that the greatest joy is in giving and not receiving. Finally, I agreed to give my new dress to Vasu. Vasu went on to do a brilliant Ph.D. in the US and has settled down there since 1964.

From then onwards, I began being called *Paropakaari* Papanna (*Paropakaari* means somebody who helps others; Papanna was my nickname at home). I am glad that I lived up to my mother's expectations. It is the habit of generosity that my mother inculcated in me that made me give 15 per cent equity of Infosys to my juniors.

I learnt much from my boss, Professor Krishnayya (JGK), at the Indian Institute of Management Ahmedabad (IIMA). Professor Krishnayya had graduated from the Massachusetts Institute of Technology (MIT) and was, perhaps, the most innovative professor at the IIMA during the late 1960s and the early 1970s. He introduced impactful new ideas in everything he did. He chose HP 2000A, a time-sharing system, for the IIMA. This was the third such system in a business school after Stanford and Harvard in 1969. It was also the first time-sharing system in India.

I learnt from JGK that glory and credit must be shared if you want your team to be enthusiastic to take up aspirational projects and work hard and smart. JGK and I had presented a paper in a conference in Rome on an advanced technical issue in real time system design and our paper was adjudged the best. JGK was generous to give the credit for the paper, which he and I worked on, entirely to me.

The manager of the session was a Frenchman who was a director in a well-known French real-time software company. He offered me a position as one of the eighteen-member team building an operating system to handle air cargo for the new Charles de Gaulle airport. An important lesson I learnt from JGK is that a good leader is generous and shares credit with his or her team. This is what I tell young entrepreneurs.

There are several other lessons I learnt from JGK. Let me mention just two that have helped in my running Infosys for more than thirty years. JGK believed in starting every transaction on a zero base and not being affected by the histories of bias from prior transactions. In other words, he started every transaction with a fully open mind to appreciate if the idea had merit.

The second was that he used data and facts to judge every transaction on its merit without considering the title, position, or the power of the party that he was starting the transaction with. These two principles, when used by me, gave everybody at Infosys confidence that data and facts alone decided each transaction and that failure in a prior transaction did not create any bias against the individual. I believe these principles are extremely important for teamwork in India.

I can go on and on with what I have learnt from my parents, my teachers, and my bosses. I can confidently say that I am a product of the values that I learnt from these people. I remain grateful to them forever.

5

Continuing to Learn

K. V. Kamath

While pursuing my mechanical engineering degree at the National Institute of Technology, Surathkal, I always thought I would have a career in business because I was already managing a small tile manufacturing unit owned by my family. However, attending the Indian Institute of Management at Ahmedabad in 1969 opened my eyes to a wider world. My journey to ICICI Bank was largely because of the initiative of one of my finance professors, who forwarded my CV to the institution. I liked what I saw, and perhaps they liked what they saw in me, and this led to a long career at ICICI.

What I learnt at ICICI's project department is foundational to everything I do today. I was privileged to be mentored by S. S. Nadkarni, then chief of the department. He taught me almost everything I know about appraising projects, conducting economic analyses, and taking a 360-degree view of any proposal that comes before me.

From project finance, he pushed me into leasing, for which he arranged a short stint at a leasing institution in London, exposing me to a wide range of financial practices. During these early years, I quickly realised that what we learnt in business school was not readily applicable in a business context. While foundational principles had been taught, their application in day-to-day situations had to be learnt on the job. There was a collaborative spirit in the institution, and this allowed me to learn how to translate foundational knowledge into practical applications. There was also a great degree of delegation, and this taught me to in turn delegate to my colleagues as I assumed leadership positions.

My first exposure to entrepreneurship was the result of setting up the leasing function at ICICI. We established this as an independent unit with its own profit line. To manage this business, which required extensive computation for each lease quote, I requested a small computer. This was my first exposure to technology, and using early 1980s desktop computers, just three or four of us ran the department as a paperless office.

My education continued when N. Vaghul joined ICICI as Chairman in 1985. He asked me to set up a strategy department, head the treasury, and induct technology into the organisation. The next three years were full of excitement as his vision for ICICI was executed by the strategy department. At the same time, the treasury function began raising resources from the global marketplace. We also made ICICI a technology-enabled organisation.

This period was as exciting as my stint in project finance at the institution. During this time, I was privileged to learn from two brilliant leaders, each with a distinctive style. I particularly remember an anecdote from when Vaghul was joining the institution. One day, he called me to discuss a leasing opportunity. Although we had been in the business for a few years, at that time we were only considering reasonably sized leases. This particular proposal was about ten times the size of our normal leasing limit, although well within our lending capacity. I mentioned this to him. He paused for a moment and very gently asked me, 'Should we then not reconsider the limit?' At that moment, I learnt that we needed to evaluate opportunities as they arise within the boundaries of risk.

I received an offer to work at the Asian Development Bank (ADB), and Vaghul suggested that I keep a lien on my job at ICICI and proceed. This was my first experience working in an international organisation. The ADB exposed me to a wide variety of cultures because of its international staffing and provided me with an in-depth look at the developmental processes in East Asia, Southeast Asia, and China. This was a valuable learning experience that proved beneficial later in my career. For example, our early move into retail lending was inspired by observing the rise of retail credit across East and Southeast Asia. I was convinced that this trend would very soon extend to India and we needed to be prepared to seize this opportunity.

In 1996, I returned to ICICI Bank at the board's invitation to become its Managing Director and CEO. This was a turbulent time, as the economy had opened up a few years earlier, presenting significant challenges to old Indian companies that were unprepared for the new competitive landscape. Reinvention was the only path to survival.

ICICI reinvented itself by first rebranding and raising resources from the public. We created a new brand identity, new colours, and launched our safety bonds. However, we realised that long-term project finance using short-term money from the marketplace was risky. The only way forward was to address the growing need for retail credit. Observing a surge in demand for retail credit in the late 1990s in India, we decided to become a universal bank, focusing on retail-facing businesses and new opportunities such as investment banking, asset management, venture capital, and insurance.

During this transformation, we recognised a pressing need for capital. With the Indian market having dried up, we proposed listing on the New York Stock Exchange and issuing American Depository Receipts (ADRs). Despite investment bankers advising us that this process would take two to three years, we wanted to accomplish it in less than three months. We worked round the clock with teams of investment bankers, lawyers, and accountants. We aligned our accounts to US GAAP, prepared the prospectus, and presented it to global investors, successfully listing on the New York Stock Exchange and raising capital within ninety days. Thus, the '90-day rule' came into being. According to this, all technology and other projects would have to be executed within ninety days.

To drive retail business, we merged the parent ICICI Ltd. and the subsidiary ICICI Bank, forming the new ICICI Bank. This structural change was crucial and supported by the Reserve Bank of India. Alongside this, we undertook massive technology induction, rolling out 1,000 ATMs (automated teller machines) in a year and creating back offices to handle branch functions. We partnered with the National Institute of Information Technology to offer a training programme for aspirants and with Manipal University for a one-year programme to train mid-management staff. These were exciting times, showcasing the power of technology and the potential of India's human capital.

India's rapid growth presented further opportunities. One was the country's internationalisation, which led us to expand globally. The second, more exciting opportunity was banking the unbanked, targeting 600 million Indians without bank access. Our strategy was to use technology to reach this large customer base, despite challenges due to issues such as data connectivity and cost-effective technology.

A core strength of ICICI has been its professional staff—a pipeline built over nearly fifty years, which is periodically replenished. Building teams taught me that one could work with professionals in their early thirties who consistently exceeded expectations. We also recognised the power of a gender-neutral organisation. I have often been asked about the effort required to build a gender-neutral organisation. The task is simple yet difficult. It starts with establishing a thought process where every job is considered gender-neutral, followed by putting in place practices that uphold this neutrality, from recruitment through evaluation to career progression. That is the simple part. The difficult part is implementing it. This you achieve by aligning everyone in the organisation to the goal.

The most important learning of this period in my career was that a leader succeeds only when the right teams are in place. It was not uncommon for me to spend a good one-third of my time on human resource matters. You do this right and a strong leadership pipeline develops.

The global financial crisis of 2008 presented a significant challenge. Despite India having no role in causing it, the country felt its impact. Looking back, India weathered the crisis fairly well.

My learning continued even after stepping down as ICICI's chief executive. I joined various national and international boards, broadening my horizons. In 2015, at the age of sixty-eight, I was invited to be the president of the New Development Bank, popularly known as the BRICS Bank. Moving to Shanghai and working with colleagues from four other countries to establish an international development bank was an entirely new learning experience. Balancing different cultures, customs, and government approaches, I had to act as both a banker and a diplomat. This experience deepened my understanding and exposed me to the development processes in emerging economies.

My greatest takeaway from my tenure at the BRICS Bank was realising the strength of collective action among nations of the South. Despite having an average credit rating of just about investment grade, collectively we achieved an AA+ rating. This taught me that the nations of the South are much stronger together than can be imagined.

Looking back, I realise I have been privileged to witness the transformation of India's financial sector, led by a growing economy, evolving technology, and demand for new products. It is hard to imagine the financial sector as it was just a few years back. With advancements such as straight-through processing, the unified payments interface (UPI), and open-source digital tools, the financial sector is poised for further transformation in the coming years.

It has been a journey of continuous learning. The greatest joy of my career has been the opportunity to learn. Looking back at all these learning experiences and the people who provided me with these experiences, I have much to be thankful for. I have learned more than I could ever hope to give back.

6

Village Teachers and Hallowed Institutions

G. N. Rao

When I look back, I feel that I have had a wonderful life—a very supportive family at every step, loving friends at all stages of my life; and excellent teachers, both formal and informal. I am also fortunate that the journey took me through different geographic, cultural, and socioeconomic milieus at various points in my life.

I spent the first ten years of my life in Edupugallu, a village in Krishna district in coastal Andhra Pradesh. My grandmother was gravely ill, and her needs occupied my mother's time. So, at a very young age, I was sent to live with my aunt and uncle. I enjoyed the love and affection of my extended family and gained an instinctive understanding of how rural communities were so close-knit. Those years gave me a strong foundation for my later years. The love and affection for each other and the simplicity of needs, sometimes combined with complex personalities, enriched my experience. This was when an understanding of our traditions and culture was ingrained into me.

I also developed some independence because I was living away from my parents. I am told that, as a young child, I would sit on the stone bench outside our home. When passers-by asked me my name, I would reply, 'Gandhi'. And so, Gandhi was the only name by which many in that village knew me.

Another aspect of growing up in a village was the close relationship with children of all communities, playing together, unmindful of backgrounds. Lunch breaks were in the farms next to the school. We would climb trees to pick fruit together. When we had to attend traditional ceremonies and events in neighbouring villages, we would travel on specially decorated bullock carts. In the school, we wrote using slates and chalk, and played games like kabbadi. These remain my cherished childhood memories.

Later in life, this background helped me empathise with people from rural areas who came to me for treatment. This shared history was critical in providing proper care to them, irrespective of their background. It also helped me while designing the rural care arm of our L. V. Prasad Eye Institute.

The next building block in my growth was my move to Guntur, an urban town, in 1955. My parents believed in the importance of a good education and being content with what life offered. My father, having struggled in his early years, highly valued a good education. Regular hours and habits were the norm at our home. Going to any destination in town by foot was another norm. Growing up with three siblings and half-a-dozen cousins at any given time, I enjoyed all the benefits of a large family—love and affection, and a caring environment. Hordes of relatives from our native villages would regularly visit us and this made for a wonderful environment to grow up in.

My father had settled in Guntur to practice as an ophthalmologist, and I was admitted to the excellent Hindu High School in 1955. Some lifelong friendships were formed at this time. The teachers there were excellent and committed. My science, Telugu, and maths teachers left a lasting impression. The English teacher liked me and made me do additional exercises in grammar. This motivated me to learn English. I began reading *The Hindu* newspaper to improve my English vocabulary and listening to the English news on All India Radio to refine my accent.

I finished school in 1959 and found myself next in the Andhra Christian College in Guntur. Here, the teachers were very good in every subject. There were teachers with doctorates, and there were teachers who were popular poets, and they all wanted to impart knowledge to students. One of them was Jandhyala Papayya Sastri, a renowned Telugu poet. With doctorates in English, Thomas and Rosaiah were superb teachers. Their instruction included every aspect of teaching a foreign language, including how to pronounce it. My appreciation of literature and my interest in writing were laid down at this stage. We admired and emulated these teachers, and, without us realising it, our spoken language improved. I was also fortunate to add to my wealth of close friends in this college where I did the pre-university course and one year of B.Sc.

The pressure began with medical college, which was quite a grind. After some struggle and uncertainty, I got into Guntur Medical College in 1963. This and the competition for entry to the All India Institute of Medical Sciences (AIIMS) for my postgraduation in 1970, acted as strong incentives to prove myself later in life.

The education in those days was very orderly, with a clear annual calendar, an undisturbed teaching schedule, and committed teachers. Most of the faculty loved their profession and that made a huge difference.

The physical ambience of Guntur Medical College, moulded by pathologist and Principal, Jagannatha Reddy (1954–1962), was very special. It was an enabling environment that nurtured both teachers and students alike. For the first time in my life, I got to know people from outside Andhra, both teachers and students, and all of this had a positive influence on me.

I studied hard and got into the AIIMS in New Delhi for my postgraduate studies. The sense of accomplishment in getting through was tremendous. At the AIIMS, for the first time, I was away from home, and had to learn to fend for myself. New Delhi was a big city, and I was at a big and renowned institution. Everything at the AIIMS was new to me, although I was among the brightest products of India's medical colleges. I thought of running back home, but fear of my father dissuaded me. Thankfully, I stayed on, survived, and later blossomed,

The AIIMS was a transformative experience. Even travelling around Delhi on crowded public transport, soaking in the sights and sounds, was a thrilling new experience to me. I acquired a large group of friends from all over India (a benefit I enjoy till today), learnt a new language, and gained the confidence to face anyone, anywhere. In four years, I matured more than in the twenty-four years of my life so far.

There was another big change—I got married to Pratibha in 1973. Her father was a renowned surgeon in Vijayawada and our families knew each other well. The years at the AIIMS taught me the value of discipline, hard work, and being consistent. They also exposed me to many bright minds, both among teachers and students, and the science of modern medicine. This set the pattern for my entire professional career. In some senses, I was now ready to face the world, and I prepared for the next big leap—to the United States.

The next twelve years in the US were full of varied experiences. The initial cultural shock—of seeing good highways, big and beautiful cars, an abundance of everything, shopping malls, diverse ethnic groups, and cuisines—was overwhelming. The first three to four years of adjustment made me stronger and helped build a firm foundation from where I could plan boldly for the future. The traditions, practices, policies, behaviours, and the environments of the American institutions that hosted me contributed to this confidence. I understood the real meanings of the words 'excellence' and 'rigour' during this time.

By now, I had a successful career and a picture postcard family with Pratibha, a son, and a daughter. However, despite all the glitter of East Coast success around us, something was amiss. Pratibha and I had always felt very strongly that people coming from families like ours should give back to our country and people. We began discussing and nurturing a dream—building a world-class academic eye care institution in India. We chose Hyderabad because of its central location, and its better chances of attracting talent from across the country.

We settled on a date to return to India despite the scepticism of our families and friends. We initially created two not-for-profit organisations, one in the US (Indo-American Eye Care Society) and one in India (the Hyderabad Eye Institute). The Andhra Pradesh government gave us land for the construction of the institute on the outskirts of Hyderabad. We raised funds in the

US for the equipment. Just about a year before our return, we were introduced to director and businessman L. V. Prasad and his family. This meeting gave our project a boost, with them donating land in Banjara Hills and a substantial sum of money. The board of the Hyderabad Eye Institute decided to name the institute after Prasad in recognition of his munificence, and the institute became popularly known as the L. V. Prasad Eye Institute.

The first phase was built in seven months, and it was inaugurated on 1 June 1987. The founding motto was 'Reconciling Excellence with Equity'. We were determined that nobody who came to the institute with an eye problem would be denied care, irrespective of their ability to pay. Everyone would receive service of the same quality. Departments to deal with education, rehabilitation, eye banking, research, and rural and community eye health were added over the next five to seven years. Product development and technology innovation have followed. Helping other organisations build capacity and actively participating in advocacy and policymaking at the national and global levels have become integral parts of the institute's activities.

We have pursued the concept of the 'road not taken' since inception, and innovation has been a part of our DNA. The L. V. Prasad Eye Institute is now one of the leading eye care organisations worldwide, and it offers the most comprehensive care, which includes prevention, promotion, and rehabilitation. The diligence and dedication of our team, coupled with the incredible generosity of supporters from all over the world, has made this possible. It has been a gratifying journey, touching the lives of millions, whose blessings continue to nurture our growth.

Indeed, it has been a full life, from rural India to the best in the West–from bullock carts to limousines, and from training under village teachers to working in hallowed international institutions. But, in the end, life is the same as it was in my early years; I am driven by the same values and tickled by the same joys. What more can I ask for? If one asks me whether I would go through life again, in the same way, my answer would be, 'Absolutely!'

7

The Joys of a Professional Career

YEZDI HIRJI MALEGAM

I started my professional career as a chartered accountant when I was eighteen years old and joined S. B. Billimoria & Co., Chartered Accountants, as an articled clerk in June 1952. All chartered accountancy firms are modelled on a pyramid structure. At the top are the partners, or the finders; in the middle are the managers, or the minders; and at the bottom are the grinders. The articled clerks formed a major part of the bottom layer. Those were the days when there were no computers or even calculators and all accounting records were handwritten. A major part of an articled clerk's work consisted of posting and totalling to ensure that the books maintained under the double entry system were balanced.

However, it was not all drudgery. S. B. Billimoria was one of the two principal auditors of the Tata Group and had a wide spectrum of other clients. It was the auditor of the Reserve Bank of India (RBI) and its subsidiaries, of the State Bank of India (SBI) and many of its subsidiaries, of the principal commercial banks, the two largest insurance companies, and a host of trading and manufacturing companies such as textile mills and pharmaceutical companies. Articled clerks were required to work in clients' locations and visit factories and travel to locations outside Mumbai. I spent almost the whole of my first year of articleship in Jamshedpur on the audits of Tata Iron and Steel and Tata Locomotive and Engineering.

The firm's policy stated that the clerk was required to visit the client's factory to understand the manufacturing process before commencing any audit. I found it fascinating to see how steel was manufactured, how coal was mined, and how iron ore was extracted, and to see how locomotives were manufactured and castings produced in the foundries. On other audits, too, I enjoyed visiting other places outside Mumbai. Audits were always conducted in teams and I enjoyed working with other clerks who came from various backgrounds and sharing accommodation with them when outside Mumbai. I also liked interacting with the client's staff.

After qualifying as an Indian chartered accountant, I spent a year in London and qualified as an English chartered accountant and on my return became a partner in S. B. Billimoria & Co. on 1 January 1958. Among the many audits entrusted to me were the principal companies in the Tata Group, the Central Bank of India, the Life Insurance Corporation (LIC), and a variety of trading and manufacturing companies, apart from other assignments. One of the interesting assignments was to certify the construction costs being paid to the Indian Steelworks Construction Co. Ltd. (ISCON) on behalf of the government. ISCON was a consortium of thirteen British firms that had supplied equipment for the Durgapur Steel Plant and was constructing the plant under a cost-plus contract. This involved frequent visits to Durgapur and it was fascinating to see the plant coming up.

During the last few years of my role as an auditor, information technology was making rapid strides. This had a significant impact on the way in which financial records were maintained and audits were conducted. I always did most of my work in the client's office, carefully scrutinising the ledgers and the journal entries, and this gave me a full picture of the client's operations. This was supplemented with discussions with various members of the client's staff to obtain the necessary explanations and affirmations. An audit necessarily involved value judgements, and interaction with the client's staff was essential to make a judgement on the level of confidence that could be placed on these explanations and affirmations.

All this has changed with the introduction of computers and accounting systems such as SAP. While much of the drudgery has disappeared and much better analysis of the data is possible, the audit has become more impersonal. The major tool of the present auditor is his laptop and communication with the client's staff is through emails. The auditor works from his office or his home and does not need to visit the client's office or discuss issues with his colleagues. I am glad that I retired before these developments took place, because I would have been uncomfortable with them.

An area of work that I found particularly interesting was the valuation of companies, mainly to determine a ratio of exchange when two companies merged. I soon specialised in this area. A valuation that gave me particular satisfaction was in the merger of Tata Oil Mills Ltd with Hindustan Lever Ltd in June 1994. The valuation was challenged in the Bombay High Court and later in the Supreme Court. I had determined the ratio of exchange using a weightage of the asset value and the income value, and the court found it difficult to understand why two different values had been used and why there was a weightage.

I therefore suggested to our counsel that we should use a simple analogy. We said, imagine that two individuals each held a government security of equal face value but with different coupon rates and wished to exchange them. If the securities were immediately due for redemption, both would agree to the exchange. If, however, the securities were non-redeemable, the holder of the security with the higher coupon rate would demand a more favourable rate of exchange. If the securities were redeemable but the redemption date was uncertain, the parties would need to consider an exchange rate determined by a weightage between the rate derived from an immediate redemption and a rate determined on the basis of a non-redeemable security. Similarly, since it was not clear if the merged company would immediately realise the assets or continue to hold onto them and realise them in the future, there was the need for weightage. This appealed to the court, which in its order discussed the valuation methodology in detail and approved it. It has since been the methodology used by most valuers.

I have always enjoyed working in committees and on the boards of companies. In 1980, I became a member, representing India, of the International Accounting Standards Committee (IASC) which had eleven members (this was later increased to thirteen), with a mandate to issue international auditing guidelines. In their approach, the members could easily be recognised as falling into three groups—(*i*) countries following English auditing practices; (*ii*) countries following American auditing practices; and (*iii*) countries following European auditing practices. The first group wanted to codify the existing practices; the second group wanted to adopt the standards they had already issued; and the third group wanted to draft new standards on first principles based on reasoning. I supported the European approach. It was interesting that although the standards were drafted in English, there were frequent disagreements on the actual wording between the first and second groups, while the third group looked to me to resolve the issue. The committee met three times a year in different locations and, apart from the discussions, I enjoyed the opportunity to visit so many countries.

In 1991, when the Government of India approached the World Bank for financial assistance, the Bank expressed some reservations about the provisioning practices of Indian development banks. I was asked to accompany S. M. Khan, IDBI's Deputy Managing Director, to Washington, DC to sort out the issue. New norms were formulated and these were later extended to commercial banks and are substantially in force even today. I was also fortunate to have been a member of almost all the major committees formed for financial-sector reforms after 1991.

One of my most interesting experiences was as a member of the Janakiraman Committee, which looked into the Harshad Mehta scam. The important lesson I learnt was that the convergence of distinct and disparate regulations could sometimes lead to a disastrous situation. First, there was the government decision to discontinue the financing of capital expenditure of public-sector enterprises (PSUs, or Public Sector Undertakings) and to ask them to obtain funds from the capital markets. This resulted in large funds with PSUs, which needed to be invested till they could be used for capital expenditure, and there was a directive that the funds had to be invested in deposits with public-sector banks. Second, there was a ceiling of 12 per cent on the interest payable on deposits, which had been imposed by the RBI. Third, there was the boom in the stock market and brokers and investors were prepared to pay an interest of 24 per cent on their borrowings.

A combination of these factors provided the opportunity for operators like Harshad Mehta to exploit the arbitrage, and they used portfolio management schemes as a vehicle to give guaranteed returns and to make settlements under the schemes. There were also purchases and sales of government paper at artificial rates. The ultimate scam was almost inevitable.

I have been a member of the boards of several large publicly quoted companies, including ICICI Ltd., where I served for more than ten years from the mid-1980s. My colleagues on the board of ICICI included some of the most eminent industrialists in the country, such as Ratan Tata, Aditya Birla, Keshab Mahindra, and others, and their collective wisdom when loan proposals were discussed was enlightening. They emphasised to me both the benefit of dissenting opinions and the need to reconcile them to obtain the best results.

I joined the board of directors of the RBI in 1994 and continued to be a director for more than twenty-one years. During this period, I have had the pleasure of interacting with five governors, each of whom had his own individual style. For me, it was a period of continued learning and I enjoyed participating in discussions that resulted in many new initiatives taken by the bank. I particularly enjoyed being a member of the committee of directors, which met each week, and my role as the Chairman of the Local Advisory Board, where I interacted with the inspecting officers. This resulted in many initiatives, of which I will describe one. The RBI used to pay commercial banks a fee for handling government work. In one of my interactions, I was informed that there was a differential fee for receipts and payments as the work involved, including calculations, was different and there was a holding cost of funds between receiving cheques and their realisation. The fees had also not been revised for several years. I pointed out that the workload would have been considerably reduced with computerisation and the fees were revised, which resulted in a significant saving in costs.

As I look back over my professional career, I realise how great a role chance has played in my life and how many of the opportunities

I obtained were because I was in the right place at the right time. My greatest joy has always been interacting with people. I must confess I am uncomfortable with online communication because I am unable to immediately clarify matters or add the information that I think is essential. However, I do realise this is because of a generation gap, and those who have grown up in the digital age may not have this difficulty.

8

Lessons for Life (And Work)

Jamal Mecklai

The most important lesson I have learned so far is that happiness/joy/pleasure, call it what you will, is the primary purpose of life, and it needs to permeate all aspects of it, including, of course, work.

A bit of history will help set the context. I had finished my B.Tech (Hons) at the Indian Institute of Technology (IIT) Bombay in 1972 and gone to Rice University in Houston to do a Ph.D. in chemical engineering that same year. But in a little over a year, life intervened and I dropped out of school. My parents were, of course, appalled, particularly because I spent the first year or so after that selling shoes. It is a long story that led to me getting my Green Card, but it was my first work experience ever. Even though it was hardly demanding, I discovered that I was a great salesman and really enjoyed my job. Loving what you do is a large part of any success story.

I moved to New York in 1975, where, of course, life was truly king-size. After another brief stint in retail sales (selling minerals, shells, butterflies, and the like), I got a corporate job at a technologically advanced marketing company. On the side, I was working (unpaid) with the Natural Resources Defence Council, an environmental advocacy group. After a while, I found I could not work directly for companies that flagrantly disregarded the environment. I told this to my boss and, to my surprise, I was fired. This was long before the environmental, social, and governance

(ESG) era, and the lesson (then and now) was that it is difficult to manage your personal morality in a corporate environment.

In addition to the environmental work, I found myself involved with a wide array of 'changing the world' activities—from anti-apartheid protests to a nutrition project for New York public schools, to helping set up the first ever alternative art space in the world (it was called Fashion MODA and was based in the impoverished South Bronx). Of course, none of these paid any, or much, money and I had to work as a temporary proofreader at law firms to pay the rent. Again, this was hardly mentally taxing work, but the continuous joy I gained from all my 'real' work made it welcome. Importantly, however, this was when I came across the idea of 'tax avoidance', which bred in me a clear (and continuing) realisation that the global expression of capitalism was fundamentally flawed. Lifelong learning can come from the most unlikely places.

Anyway, around 1980, I came back to India for a visit and my mother suggested I go visit Homi Sethna, who used to be a neighbour and was now fairly renowned as a documentary filmmaker. I guess she thought we would enjoy each other's company. We got along famously, and at one point in one of our conversations, he said, 'I want to read you something from the Bhagvad Gita: "The only thing is to do the work and not even look at the result".'

It hit me like a thunderbolt—it was the most liberating thing I had ever heard, and I immediately found myself in the smiling company of God. Like most 'cool' people, I had always been an intellectual agnostic, but this experience turned me instantly into a complete believer. And, most joyously, I realised that God (who, by all 'believer' accounts, is all-knowing, all-loving, and so on) could only have put me—and, to be sure, everybody else—on this earth to be happy. The genesis of Lesson 1.

I returned to New York happier than ever and even more on fire than before. Things had been working out—apartheid had been dismantled, Fashion MODA was doing very well, and, by then, I had developed more effective skills at raising money for 'change the world' projects. I worked on a series of projects and then, through a tenuous connection, embarked on perhaps my most quixotic effort ever—to build people-to-people friendship between the US and the Soviet Union.

I travelled to the Soviet Union two times and, despite the roadblocks created by the system, met several wonderful people there—a couple of whom are still close friends. At the end of the second visit in 1981, I smuggled some Soviet rock 'n' roll music out of the country and, with that as a peg, tried to create a bridge between young people in the two countries using the common language of art, performance, and rock music. Partnering with a magazine called *Semiotext*, I developed a parallel presidential election billed as 'The Only Truly Democratic Election in America—President by Lottery', which we launched at a nightclub on 6 November 1984, the evening of the US presidential election.

The night before the election, I spoke with the producers of ABC, CBS, and NBC news, pointing out that with voter turnout at an all-time low, democracy was hardly working; it was time for something radical as we were planning, and if the media were to meaningfully cover the event, the power of their coverage could make the winner of the lottery the real President—we had already arranged a phone call from Moscow at midnight and would be sending 'the real President' to the Soviet Union for celebrations the following week. Despite being extremely strapped for time, they listened to me, but they did not cover our election.

Many people found the event to be a great success but, despite my best efforts, I felt it had failed. (I would point out, though, that a few years later, the Berlin Wall fell and the Soviet Union changed in the direction I [and, no doubt, millions of others] had been pushing.) The very difficult lesson I learnt is that Cervantes notwithstanding, tilting at windmills will only serve to exhaust you.

I was exhausted by this effort and began to feel that I should return to India. I came back in 1985 to see how I could fit into the family business, which was interbank foreign exchange broking. My father had started a foreign exchange information service in the late 1970s, and by 1985, it had developed a respectable following in the Indian corporate sector.

I had neither a background in economics nor any knowledge of financial markets, but I plunged in, learning as fast as an eager child. I liked to write, I wore bright shirts (which remains very unusual in the financial sector), and was one of the few people thinking about the foreign exchange market at the time. As a result, it was relatively easy to expand the brand. In fact, the reason I am in this set of essays is that early in my finance career (probably 1986), Y. V. Reddy, who was then at the Ministry of Finance, must have read something I had written and invited me to meet him in Delhi, which marked the start of a beautiful friendship.

By the time of the 1987 Wall Street crash, I had become something of a forex guru. I remember when the market opened the next day, the phone(s) were ringing off the wall—it seemed like everybody wanted me to tell them what was going to happen to the dollar. I had no idea, of course, and I told people that. But the pressure stayed—people I had never even heard of were calling me, asking what I thought. While at one level it was all very flattering, it was also overwhelming.

I remember I went down for a smoke—I still smoked in those days—and while I was leaning against the building thinking about it, the *chanawala* (chickpea seller) who worked off the pavement there came up to me and said, '*Sah'b, pachas rupiya chahiye*' ('Sah'b, I need 50 rupees').

He was a cheerful guy and we often chatted about this and that, but I was thoroughly preoccupied, so I shooed him away. And as I smoked and thought, it suddenly hit me. I called him over and asked him, '*Bolo kya hone wala hai—dollar upar jayega ke neeche?*' ('Tell me what is going to happen, will the dollar go up or down?').

He was shocked. He said, '*Sah'b mujhe kya pata?*' ('Sah'b, what do I know?')

'*Pachas rupiya chahiye?*' ('You need 50 rupees?')

He nodded and said something to please me. I gave him the Rs 50. I do not remember what he told me, but I went back upstairs and told all subsequent callers what he had said. I do not remember whether it turned out to be right or not, but it was a critical lesson in markets—after an unprecedented event, nobody has any clue as to what will happen; the chanawala's view is as good as any expert's.

A much later extension of this particular lesson is that while details (of anything in life) are often critical, it is important to know when the details are not worth the time. Over a couple of decades, I must have spent months (probably years) working away at building models to try and outperform markets, till I learnt a fundamental truth—it is impossible to beat the market consistently. Put another way, nobody has any clue as to what will happen to the market at all times. Put yet another way, you can forecast a level or a timeline, but not both.

By 1991, with the rupee devaluation and partial convertibility, our business was doing very well. The brand was doing even better. I remember for Manmohan Singh's budget in 1992, I had written an article that described the Indian economy as 'champagne and vada pao' and had a party at a restaurant where we only served champagne and *vada pao*. Indeed, we had champagne and vada pao parties for several budgets after that where I (and a few others) wore turbans to celebrate. When P. Chidambaram became Finance Minister in 2004, the head of Merrill Lynch came to the party in a *veshti*.

All this, plus my bright colours, loud ties, and printed shirts had everyone I knew (and many I did not) assuming—correctly—that I was having a great time. And, as the world was more and more convinced that I was always having a great time, I ended up always having a great time. The lesson here is something I read in the introduction to a novel—it is impossible not to become what the world thinks you are.

It was probably about this time that I coined my catchphrase—business is pleasure; work is play—which decorates both my company website and my CV.

While things were going swimmingly, I knew—and have always realised—that I was extremely lucky (Lesson: I'll take luck over brains every time; after all, the brain is like a toothbrush—an admirable instrument for certain activities, but hardly of any value in deciphering how to find joy in life) and that my successes (such as they are) and joys were supported—and often built—by hundreds of people I may not have known or even heard of. I often quote Blanche Dubois, the beautiful anti-hero of Tennessee Williams' *A Streetcar named Desire*, who pointed out, 'Ah've always depended on the kindness of strangers.' To my mind, this is one of the most important lines (and lessons) in all of contemporary American literature.

Of course, there are some teachers whom I do remember well. Once I was visiting Deputy Governor Y. V. Reddy at the Reserve Bank of India. While I was sitting in the waiting room, I picked up a couple of newspapers and magazines lying there and was horrified to see that they were several weeks old. When I was called in, I told him about it. He smiled apologetically and said, 'From tomorrow, I'll bring my own newspapers in and have them put in the waiting area; perhaps that will bring about a change.' Even in the smallest things, lead by example.

Another lesson that I am (in retrospect) grateful for was how to deal with failure. In 1998 (or 1999) a young venture capitalist, Abhay Havaldar, showed up at my doorstep, just as the internet was arriving in India. He delighted me so much about the prospects of the new world that I remember once telling him, 'You excite me so much, I'm so glad you're not a woman; it might end up testing my joyous marriage.'

To cut a long story short, I bought the snake oil and built a grand scheme where eMecklai would be the only global trading platform for all emerging market currencies (and other illiquid assets). As it happened, we were a dozen years or so ahead of time, both in terms of technology and user awareness, but were perfectly tuned to investor fear of missing out. We attracted a large amount of capital (relative to our scale) and, for a couple of years, tried to build the pipe dream.

Business slowly ceased to be a pleasure and the work became hugely difficult. We lost most of the capital, the investors (understandably) turned vicious, and I had to fire about 100 people individually. What I learnt—and am still learning—is that empathy is *the* most important emotion when anyone's chips are down. The good news is that even today I am in contact with several of the people who were with eMecklai, all of whom are doing reasonably well despite having had to start again. Indeed, there is a Mecklai-Vintage WhatsApp group with around thirty-five members, most of whom worked with me around that time.

Another lesson from this was that after a certain amount of time, there is always good news. My father had a chart behind his desk, headlined 'Depressions never last forever' (it was from the 1929 Wall Street crash). Markets (and, indeed, everything in life) always turn around. Anyway, it took a few years of licking my wounds to get started again and, delight of delights, the brand turned out to be strong enough to (more than) survive the collapse—like I've said over and over, wear a bright shirt.

And finally, to find happiness/joy/pleasure in all aspects of life (including work), you have to openheartedly touch as many people as you encounter in your life. Now I know that sustaining any relationship takes time and energy, which is why many behavioural (and business) gurus have cut-offs for the number of close friends (reports) you can have. However, a more important truth is that a smile does not take any time or energy at all; rather, every time you smile at someone, you get more joy or energy in return. In particular, when you encounter somebody in a wheelchair, be sure to smile and ask them if they've come for the dance classes—their joy will bless you a hundred times over.

So, if you run into an older guy in brightly coloured clothes smiling apparently foolishly at everyone, smile back. It's probably me.

9

To Thine Own Self Be True

Joydeep Mukherji

Shakespeare unwittingly summarised the Upanishads when he wrote the following words in *Hamlet*–'To thine own self be true'. How do you discover what your own self is? Mystics may go to the mountains to discover themselves, but most of us make many of our discoveries through what we call 'work'.

Work involves meeting people and being influenced by them, and influencing them. The human interaction can change how you feel about your work, whether it is perceived as a pleasure or a pain. Engaging in work gradually helps reveal what motivates you and the pattern of your thinking and behaviour. Through work, we also create common bonds that encourage people to shed their narrow identities and discover our shared humanity.

Like many students, I entered the University of Toronto with only a vague idea of what I wanted to study and what kind of job I would enjoy. However, soon after beginning classes, I developed a strong interest in economics as it seemed to be a powerful tool for both analysing the world and trying to change it. Fortunately, there were some experienced professors in the economics department who had worked outside academia, either in government or other institutions, who impressed upon me the need to place abstract economic theory within a political and historical context. Academic knowledge is not enough to understand how we make public policies.

Based on this insight, I applied for and received an internship in the legislature of the Canadian province of Ontario after graduating from college in 1984. As one of eight such interns, I worked for elected members as part of their regular staff, doing a wide range of tasks (such as preparing speeches, drafting questions to be raised in Parliament, and addressing the problems of the people who lived in their constituency). The legislators were politicians who gave smooth speeches and never deviated from the party line. It was hard not to be cynical about such people, at least until I started working with a member of the legislative assembly named Jim McGuigan.

Jim was a philosophical, soft-spoken farmer around sixty-five years of age. In my interview for the internship, he said he would like his intern to leave Toronto and work with him in his rural constituency during the upcoming elections. In the 1980s, rural Ontario was almost all white. I asked him if the presence of an Indian alongside him during the election campaign would lose him any votes (the West was less welcoming of Indians back then). He replied that he had lived his life based on his own beliefs and was not afraid of the opinion of others. 'If I lose any votes because of your presence, I don't want those votes,' he told me. His sincerity and decency were apparent.

I went with Jim throughout his constituency, meeting people who sought his help with some provincial government matters or wanted to persuade him to change some policy. The work exposed me to the practical nature of politics and policies. Politicians like Jim had to make decisions based on the actual circumstances facing them, not on abstract notions based on ideology and elegant theories. I saw that individual politicians also had limited powers, as most decisions depend upon the cooperation of many other people. During those travels, Jim and I became good friends, despite the differences in age and background.

There were no cell phones back then. Working on an election campaign meant living in the area. Hence, I spent almost a month living in Jim's farmhouse and working long days, while his wife took care to feed me. The work was hard and posed many challenges, as I was dealing with villagers and farmers for the first time in my life. However, the personal bond that we had developed motivated my work because I wanted Jim McGuigan to win re-election. As the campaign advanced, I felt that I was happily fulfilling my duty to a friend, rather than doing some unpleasant thing called 'work'.

There is a quiet inner satisfaction in feeling that you are useful because your work could make a small difference to the lives of other people. Under such circumstances, political ideology begins to recede, but not disappear, as you have more and more personal interactions with many people who seek practical help for their problems.

Jim won the election and I soon returned to his office in Toronto and resumed working on problems faced by his constituents. The constituency work became nicer and my motivation stronger than before the election because I now knew many of the local people whom I was trying to help. Personal relationships can sometimes change how you see your daily tasks, either as a pleasurable duty to be cheerfully fulfilled or a dreaded chore that must be done because you are being paid to do so. The context and the people make all the difference.

After the legislative internship, I went to graduate school in Princeton, New Jersey, in 1986. I wanted to focus on applying academic knowledge to public policy, deepening my experiences in the Ontario legislature. Soon after the classes started, I noticed the difference between my fellow students in the Master's programme who had already worked in some policymaking institution before going to graduate school and those with no such experience. The former were usually more sceptical than the latter about abstract ideas, thanks to their own experiences in the practical world of work. Some of the people teaching us were former government officials from various countries, who could combine both academic knowledge and immense practical experience. Looking back after many decades of my own work, I now realise how difficult it was for those officials to fully convey their knowledge to us young students.

After finishing graduate school, I found a job with a large Canadian bank, starting as a management trainee. Having worked in politics, I was curious to learn about the private sector as well. I worked in the bank for five years in corporate lending and later in investment banking (in the field of asset securitisation). Despite working with many smart and pleasant colleagues, I found the job increasingly unsatisfying from a personal angle. The work was challenging, but over time it became less interesting. Undertaking similar business transactions over and over again could be lucrative, but not very motivating, at least for me. It was clear that my calling was not to be a banker, regardless of the material comforts that came from the salary. Personal motivation comes from more than just money.

I left the banking job in 1994 and decided to travel in Latin America and learn Spanish. I had long wanted to learn that language and thereby increase my knowledge of Latin America and improve my experience of it, but had not done anything about it until then. I did not start the journey with a defined destination or a specific new job in mind. I simply hoped that a new language would make it easier to eventually find a job related to international matters, as I wanted to broaden my horizons. Having worked in various jobs that were suitable and unsuitable for my own nature, I would hopefully be in a better position to discern what future jobs would be good for me.

I was lucky. After travelling and doing some odd jobs for a couple of years, I joined a credit rating agency in New York City in 1996 to work on sovereign ratings. A large part of my new work was to analyse the political and economic realities of a country, a task that was closer to my own interests and character than banking. I was naturally interested in solving the work-related challenges that arose every day, happily going beyond the minimum work needed for the task.

As a rating analyst, I would meet regularly with a wide range of officials in countries that we rated, asking questions and gathering information. Through this interaction, I was pleasantly surprised to realise how many hardworking, bright people around the world were working in government, trying to do the right thing, even while facing serious political and institutional constraints. It is easy to be cynical of government and bureaucrats, but there are admirable people in the public sector who try to do their best.

I worked for several years on India's credit rating, which gave me the opportunity to meet many Indian government officials. One of them, a senior officer, met with us regularly and made persuasive presentations. He immediately struck me as being different from the rest, with a respectful, gentle manner that instantly created a sympathetic bond with people, regardless of whether he agreed or disagreed with them. His behaviour during our many meetings demonstrated how it was possible to foster friendship and personal respect while often disagreeing in a professional manner (I later learnt that those personal qualities had made him a very efficient officer, more capable of getting things done in his work than most people).

Inspired by his example, I began to experiment by changing my own thinking and approach in settings where disagreements were inevitable. Slowly but surely, I discovered that it was possible to disagree on important matters while maintaining cordiality, if you listen better to understand their message, show genuine respect for others, and consciously prevent impersonal issues from creating personal animosity. Not all disagreement needs to become personal.

My job as a credit rating analyst meant that I often had to deliver bad news about a ratings downgrade to government officials. Of course, they would not be happy with the bad news just because of a change in style and approach on my part. However, they would often respect us more at the personal level, despite the unfavourable news, if they could see that we genuinely did our work and tried to be fair. Trying to bring the best out of other people sometimes depends on bringing the best out of yourself, a valuable lesson I learnt from this Indian official.

Many officials in public life need to make very difficult decisions with great uncertainty about the outcome, a very lonely process. The senior Indian official whom I had come to know was soon in such a position, under pressure from various quarters to make some very tough decisions. Although the subject matter of his decisions was not directly connected to my own work, I felt that he deserved some support. Good people need to be encouraged to do what they think is good. A feeling of personal duty and sympathy compelled me to say something, urging him to do the proper thing. Although the internet had appeared by then, I decided to write informal letters to him on paper, a more personal medium, expressing my hope that he would rely on his inner judgement to do the right thing without worrying about the consequences.

Why did I write those letters, going beyond the limits of professional work and running the risk of offending a senior figure through personal correspondence? I had changed in some ways from meeting him and aspects of my life had become easier because of his example. My interaction with him had convinced me that it was my duty, in a personal and not business sense, to communicate with him in this difficult moment, regardless of the outcome. After sending him a couple of such letters, I met the Indian official one day in the US. He happily told me that he appreciated my letters very much (perhaps because they nudged him to do what he was going to do anyway?). We have remained good friends ever since, thanks to the mutual sympathy and understanding that arose from these incidents.

The immense improvement in technology during my life did not change how I interpreted my role and duty during these memorable moments. Technology can raise productivity and make work easier in many ways. However, better technology will not transform an uninteresting job into an interesting one if your own nature is not suitable for that type of work. Conversely, better technology may transform an interesting job into a more productive job as well.

Interaction with other people through work gives more meaning to life and opens the door to self-understanding. Work takes up so much time that it can come to define you. But, you can also define what work is based on your mindset. Work can feel like misery or pleasure, based on how you interpret your role and actions.

These episodes taught me something about myself and not just about the other person, as my behaviour revealed a hidden part of my own nature. My strongest recollections from these episodes are the people, the lessons learnt, and the gradual revelation of what motivates me and hence who I am.

The revelations that emerge from working and introspecting can help us to discern the most appropriate goals in life, avoiding seemingly seductive goals that may be good for others but which clash with your own nature. Work is important, not only for creating a career and enjoying material comforts, but also for understanding concepts such as dharma through both outer and inner experiences. Gradual self-understanding, not technology, helps us find a personal path towards contentment. Shakespeare understood that.

Part III

Public Policy

10

Work and Life

Shankar Acharya

Above the main entrance to the Auschwitz-Birkenau complex of concentration camps in south Poland (which exterminated 1.1 million inmates—mostly Jews—in the 1940s under the Nazis) is carved 'Arbeit Macht Frei', meaning 'work sets you free'. Ironically, there is much truth to the phrase, even though in Auschwitz 'liberation' was mainly attained through gas chambers. In the seventy-eight years since World War II, work has remained a central element of life for humans. For the poor and dispossessed, it has often entailed hard, relentless, back-breaking labour in fields, factories, and homes. For a fortunate minority (at least in India) like us, work has conferred dignity, fulfilment, and pleasure. What follows is a snapshot of my working life, which, because of parental circumstances, was spread over three countries and continents.

My first paid job was in 1964, when I was eighteen. While studying for a year at the London School of Economics, I worked in London as a part-time home cleaner. The elderly English lady for whom I cleaned did not treat me as a menial, but rather as someone she could chat with in her lonely life, never forgetting to give me a cup of tea and biscuits at work's end. During the winter break from studies, I emulated many other students to earn a few extra pounds by working for the post office, delivering the surge in Christmas parcels across parts of north London, driven around by our very pleasant supervisor-driver. The big lesson I took away was that in a reasonably well-functioning democratic society, doing menial physical work did not necessarily mean being treated badly by the employer or by society, more generally. One's dignity as a human being was not threatened.

Over the next seven years, I proceeded to acquire the credentials of a well-trained economist—three years for a BA in Politics, Philosophy and Economics at Oxford, followed by four years earning a Ph.D. in Economics at Harvard in 1972. (In Oxford, I formed some lifelong friendships with people such as Aung San Suu Kyi and Montek Ahluwalia, and also courted and married my wife of fifty-five years, Gayatri Dasgupta.) Although I did do some paid work as a teaching fellow in a couple of graduate courses at Harvard, my first real job was as a World Bank economist from 1971. That is where I learnt both real world economic analysis and teamwork, both as a member of economic 'mission' teams to different countries such as Sudan, Zambia, Yugoslavia, and the Commonwealth Caribbean, and as team leader ('mission chief') to nations such as Tanzania, at quite a young age of thirty.

All this was happening in the 1970s, decades before emails, the internet, mobile phones, and even word processing. On missions (typically three to five weeks) one got to know one's colleagues closely and learnt a central lesson—it was always better to cooperate with colleagues than be antagonistic to them. The essence of our work entailed a great deal of face-to-face human interactions, in sharp contrast to the current plethora of social messaging apps, emails, and mobile telephony.

In 1977, World Bank President Robert McNamara started the globally well-known flagship series of annual World Development Reports. I was privileged to be a member of the first 'core team' for World Development Report 1978 and a leader of the second team for World Development Report 1979. Aside from coordinating the writing of a large number of good quality background papers by Bank staff from other parts of the institution and consultants, and then distilling a coherent final report, the exercise involved monthly meetings with McNamara, an impressive and domineering personality, with only two or three vice-presidents present. I learnt a great deal about the importance of cultivating productive work relationships with peers, subordinates, and superiors in a large international organisation. This experience would stand me in good stead for my subsequent sixteen years with the Government of India (1985–2001) and fifteen years on the board of Kotak Mahindra Bank (2003–2018), where I served the last twelve years as non-executive chairman.

My first six years with the government began in early 1985 as Economic Adviser in the Ministry of Finance. It was a learning experience—of not only work but also the (sometimes mysterious) ways and modalities of the Indian government. While the first two years were quite exciting during V. P. Singh's tax-reforming phase (when direct tax rates were reduced and a modified value-added tax was introduced), the remaining four with Ministers Narayan Dutt Tiwari, S. B. Chavan, and Madhu Dandavate were less so.

During the V. P. Singh years, I had the privilege of being the coordinating author of a policy document (laid in Parliament in December 1985) called the Long Term Fiscal Policy. Among other initiatives, it laid the foundation for introducing the modified value-added tax (MODVAT) in 1986 for central excise duty, which later formed the basis for transitioning to the goods and services tax (GST) in 2017. The time spent was valuable in forming good working relations with additional secretaries, joint secretaries, other economic advisers and directors, as well as with deputy governor C. Rangarajan at the Reserve Bank of India (RBI) and his executive director S. S. Tarapore, not to mention old friend Montek at the Prime Minister's Office (PMO). In many ways, it was a necessary and valuable apprenticeship to my eight years (1993–2001) as Chief Economic Adviser, following a deputation abroad in 1991–1992.

Those were heady reform years across the governments of Narasimha Rao (Congress), with Manmohan Singh as finance minister, and A. B. Vajpayee (BJP/NDA) with Yashwant Sinha as finance minister, with a two-year interregnum (1996–1998) of the United Front government, with P. Chidambaram as finance minister. It was a pleasure and privilege to work with these three unusually talented and dedicated ministers and the strong official team at the finance ministry, including Ahluwalia, N. K. Singh, Vijay Kelkar, and Y. Venugopal Reddy. So too with Rangarajan, who was heading the RBI and supported by very able deputy governors such as Tarapore and, later, Venugopal Reddy.

Throughout the reforming 1990s, the collegial and mutually respectful relations between the finance ministry and the RBI greatly aided the conception, execution, and articulation of macroeconomic policy in a manner that may not have been replicated as well, either before or thereafter. Frequent face-to-face interactions between all protagonists (and innumerable phone calls) oiled the wheels of policymaking.

In 2001, I left the government on early retirement and joined the Indian Council for Research on International Economic Relations (ICRIER), a think tank headed by the dynamic Isher Judge Ahluwalia. I engaged myself in writing policy-oriented research papers and books, while contributing a monthly column to the *Business Standard* led by T. N. Ninan, one of India's best newspaper editors. I regularly attended their Monday morning editorial brainstorming meetings, where I learnt about breaking news stories and was able to contribute suggestions for editorials.

From 2003, I accepted Uday Kotak's invitation to join the board of his fledgling bank, going on to serve as chairman for twelve years (2006–2018) and thereby learning enormously about how a truly well-run private firm can prosper, generate tens of thousands of productive jobs, and become a favourite of the stock market, all without sacrificing good governance and integrity. During this time, I was also a member of the Twelfth Finance Commission (2004), the National Security Advisory Board (2009–2013), and the Reserve Bank's Technical Advisory Committee on Monetary Policy (2005–2016).

I have been very fortunate with my work opportunities—and the life that went with them.

11

Reflections on a Career in the Civil Service

In a Season of Mists and Mellow Fruitfulness

SHEELA BHIDE

On 7 July 2023, my batch, the 1973 batch of the Indian Administrative Service (IAS), celebrated its fiftieth anniversary. It was a landmark event in our lives. Looking back over my thirty-six years of service, I ask myself, 'What do I take away from all this time in public service? What are the memories of events and people that I cherish the most? What were the lessons that I learnt while implementing various developmental programmes?' The answers are many, but I shall mention only a few of the most significant, which have left a lasting impression on me.

Cadre Camaraderie

After our joining the Andhra Pradesh cadre, my husband, Pradeep Bhide, and I called on Chief Secretary Bhagwan Das. He welcomed us warmly but commented with a loud guffaw, 'So you are the couple that is going to give me all the trouble, right?' We were the first IAS couple in the cadre and he was perhaps expressing his anxiety about the problems he would face to accommodate both of us in the same districts or, at least, in nearby districts. Fortunately for us, Bhagwan Das and the other chief secretaries who followed him were extremely considerate and gave us convenient postings.

Looking back, I realise that it was such gestures of kindness and consideration for colleagues that really helped in creating a bond among all those who were cadre mates. It was only later on, when we went to the Government of India on deputation, that we realised what it meant to be a cadre mate. It is a special bond that binds IAS officers from the same state cadre, and it not only helped in official interactions among officers but also in interactions between their families. This was, indeed, a very comforting thought for young officers facing the vast ocean of the Central government's bureaucracy for the first time.

Lifelong Impact of Training

When an IAS officer is fresh in a district and is learning the nitty-gritty of district administration, the influence of the district collector on her/him is decisive. The theoretical part of training in the academy soon recedes into the background, and the young officer becomes keen on learning what the ground reality of district administration is all about. I used to make a mental note of every word the collector said, his gestures, and the way he interacted with the subordinate staff and local politicians.

I was very fortunate to have Kosal Ram as the 'Training Collector' in Kurnool. He had the unenviable task of getting me through a specially designed capsule training course of just four months against the prescribed period of one year, because I had changed my cadre from Gujarat to Andhra Pradesh half-way during the field training period. He was very thorough in his knowledge of district administration and took great pains to ensure that I got an exposure to all aspects of it in the brief period available. His wife, Priya, was a very friendly person and invited us frequently to their house for chats and homemade meals. Admittedly, I had only rudimentary culinary skills in those days and we were tired of the fare that came in tiffin carriers from local restaurants. In the evenings, Pradeep and I used to sit discussing 'official matters' with the collector for as long as possible till Priya had no choice but to invite us to stay on for dinner. We gratefully (and very promptly) accepted the invitation. Our friendship with the family continues till today.

B. N. Yugandhar, who had been collector and district magistrate of Srikakulam district at the height of the Naxalite uprising in the late 1960s, came to the National Academy of Administration in Mussoorie and was our course director in October 1973. He inspired all the probationers with his stirring speeches on how we were expected to serve the weaker sections of society and protect them from exploitation by the well-entrenched upper classes. He once told us in the academy, 'I want to break the shackles of your mind and remove all the cobwebs that have clogged it.' It was not surprising that after such inspiring words, we left the academy to take up our assignments as sub-collectors flush with idealism, with a desire to ensure fair play and justice for the weaker sections, and to improve their socioeconomic status. It is said that an IAS officer's initial years in a district are the most socially committed and productive period in her/his service. From my own experience, I fully endorse this view.

Indelible Impressions

When I worked as sub-collector in Ranga Reddy district from 1975–1977, I was very fortunate to have Raghavendra Rao and, later, Venugopal Reddy as my collectors. Both were extraordinary officers, two of the finest in the Indian Administrative Service. I soon realised that both of them were successful as collectors because they understood the pulse of the people. They had a deep understanding of what the people of the district needed and how best the district administration could deliver the government's services and welfare schemes to them. What impressed me the most was the way both of them dealt with local politicians. There was a very cordial relationship between them and the local elected representatives. They listened carefully to the politicians and gave due weight to what they had to say. The politicians, in turn, respected them for their wisdom and understanding of how the district administration should conduct itself.

When I read in the news these days of head-on confrontations between bureaucrats and politicians, I recollect what I learnt during my sub-collector days from these collectors. They impressed upon me that politicians and bureaucrats have both been entrusted with responsibilities under the democratic system in the country, and both have to carry out their duties in as harmonious a manner as possible. There is no need for either of them to turn to the Constitution or to the courts to assert their authority over the other. Both parties have to only bear in mind that they have an equal responsibility to achieve the common goals of welfare of the people and progress of the country.

Magisterial Responsibilities

The primary responsibility of an IAS officer in the district is carrying out certain magisterial duties. Two of the important ones are the holding of elections and maintaining law and order. I had interesting experiences with both.

During my tenure as Joint Collector in Khammam district between 1979 and 1980, the national election was to be held in January 1980. I was the Returning Officer for the Khammam parliamentary constituency, the largest in the country in terms of area, covering all the tribal areas of the five contiguous districts of Khammam, East Godavari, West Godavari, Srikakulam, and Vizianagaram. It was a reserved constituency for tribals. When the nominations were received, alarm bells began ringing in the Home Ministry in New Delhi and in the state government. One of the candidates was a convicted Naxalite leader who had spent several years in jail, having been convicted on various charges of murder and attempts to overthrow duly elected governments. Rumours spread that he intended to get elected to Parliament and then subvert parliamentary institutions from within. I received several phone calls from a few senior officials in the Home Ministry, advising me to reject his nomination on some pretext or the other.

I studied the case carefully. It was true that he had been sentenced to rigorous imprisonment for a period of six years. However, this period of imprisonment included the years he had spent as an undertrial. His six-year ban on participating in elections had got over much before January 1980. According to the Representation of the People Act, 1951, read with the relevant election rules and regulations, he was eligible to stand for the election in January 1980. I made enquiries with the superintendents of police in all the five districts about whether there were reports of this candidate intending to subvert the election process. None of them had any such information.

It was a very difficult decision to make. The Returning Officer has to exercise her/his judgement in such matters and cannot seek any external opinion. If, after getting elected to Parliament, the former Naxalite leader indulged in violence and extra-constitutional activities, I would surely be blamed for my negligence and disregard for warnings given informally by senior officials in the Home Ministry. If, on the other hand, I rejected his nomination on unfounded allegations, it would be a travesty of justice. It could possibly incite the Naxalites to intensify their insurgency. After weighing all these factors, I decided to accept the nomination, and wrote, in my own hand, a detailed justification for my decision.

On the eve of the election, a large number of tribals gathered in the office compound of the Joint Collector. All night long, they sang revolutionary songs, led by Gummadi Vittal Rao, a balladeer popularly known as Gaddar. To our great surprise, they also sang songs in praise of the district administration for upholding the fundamental rights of their candidate. However, I spent a sleepless night, wondering what was in store for us the next day when polling began. I sent a confidential message to all the superintendents of police and tahsildars to be on their guard.

The election, mercifully, went off peacefully. The Naxalite leader lost and a tribal woman of the Congress party won the election. There was all-round relief. After a few weeks, I received a letter from the Ministry of Home, Government of India, forwarded to me by the Chief Secretary of Andhra Pradesh, appreciating the manner in which I, as the Returning Officer, had conducted the election in a peaceful manner. It was heartening to know that the path of following the rule of law and respecting the fundamental rights of a common citizen had paid dividends.

When I worked as Collector of Nizamabad district from 1982 to 1983, I faced many crises—floods, drought, students' agitations, disputes over the sharing of irrigation water, and communal violence, to name just a few. To handle these problems, I had to first properly understand the situation at the ground level by making frequent tours through the district and interacting directly with the people. I had to judge each situation myself and try to deal with it as tactfully as possible. For instance, communal violence erupted during the immersion of Ganesh idols on the last day of the Ganesh Chaturthi festival in September 1983. Although an understanding had been worked out by the Superintendent of Police with the organisers of the festival on the modalities of regulating the procession, this understanding was breached by both sides. Violence erupted, and prohibitory orders under Section 144 of the Code of Criminal Procedure were imposed. The people involved in the disturbance were dispersed.

It began raining incessantly and the power in the entire city went off. We realised that the abandoned idols were getting damaged in the heavy rain. Fearing that emotions would be aroused if people saw the disfigured idols the next morning, I requested the Assistant Collector under training, V. Bhaskar, to seek the help of the headquarters tahsildar and his staff to swiftly move the idols and quietly immerse them in the nearby river—all under cover of darkness.

The next day, some leaders came to meet the Superintendent of Police and me to protest against the high-handedness of the administration in removing their idols from the carts on the roads without their permission. When they saw that the Collector and the Superintendent of Police were firm and united in justifying their actions on the grounds of maintaining law and order, they agreed to a compromise solution—only one idol would be taken as a token for immersion, with a strict police escort. The neutrality of the administration and the timely action taken by it to control the situation sent a message to all the parties concerned—no mischief from any quarter would be tolerated. There were no communal incidents for the rest of my tenure in the district.

Some Hard Lessons

My tenure as a Project Officer of the Integrated Tribal Development Agency (ITDA) in Vizianagaram district during 1980–1981 was a period of hard learning because I had never before been exposed to the unique culture and social norms of the tribal people. I realised very soon that I would have to be really creative in adapting the development schemes of the government to the special socioeconomic situation of the tribal areas. Inevitably, in this process of adaptation, some mistakes were made.

We were expected to take up minor irrigation check dam projects across seasonal rivulets that flowed during the monsoon so that tribals could irrigate their nearby fields in the dry season. According to government rules, we had to follow an open competitive bidding procedure and call for tenders by publishing the notification in three local newspapers. The contractor was to be selected on the basis of his low bid and his experience in executing similar projects. I followed this scrupulously, but soon realised there were flaws in the system. No printed daily newspapers were available in the tribal areas and the tribals were not literate enough to read them. The daily newspapers were published and distributed in the non-tribal areas of Vizianagaram district. Not surprisingly, the contractors who submitted bids for such minor irrigation projects were non-tribals. They did not reside in tribal areas and had no idea of the geo-physical contours of the region. The check dams that they constructed did not even last a season, and the cement they used was substandard. Those days, there was an acute shortage of cement in the open market and contractors sold the cement that was provided to them by the ITDA at black market rates. I was quite disturbed to see the large-scale failure of our minor irrigation schemes, but it was only after some time that I realised the folly of our administration.

In December 1980, soon after I had joined as a Project Officer, ITDA in Vizianagaram district, a young tribal leader in Bhadragiri block met me and explained to me why he thought these projects had failed. He said that the non-tribal contractors did not live in the area and had no idea about the terrain they were working in. They ended up constructing check dams in the wrong places and these were washed away when the current became strong. Second, they did not use adequate cement and the mud check dams were easily broken by the flow of water. He showed me an ideal spot where a check dam ought to be constructed and gave me a plausible explanation of why he felt so. I was quite impressed with his knowledge of local conditions, his innate technical acumen, and his sincerity. I spoke to the Commissioner of Tribal Welfare about deviating from the rules so that such contracts could be awarded on a nomination basis to local tribals. He was hesitant at first, but later agreed to allow the process of nomination for only two projects on an experimental basis. I was excited about this fresh approach to tribal area development. Would the experiment work? With bated breath, we awaited the completion of the projects.

To the amazement of all the officials in the ITDA, the tribal leader and his team implemented the two projects in record time, accounting fully for the cement and funds provided by us. After observing that the check dams withstood strong currents very well during the ensuing monsoon, we requested a senior irrigation engineer to inspect them and certify whether they met the technical specifications set by the department of minor irrigation. The engineer certified that the two check dams were well up to standards. We were delighted with the success of the experiment, and the tribals celebrated by dancing all night long. However, the celebration was short-lived.

We were told that the special permission given for nominating the local tribal leader as the 'implementing agency' in two projects could not be made a norm because the rules did not allow field officers to exercise such discretionary powers. We realised soon enough that the non-tribal contractors were a powerful lobby, and this had ensured that such a relaxation of rules was never going be allowed to take place on a regular basis. For me, it was a sad realisation that even in the face of clearly flawed development strategies for tribal areas, very little could be done by someone wanting to change the system.

Another failure that I faced was in the implementation of a programme for imparting technical training to tribal youth in different fields such as masonry, woodwork, welding, and plumbing. A special Industrial Training Institute (ITI) for tribal youth had been set up in Khammam district in the mid-1970s. With great enthusiasm, I collected ten applications from tribal boys who were willing to undergo such training, and, in the course of time, all of them graduated from their respective courses.

The next problem was finding suitable jobs for them. There were no job openings for technically qualified people in the tribal areas of Vizianagaram. However, there were many large industrial units in Vishakhapatnam city ('Vizag' for short), which was in the neighbouring district. One of them, Bharat Heavy Plates and Vessels Ltd. (BHPV), a public-sector undertaking, agreed to give the trained tribal boys jobs in their plant in 1981. We were happy that the boys had obtained regular employment, that too in a well-established public-sector concern. After a few months, we enquired with the management of BHPV how the tribal boys were doing. We were in for a very rude shock! All the boys, one by one, had run away, returning to their tribal homes in the forests of Vizianagaram. They said that the boys had not been able to adjust to life in a large metropolis and had felt disoriented. We had no clue as to how to facilitate their social adjustment to a new urban environment. It was a difficult conundrum for me, which left me saddened and confused.

Making a Difference

A district collector is the head of all the government's development and welfare departments at the district level. With considerable financial and manpower resources at her/his command, s/he has a great opportunity to take up development schemes that can change the lives of the people for the better. I would like to mention a few of the initiatives taken by me as the Collector in Nizamabad between 1982 and 1983.

Nizamabad was well-known for growing good turmeric, which was prized for its high curcumin content. The marketing of the turmeric was not well-organised and the farmers did not get a remunerative price for their produce. We decided to organise a regulated wholesale market to eliminate the middlemen, who used to buy directly from the farmers at very low prices. The District Cooperative Marketing Society (DCMS) was strengthened and a system of open auctions was introduced. Wholesale buyers from all over the country began attending these auctions and Nizamabad soon became the most important wholesale market for turmeric in the country. The farmers got much higher prices in these auctions, and funds were provided by me to the DCMS to construct godowns so that some of the turmeric could be stored to be sold in the offseason at a higher price.

The farmers were also encouraged to go in for organic farming. Certified organic turmeric was in high demand in global markets and the export of turmeric from Nizamabad brought even greater returns to the farmers. We also encouraged manufacturers of turmeric-based herbal medicines and beauty products to set up their units in Nizamabad. This not only created high local demand for the raw produce, but also provided employment to the local youth. The district administration's strategy for developing the production of high-quality organic turmeric in Nizamabad was a success and resulted in much higher incomes to local farmers. Nizamabad soon became the most important turmeric producing district in the country and the leading wholesale market for turmeric.

Another initiative taken by the district administration was upgrading the status of traditional workers such as masons, plumbers, electricians, welders, and carpenters, who had learnt their skills from family elders. These skilled workers were in high demand in the Middle East. However, they did not get remunerative wages because they did not have any certificates or diplomas from recognised institutes. They were thus at the mercy of unscrupulous labour contractors who demanded huge upfront payments for getting them jobs in the Middle East.

We decided to send some young boys who had learnt basic technical skills from elders in their families and had also passed the twelfth standard to an Industrial Training Institute. The young people were admitted to courses for one or two years and were awarded certificates once they had completed them. This improved their job prospects in the Middle East. We also requested the consulates of some of the Middle Eastern countries to screen the agents and empanel them as recognised agencies for the recruitment of qualified technical people. This substantially brought down the level of exploitation of these people. Very soon, foreign exchange remittances from these workers in the Middle East started to flow to their families in Nizamabad district, and brought in a prosperity that the people there had never seen before.

Introducing Technology

From the mid-1990s, there was a great deal of focus in Andhra Pradesh on introducing technology in government. Chief Minister N. Chandrababu Naidu was keen on industrialising the state. He realised that it would be difficult to compete with states such as Maharashtra, Tamil Nadu, Gujarat, and Karnataka in traditional heavy industries because they already had a lead in this field. He therefore wanted a thrust to be given to new emerging tech industries such as information technology (IT), IT-enabled services, biotechnology, pharmaceuticals, and specialty chemicals—all sectors in which people from Andhra Pradesh had excelled in the US. He expected civil servants to become familiar with these new emerging technologies and to adopt new strategies to promote investments in these emerging sectors in the state.

I was Secretary, Industries between 1995 and 2001 and found the task very challenging. This required a completely different orientation and approach to industrial development on the part of civil servants. Specialised industrial parks for high-tech industries, such as information technology at Madhapur and biotechnology at Shamirpet, were set up. The chief minister called himself the CEO of the state and marketed the state as an attractive investment destination. New institutes for training specialised manpower were set up to serve these new industries. Uninterrupted power supply, good quality piped water, internet facilities, and well-developed industrial plots were made available to new investors in these industrial parks. Andhra Pradesh became the fastest industrialising state in the late 1990s, ranking fourth in the country for attracting new investments. A combination of de-regulation of industries, encouragement to foreign investments, a dynamic political leadership at the state level, good teamwork among senior state government officials, and the support of Telugu non-resident Indians contributed to the rapid industrialisation of the state from the mid-1990s onwards.

One of the important factors in Hyderabad becoming an IT hub was that political leaders and senior bureaucrats in Andhra Pradesh approached their relationship with industry in a new spirit of partnership, rather than trying to regulate and control. The true spirit of entrepreneurship and the latent talent of the people were allowed to blossom. This was the driving spirit behind Hyderabad's IT journey.

Looking back on the experience of promoting the IT industry in Hyderabad, I am of the view that one of the main reasons why information technology took off in the country in the 1990s was that there were no significant government regulations in place. Government officials were not yet exposed to the IT industry and were not aware of what rules and regulations were required to be put in place. India was emerging out of the licence and permit raj, and the IT revolution happened at the right time as a new spirit of liberalisation was sweeping the country.

Further, with liberalisation, the IT industry had the opportunity to develop its own strategies to face many challenges. The industry association, the National Association of Software and Service Companies (NASSCOM), had been set up in 1988. It provided a forum to the leaders of the nascent industry to discuss issues and resolve problems within the industry circles. NASSCOM presidents such as Dewang Mehta, Kiran Karnik, and Som Mittal provided leadership to the industry. The newly established Hyderabad Software Exporters' Association (HYSEA) encouraged the city's IT companies to globalise their operations. In the late 1990s, the Y2K problem presented a great opportunity for Indian IT companies to set right computers in offices the world over.

Modernisation of the state inevitably required modernisation of the government's functioning. All officers in the secretariat were provided computers and had to undergo training in using them. All secretariat processes were digitised and decisions were taken online. Those were exhilarating times for all of us. No more dusty, bulky files being moved from one office to another by peons. The pace of decision-making quickened and there was greater transparency and accountability. Attendance in offices was marked by swiping identity cards on recording machines at the office entrance. This was mandatory for all—the chief minister, ministers, officials, and secretariat staff. Attendance improved, and so did efficiency. Civil servants were encouraged to become tech-savvy and to put in place a technology-driven administration so as to provide citizens with direct access to all government development schemes. Most of the government schemes were made accessible online to the public. For instance, they could apply for ration cards online and buy bus and train tickets at kiosks. The common citizen was, in a sense, empowered because there was much greater ease of dealing with government agencies.

Of course, digitisation of government processes had some negative fallout. Officers hardly had informal chats over lunch or tea any more. Most of the meetings were conducted virtually between senior secretariat officials and the field staff. Personal interactions between officials, which had earlier enabled them to sort out many problems, became limited.

Industry-Government Partnership

Modernisation and computerisation of government activities is very crucial in an evolving tech-driven world. It is inevitable if the administration has to move with the times. However, we have to bear in mind that technology is a tool to deliver government services to the people as efficiently as possible. It is important to examine how the digitisation of government processes will affect different segments of the people and to convince them that the change will benefit them. I say this from personal experience. As a Joint Secretary in the Ministry of Corporate Affairs in 2002, I was made the Project Officer to implement Project MCA21, an initiative to computerise and modernise the Ministry of Corporate Affairs to make it ready for the twenty-first century. It was the first major computerisation project of the Government of India, covering all the functions of the field offices of the registrars of companies and the secretariat. It required an outlay of Rs 487 crore, a sum unheard of for such projects in those days.

I visited some important registrar of company offices to understand the problems faced by company representatives in filing their documents physically. We soon realised that only experienced private IT companies would have the technical know-how and nationwide capability to implement such a large project. At that time, the government did not have in-house expertise for this. We created an advisory committee of eminent IT experts headed by Kiran Karnik, former chairman of NASSCOM, to guide us in taking the pioneering initiative forward.

Initially, there was tremendous opposition to the project from various stakeholders. The company secretaries thought their relevance to their clients would be diminished. The registrars of companies thought their importance in the system and their opportunity to make under-the-table income would diminish. The small companies felt that they did not have the resources to digitise all their records. Moreover, several of them used to file documents based on unauthenticated financial data and had an arrangement with officials of the Registrar of Companies to ensure that their files were 'misplaced' in the dusty record rooms. Digitisation of records and making them available to the public online would have exposed them sooner or later.

The Planning Commission opposed it vigorously on the ground that it was being outsourced for implementation to a private agency when there was enough in-house capability within the National Informatics Centre (NIC) to implement it. The finance ministry insisted that it did not have the resources to fund such a project in a single year. It said that it could provide only Rs 20 crore a year, and that computerisation should proceed in an incremental manner.

To introduce new technologies on a significant scale, it is necessary to first convince all the parties likely to be affected that it will be in their interest to cooperate in implementing the project. Company secretaries were allowed to file documents on behalf of the owners of companies and found that new career prospects opened up for them. An effective system of reward and punishment was introduced for the registrars of companies and their key staff members, and they felt that it was better to fall in line. The companies saved a lot of time and money by filing their documents online.

Jaswant Singh, the Finance Minister in 2002, was also the Minister for Corporate Affairs. He overruled the finance ministry and Planning Commission officials and sanctioned the entire amount for the project upfront. The result was that the entire project could be completed in three years, with funds being released to the identified private implementing agency as and when required. The level of compliance went up several-fold and the government's revenues from filing fees went up substantially. Finance ministry officials were delighted that the increased revenue from filing fees in the first three years far exceeded the entire amount spent on the project.

The banks were very happy with the project because they had easy online access to all the property documents of the companies they wished to finance. There was no longer a need to sit in dusty record rooms of registrars' offices to hunt out old physical documents in various stages of disintegration. They were also no longer at the mercy of record-keepers who refused to cooperate unless they were paid under the table.

The implementing agency, which was selected by fair, open competitive bidding, was experienced and implemented the project without any glitches in two years. In appreciation of the successful implementation of the first major computerisation project for the Government of India, the project team received the Prime Minister's Award for Excellence in Public Administration in 2007. The 24/7 online facility for filing documents eased the process of the statutory annual filing of documents by companies. It reduced transactional costs, eliminated corruption, and improved levels of compliance.

What Lies Ahead?

Artificial intelligence, machine learning, the internet of things (IoT), data analytics, virtual reality, augmented reality, blockchain, and robotic process automation are some of the buzz words we hear these days. At times, we feel overwhelmed by these rapid technological changes, but the government will have to adapt itself to them. The experience of implementing the MCA21 project made me realise that although introducing technology in the administration was critical to improving efficiencies in governance, technology, per se, was not neutral.

It can impact different people in different ways. It can also be divisive and create new classes in society—those who are tech savvy and those who are not, those who have access to computers and the internet and those who do not. Therefore, such projects have to be taken up by civil servants after considerable thought and planning. The officers have to be trained to understand the basics of the technology and the modalities of using it effectively in administration. Only then can we hope to implement such technology-based projects in the government in a smooth and efficient manner.

While technology is an important tool for achieving efficiencies and transparencies in governance, civil servants must not forget that their primary responsibility is to ensure that people's lives are made better by such interventions. Therefore, development projects must always be people-centric, with technology serving as an instrument to achieve their goals as efficiently as possible.

12

Unity and Diversity

NITIN DESAI

Looking back on one's working life, what usually looks most interesting is one's path from one job to another. This requires an explanation of why and how one moved, and that often involves rather specific anecdotes. But looking back upon episodes from one's working life, one can also ask whether there was some continuity of aims and ability amid the changes. Is there something that lent unity to a diverse career?

In my case, a shift came at the very beginning. I came from a legal family and the intention was that although I would go to the London School of Economics, I would also qualify as a barrister-at-law. What happened there reflected my academic ability and I ended up as a postgraduate, eligible and well-qualified for academia. My image of myself had always stressed my academic ability and I was readily persuaded to change my goal from law to academia. In some ways, this was what brought unity to my diverse career, which, if I had to describe it in terms applicable to all my jobs, focused on the capacity and desire to connect economic theory and development practice. My working life began in 1965 as a faculty member in Liverpool and Southampton University.

After working as an academic in Britain for five years, I felt a desire to return to India. There was no clear indication that I would obtain a university post in India. Moreover, after five years of teaching economic theory, I was diffident about my ability to make new contributions in this area. I felt I needed to move over to the application of economic theory to practical policy analysis.

This is what happened when I returned to India and joined Tata Economic Consultancy Service (TECS) in 1970 in Mumbai. A major opportunity for me to connect my knowledge of economic theory to practical development came when TECS got a contract from the City and Industrial Development Corporation (CIDCO), Mumbai, to do a formal study for an industrial location policy for Navi Mumbai, a new city that was coming up across the water from the island city of Mumbai.

I carried out this study in collaboration with several other TECS staffers, using a very structured and formal model of two-region growth and some innovative ideas on the role of agglomeration economies in urban development. My one regret is that this good study is still not publicly accessible. Perhaps because of my youth and because TECS was not an academic organisation, the CIDCO set up an advisory committee to oversee the preparation of the study, which included economist Sukhamoy Chakravarthy. Chakravarthy was impressed by the theoretical rigour of the model, the way we used it despite gaps in data availability, and my vigorous defence of our proposed approach at advisory committee meetings. This contact with him led to the next unpredictable twist in my career.

In 1971, Chakravarthy was appointed as a member of the Planning Commission, which the new government opened up for lateral recruitment, in order to strengthen it. On Chakravarthy's advice, I was inducted in 1973 into the newly formed Project Appraisal Division (PAD), which I ended up heading informally in 1977 and formally in 1979. This appraisal of public investment involved the development of a workable cost-benefit analysis based on the theoretical work in welfare economics. Later, I was involved a little more in the formulation of broader development strategy.

This shift from the academic world to private consulting, and from private consulting to national civil service involved contacts with influential persons and my willingness to leave a safe and satisfying job for a challenging one. The first shift happened because of my contact with Freddie Mehta, a director in Tata who recruited me to TECS. But perhaps more significant was the contact with Chakravarthy, who recruited me to the Planning Commission. Each of these jobs involved a change in my occupational ambition and in my knowledge and understanding of practical economics. They also changed my capacity for teamwork and for writing presentations that would convince others who were less well-versed in economic theory. More importantly, the exposure to the problems and challenges of the real economy and politics made me reinterpret much of academic economics.

The final step in my career was a shift to international civil service. This began with my induction as a Senior Adviser to the World Commission on Environment and Development (better known now as the Brundtland Commission). In 1985, I was brought in to bridge the gap between the members from developing countries, who saw a global push for environmental goals as an obstacle to growth and poverty reduction, and the environmentalists, mainly from the developed world, who saw the priority for growth as a major challenge to the future of the environment. This is where I introduced the concept of sustainable development as an idea that could connect development aspirations and environmental protection. This was well received, and it also greatly improved the impact of the Brundtland Commission on the global development dialogue.

The recognition of my contribution to the outcome of the Brundtland Commission shaped the rest of my career. A senior and active member of the Commission, Janos Stanovnik, who later became the President of Slovenia, stated, 'The Brundtland Commission has had tremendous impact on governmental policy thinking. Documents of my little country's government now always speak of "sustainable development". I think that the "father" of this thinking is Nitin Desai, who was economic adviser to the commission.' Secretary-General of the Commission Jim MacNeill wrote in the copy of the final report that he gave me, 'To Nitin Desai, Without whose knowledge, wisdom, penmanship and steadfast support, we would never have made it.'

I came back in 1987 as a special secretary in the Planning Commission and then as secretary and chief economic adviser (CEA) in the finance ministry. But the short stint as CEA turned out to be a diversion from a career that had become a continuation of my work in the Brundtland Commission. In 1990, the United

Nations decided to hold a World Conference on Environment and Development (WCED) and named Maurice Strong, a well-known environmentalist and businessman, as its Secretary-General. Strong, who had been an active member of the Brundtland Commission, knew me and had seen the effectiveness of my work there. He asked me to join and I was appointed Deputy Secretary-General of the WCED.

My role in the WCED was to lead the substantive preparations and partner the chairman of the preparatory committee, Tommy Koh, in managing the negotiations. I believe the competence I had built up in the Government of India to draft policies and proposals to both influence and reflect the views of Planning Commission members and of the committee of secretaries helped me greatly to support the global negotiating process. It is crucial to connect personal mastery over substantive issues with a capacity to listen and take the views of decision-makers into account in international organisations.

The success of the WCED, which met in June 1992 at Rio de Janeiro, was widely recognised by diplomats and UN Secretary-General Boutros Boutros-Ghali. My personal engagement with the substantive preparations and the negotiating process led to much of the credit for the success of the Rio Earth Summit being attributed to me. This led to another major twist in my career—the Secretary-General appointed me as an Under Secretary-General of the Department for Policy Coordination and Sustainable Development in February 1993. I continued as Under Secretary-General for Economic and Social Affairs when Kofi Annan took over as Secretary-General of the UN at the end of 1996, and remained in that role till August 2003.

In a way, my ten years at the UN were more or less a continuation of what I had done for the Rio conference, but with a wider remit. What mattered was my competence in economic and social affairs, my sensitivity to the views of country representatives, and my active engagement with non-governmental organisations that brought issue-oriented concerns into the discussion and negotiation processes. This diluted the standard focus on finding a compromise between divergent national interests and concerns.

My formal career ended in 2003, but I have continued my association with the UN. In 2010, the Secretary-General appointed me as a Special Adviser on Internet Governance, which was not a full-time position but one where I contributed when required. The main achievement was the establishment of the Internet Governance Forum in the UN, which continues to this day and has drawn governments and other stakeholders of the internet together for a constructive dialogue.

In the years since my retirement from the UN, I have lived in New Delhi and have been occasionally involved in policy dialogue and advice, mainly when Manmohan Singh was prime minister. I have been on the board of several research and non-governmental organisations. Much of my involvement is based on my standing as a promoter of sustainable development and environmental protection.

This narrative of my career shows the diversity of the employers I have had—in academia, the private sector, the national government, and international organisations. It also shows the consistency I provided in connecting economic understanding and practical application. But the jobs differed in some respects and that must also be mentioned.

In academia, one is quite independent as a faculty member and not under the tight control of a departmental head or vice-chancellor. In the private sector, your relationship with your superiors is determined largely by their perception of your commercial value. In governments, your bureaucratic superiors share their authority over you with their political masters, and this can sometimes lead to a distortion in hierarchical norms. In international organisations, departmental heads are very independent and control by political participants is much more diffuse than in national governments. The key to impact and success is how tactfully you balance your independent position and views with your need to work as part of a team where others also hold independent positions.

The other difference worth looking at is the physical basis of work, which changed dramatically between 1965, when I started working, and 2003, when my career ended. At the start of my working life, the process of acquiring information was time-consuming and the data was often rare or old. Preparing drafts involved typewriters, and redrafts required retyping. Everything had to be stored on paper. This has changed substantially with the development of calculators, computers, and the internet, which came to be used widely in the 1970s, 1980s, and 1990s, respectively. This has made acquiring data and information much easier and less time-consuming than in the past, and allows one to concentrate more on thinking. This too will be affected, hopefully in a positive way, by the rapid development of artificial intelligence (AI).

Thus, the way in which today's job seekers have to work is very different from how we worked. But the basic principle behind seeking a job or changing one remains the same—one must always do what one's knowledge and interest are best for, and jump at new opportunities to use these more effectively.

13

Abiding Friendship, Building Trust

N. K. Singh

As I look back on my life, it is a mix of successes, failures, excitement, and disappointment. I can reach no uniform conclusion. It has been a long, sometimes unexpected, and even often arduous journey, but on the whole, there has been an extraordinary joy of working. What has been one continuous thread over the eight decades of my life? It has been the power of abiding friendships and building trust.

In my early years, under the guidance of my father, I identified economics as the subject I was interested in. Having completed my postgraduation from the Delhi School of Economics, I was greatly inspired by the intellectual prowess and humility of Jagdish Bhagwati, Amartya Sen, Padma Desai, and K. N. Raj, to mention a few. Therefore, when I got a job as a lecturer of economics at St. Stephen's College in 1963, I grabbed it with great excitement.

At that stage, I was not too enamoured with taking the examination for the civil services. My father's experience in the Indian Civil Services (ICS), notwithstanding the success he achieved, was a mixed one. The guiding philosophy of the ICS was that you had to be politically neutral, carry out the decisions of the elected representatives, and, most importantly, fearlessly tender such advice as you considered appropriate. In practice, however, what he said on bank nationalisation was not appreciated. I then learned that encounters with the truth could be a mixed blessing.

Under these circumstances, it took quite a bit of persuasion from my parents for me to take the examination for the civil services. It was agreed that, if successful, I would join the Indian Foreign Service (IFS). I got into the Foreign Service and joined as a probationer in 1964. Then, under repeated pressure, particularly from my mother, I crossed over to the Indian Administrative Service (IAS) in the same year. In the service for more than fifty years, the experience was always educative and, very often, hilarious, but always sustained by personal relationships, which had their own twists and turns.

I will recount four such instances.

After some years in Bihar, in 1969, I joined the Ministry of Commerce, which was presided over by the one and only K. B. Lall, jocularly referred to as '*Khudha Miya*' because he always had the last word. Within three days of my joining as Under Secretary in the International Trade Policy Division, he summoned me to his room and said that he would like me to prepare a few pages of a speech for Foreign Minister Dinesh Singh, to be delivered at a United Nations conference. I told him that I was hardly a week old and this was a tall order. He rebuked me, which shook me up. He said that I had to learn some time, and it better be now. It was really a baptism by fire.

Chastened, for the next two days, I read as much as I could and produced a three-page draft on commercial and trade policy issues. I went back to Lall. He took a careful look at my draft, asked me to sit down, and began dictating. As he proceeded, my face fell more and more, as I realised that it had no relation whatsoever with what I had proposed. He then looked up with a smile and said, 'Do not feel disappointed. I have, after all, used two words from your draft.' This hardly put me at ease, but the episode ended. But my baptism by fire continued.

In a few months, I had acquired some familiarity with the language and verbiage of multilateral negotiations. Lall asked me to prepare myself for an important conference of non-aligned countries in Lusaka, Zambia in 1970. Prime Minister Indira Gandhi was to arrive later and I was to be part of an advance preparatory team. Since he was reposing trust in me, I asked him for some guidance on the brief that I had prepared. He looked at me and said, 'I hadn't thought about it, but on your way to the airport, please drop by at my house.' I dutifully did so and again asked him for his guidance.

He said, 'Go and create confusion.' I was taken aback. Lall laughed and said, 'Unless you create confusion and problems, what will I solve when I come later?'

I went to Lusaka for the conference and circulated several drafts of possible agreements among countries in the non-aligned movement. I also went to the Yugoslavian mission, and a few developing countries began a debate on two possible drafts.

Soon after, I went to receive Lall, who was accompanying the prime minister, at the airport. He asked me to ride with him, and enquired about the scene at the conference. I told him there was utter confusion—I had circulated several drafts, which some delegates even thought were their own. He smiled, and asked, 'Where is the real one?' I took a script out of my pocket and handed it over, which pleased him. I had won his confidence and trust. This paid off soon, in that he gave me many opportunities to prove myself in various meetings of the General Agreement on Tariffs and Trade (GATT). (At that time, there was no World Trade Organization [WTO], IMF, or the UN Conference on Trade and Development [UNCTAD].)

Not much later, I was asked to attend an UNCTAD meeting in Geneva. I was preparing for the meeting when I was asked by the Ambassador of India in Brussels, who also looked after UNCTAD, to order a top-class lunch at Hotel Du Rhone, a well-regarded establishment at that time. UNCTAD Secretary General Manuel Pérez-Guerrero would be at the lunch. He also asked me to order some good quality wine. On reaching the hotel, I asked for the menu and the wine list. When it came to wines, I was confidently told by the manager that every kind of wine was available—French, Italian, and even fresh Swiss wine. If I was not particularly interested in red meat, they could give me chicken or prawn cocktails. These, I ordered. The ambassador and the secretary general arrived, and the lunch commenced. The ambassador took two sips of the wine and called me. He asked me what wine I had ordered. I told him that I had ordered fresh Swiss wine. He looked angry and perturbed.

He cancelled my order and asked for some decent French wine. It did not stop there. He sent a classified telegram to Delhi, in which he pointed out that the next time the ministry sent representatives to such meetings, it should ensure that they had a minimum understanding of diplomatic obligations.

This rebuke was taken note of. Lall laughed about it and said that I must learn about wines, generously sending me a book on wines. It took some time to acquire a respectable knowledge of wines and vintage years. The trust Lall reposed in me helped during this awkward incident.

Another incident relates to an identity crisis–the state administration mistook me for someone who had the same name as me. When I returned to Bihar in 1977, I was appointed as Special Secretary, Irrigation and Power. A little later, the chairman of the Bihar State Electricity Board (BSEB), Brigadier S. P. Kochhar, lost the trust of the new government headed by Chief Minister Ram Sundar Das. An interim arrangement for the chairman of the electricity board needed to be made. The mentors of the chief minister advised him to appoint N. K. Singh as the acting chairman. Yashwant Sinha was the principal secretary to the chief minister.

Sinha congratulated me on my additional assignment as the acting chairman of the BSEB, which was in a colossal mess. Two days later, he told me a problem had arisen because the chief minister had asked him how and why Nandu Babu, which was my nickname, had become chairman of the electricity board. Sinha was very surprised, and said, 'That's what you had said.' The chief minister then clarified that the person he had meant was N. K. Singh Jr., another officer with the same name. Although this identity crisis caused great amusement, I continued as the BSEB chairman till my return to Delhi in 1980.

I was transferred to the Indian Embassy in Tokyo as First Minister, Economic and Commercial Affairs in 1980. During that assignment, I realised that it was difficult to gain the confidence of the Japanese, who are, by nature, somewhat reticent. But I cultivated some people in vantage positions in the ministry of finance, and realised that once a person accepted you as a trusted friend, the relationship would last long.

Three clear instances come to mind. The first was in 1985, when India wanted to borrow from the Asian Development Bank (ADB). I approached Toyoo Gyohten, who was then vice minister of the ministry of finance, and made the request. He laughed, and said I must be joking. India was an important equity partner and it would destroy the *raison d'être* of the regional development bank if a large country like India were to become a borrower. The purpose of this regional bank was to bolster the economic development of much smaller countries. I persisted with my request during two subsequent meetings. Then, at a lunch at my house, he laughed and said, 'All right, please become a borrower. It comes with the condition that you give up your automatic right to the vice chairman's chair,' a position that India had traditionally enjoyed.

The second instance that I recall is my friendship with Shigemitsu Sugisaki, who was in a high position in the ministry of finance. We had become good friends, and in 1990–1991, during the balance of payments crisis, we needed both friends and accommodation. Finance Secretary S. P. Shukla and Chief Economic Advisor Deepak Nayyar realised that the sums likely to be pledged would not add up to investor expectations. They told me that one way in which the gap could be bridged was if the Japanese could significantly enhance their pledge, and asked me if I could use my own links in Japan to achieve this. Time was short because the pledges had to be made the very next day.

I rang up Sugisaki at some unearthly hour, and made this request. He was taken aback, but understood my plight and wanted to help. The instructions were altered overnight. The next day, the Japanese made a very robust pledge and the arithmetic added up. My trust was repaid in ample measure.

The third important instance was in 1991 when Michel Camdessus had come to India to assess if our structural reform programme was on track. During my successive visits to the IMF, I had developed a reasonable familiarity with him. I looked after Camdessus, and accompanied him to the Mehrangarh Fort in Jodhpur for a private lunch hosted by the former Maharaja of Jodhpur in the fort's coronation room. This left a deep imprint on his mind. He exclaimed that the legacy and history of this country needed to be preserved. The country had run into a balance of payments crisis, but international multilateral entities would do their very best to help us out, he implied.

I also had the privilege of working with Manmohan Singh in multiple capacities. I had known him from the time he joined the government as economic advisor in the ministry of commerce. We developed a strong rapport and this continued over a long period.

One hilarious incident, which was a bit bewildering to us all, was when, during the balance of payments crisis, I went with Manmohan Singh to Bangkok in 1991 for the annual meetings of the IMF and the World Bank. We were a bit tense, since it was a critical moment in securing international support. We were in his suite in the Oriental Hotel in Bangkok in the evening with other members of the delegation, discussing the country's position, when the room bell rang. This was followed by a knock on the door. He asked his private secretary, Rahul Khullar, to check who it was.

To our surprise, it was the Hinduja brothers, Srichand and Gopichand. They handed a letter over to Khullar, which had 'For your eyes only' on it. Curiosity ran high among the members of the delegation. Manmohan Singh opened the letter and found it had nothing surprising or consequential in it. It only contained routine information on what IMF President Lewis T. Preston would tell him at their bilateral meeting the next day. A sense of relief washed over the delegation.

Perhaps the most important instance of an abiding friendship and trust relates to Atal Bihari Vajpayee. He visited Japan when he was not a Member of Parliament. He was not technically entitled to be received by the Indian mission, but considering his association with my father and his standing in political life, I decided to drive a long distance to receive him at Narita Airport. This touched him. Much later, when he became the prime minister and appointed me as secretary of his office, he jocularly remarked that he had not forgotten the car ride from Narita Airport to his place of stay in Tokyo. He also enquired whether that car in which I had received him was still with me. As it happened, I had not sold the car. I have not done so till date because it holds so many memories.

Investing in people and places, and winning their genuine affection has a long-term value. Not least is the joy of unexpected insights and creativity, which can only come from collaboration. No internet of things or artificial intelligence can teach you this.

People Matter

K. SUJATHA RAO

I was brought up in Delhi. It was a lovely, safe city. I had a happy childhood, unaware of the fissures and cleavages, the daily deprivations and poverty of a majority of our citizens. But when I went to college in 1968, the air was rent with news of student rebellions everywhere, particularly in France and the US—against militarisation, insensitive bureaucracies, and the Vietnam War. Closer home, the Delhi University coffee shop was always full of young students fired with a desire to change the world into a more equal one. With China as their model, we heard of the birth of Naxalism, and many of our top students joined extremist movements to fight feudalism. In discussions among ourselves, we used all these words, but hardly understood what they meant. Even so, the times seeded our impressionable minds with ideas of injustice, poverty, exploitation, unfairness, and inequality. And as was the norm in many middle-class families, on completion of my MA, I sat for the Indian Administrative Service (IAS) examination and joined that service in 1974.

For my training, I was posted to the bubbling, cosmopolitan city of Visakhapatnam. It was, however, my visits to the rural parts of the district that exposed me to poverty and want. After my two-year training, I was posted as Sub-collector in the Vizianagaram subdivision. I was also the magistrate of the scheduled areas. Vizianagaram had large tracts of scheduled areas where tribals lived, many in a time warp of their own, suspicious and afraid of us. As opposed to the ready justice of village elders, the tribals were now confronted with formal systems of law and its trappings—a magistrate, black-robed lawyers, a witness box—all talking a language they did not understand.

I held court every Friday. To my amazement, I found cases that had been pending for years together. The poor tribals would travel a whole day—walking 10 miles to the bus stop, undertaking an arduous seven-hour bus journey, and then wending their way to my office, only to be told that the case was adjourned. This was happening as a result of collusion between lawyers.

To solve this problem, I decided to hold court in a very remote place called Munchingput. That place had just a one-room travellers' bungalow and a small tea shop, with a bus that came there at 10 AM and 4 PM every day. When I posted the case there, the lawyers were very excited at the thought of going to a new place.

On the court day, I busied myself with other work and called the lawyers at 3.30 PM and kept them waiting till the 4 PM bus had left. I posted the case at the same place the following week. Forced to stay the night in a less than hospitable place, I found at the next hearing that most of the cases had been settled out of court! It was as a sub-collector, full of idealism and a desire to solve the people's grievances, that I learnt that even in rule-bound, impersonal bureaucracies one can find solutions by being innovative.

My second posting was in the Department of Social Welfare in 1978 under an officer who had mentored many. He guided us to see the IAS as a catalyst for social change, aiming to break down barriers and achieve a more equitable society. Our conversations were important and had an effect on not just myself, but on a generation of us—on the way we worked and on our attitudes towards marginalised people.

One week after joining the department, I received a file dealing with a request from some very poor people, which the district authorities had rejected on the grounds of being against the rules. I studied the rules and regulations thoroughly and wrote a detailed note that, in short, upheld the field reports and submitted the file to the Secretary. The next day I was asked to meet him. I was expecting praise for the hard work I had put in on the vexatious matter. He sat me down and said that if citing rules was the objective of disposing of an issue, there were clerks who knew the rules far better than me. An IAS officer, on the other hand, he explained, was expected to examine how to interpret the rules and laws to ensure justice and help the poor. That advice and several conversations that followed were very important to shaping my understanding of myself as an administrator.

After the initial years in the field, which were highly rewarding, I was posted to the finance and planning department in 1985. Besides having to prepare a plan for the long coastline of Andhra Pradesh, I was also asked to work on using computer technology to improve efficiencies. Computers were then an innovation and there was much cynicism about their utility. My colleague in the department, who was in charge of data and statistics, distrusted computers deeply. He insisted on doing all calculations manually to make sure the machine was right!

I knew little about computers, but began to understand them better as I was given the responsibility of establishing Andhra Pradesh Technology Services (APTS), a government-owned company responsible for providing computers to all departments, as well as for training and assistance in using them. After APTS had been registered as a society, personnel had to be hired, computers and servers had to be bought, and the space to put them all in had to be found. The APTS was the first of its kind in the country and it led to the use of computers, which have become indispensable today, in all government departments. Looking back, it seems as if those were days from another time altogether. My superiors who guided me in all this were visionaries, ahead of their time in understanding the importance of technology.

In 1987, I was posted as Commissioner of School Education. I was the first IAS officer to be appointed to that post. It was a remarkable experience as I was deeply engaged with the implementation of the National Education Policy of 1984. Most primary schools had only one teacher and one classroom, with five classes being run in that room and the verandah. Under the 'Operation Black Board scheme', the states were to ensure a minimum of two teachers and two classrooms to be eligible for a grant-in-aid from the Union government. This meant that almost six times the routine budget had to be expended on constructing additional classrooms. I approached the secretary to the chief minister as no one was helping me with my proposal for an increased budget.

One morning, I got a call from the chief minister at 5 AM, asking me to come over to his house for a meeting. By the time I got there, senior leaders like Jana Reddy and Chandrababu Naidu were already there. The chief minister introduced the subject of enhancing the school building budget, but said that would mean reducing the money for internal roads. All opposed the proposal. I had tears welling up in my eyes. The chief minister took one look at me and announced that the money for constructing classrooms would be allotted. That chief minister was N. T. Rama Rao. While coming out after the meeting, one senior politician looked at me angrily and hissed, 'How do you think we will win elections?'

That was also the time of my first experience with technology. NTR had the idea that children would gain a better grasp of concepts and mathematics if audio-visual media were employed. A well-known film scriptwriter was hired to create classroom lessons that explained concepts in an engaging manner. These audio-visual lessons were then transmitted to TV sets that we supplied to all primary schools. Besides the films, it also meant training teachers on how to use these teaching aids and supplement lessons with them in the classroom. Since then, the Central government has set up audio-visual studios and sought to expand learning and standardise learning inputs through the use of technology. Today, we have computers that give access to excellent learning materials.

I spent two decades, from 1988–2010, in the health sector, with some breaks. Here, again, I saw how technology helped to save lives. I recall the hug of gratitude when sight was restored to an elderly woman after an intraocular lens (IOL), or cataract, operation. An IOL operation was beyond the reach of common people in those days. In 1996, the Government of India took a World Bank loan to provide free IOL surgeries. This stimulated the local industry to manufacture lenses domestically, bringing down prices drastically. I was posted as Joint Secretary in the Ministry of Health and Family Welfare in 1998 and was in charge of the National Blindness Control Programme. Under this programme, we expanded the number of people who received free eye surgeries from less than a million a year to more than four million in three years. No country at that time was providing free IOL surgeries on such a scale. I am now amazed at how routine cataract surgeries have become—a mere 10-minute procedure against the five days of hospitalisation required earlier.

I had a similar experience as Director General of the National AIDS Control Organisation (NACO) when we introduced free treatment for HIV-infected persons. HIV has no cure and those were the days when drugs cost US$ 12,000 a year for one patient. Fierce battles around the world forced pharma companies to reduce their price to US$ 1,000. But even that was not affordable. One day, Mumbai-based Cipla entered the market with generic versions of the drugs at Rs 140 a year for one patient, enabling us to rapidly expand coverage and save many from certain death. Within a year, we had expanded the coverage to more than 100,000 people. Today, more than1.5 million affected people get free treatment.

The NACO posting, from December 2006–September 2009, was a highlight of my life and truly humbling. Interacting with the underbelly of India's society—with sex workers, drug users, and homosexuals—I witnessed discrimination, irrational social prejudice, and denial in a manner I had never seen before. Increasing the budget five-fold, we mounted a massive offensive to combat HIV/AIDS. India achieved a 57 per cent reduction in incidence, the highest in the world, partly due to our inclusive policies and partly because of scientific advances in drugs and medical devices, which enabled us to diagnose HIV early and begin treating it, prolonging both the well-being and lives of patients.

Technological advances have opened up a plethora of unexpected possibilities, including the scope for near accurate diagnosis and personalised medicine in the health sector. Artificial intelligence (AI) will change the way we teach and practice patient care remarkably, even while classroom instructions are being replaced by distance learning. There are universities that do not require students to attend classes or have face-to-face interactions, much like the work-from-home routines that Covid-19 forced us into. Such 'conveniences' that technology provides come with their challenges—we have to reorganise our work, education, and health systems, and adapt to a new normal of a greater dependence on technology without allowing it to compromise our intuition. There was a time when I could remember all the phone numbers I needed to use regularly. With the coming of cell phones, I barely remember my own. So I do worry about whether technology will become a substitute for our mental faculties—our memory, our intuitions. What will the balance be? How do we achieve it? These will be the questions that tomorrow's society will have to ponder.

As I try to imagine and visualise tomorrow's educational and health systems, which may not need a face-to-face meeting with a doctor or a teacher, it seems scary and overwhelming. For, all said and done, the human touch, the tap on the shoulder, a smile of reassurance, and some emotional empathy do go a long way in our growth and development. They help us learn the importance of values such as compassion, communication, and empathy in a way that technology cannot. I think of how much I learnt from my teachers and how safe I felt when the doctor assured me that nothing was the matter and all would be well. And all that I learnt from sharing, listening, and participating in discussions and debates around ideas.

An important challenge in the future will be addressing the growing technological divide between countries and between different classes of people within countries. How do we take technology, scientific discoveries, and breakthroughs over to the other side? Will technological and scientific advances be equalisers and levellers, or will they polarise societies more sharply? Questions of justice and equality also loom larger than before. These two issues should guide the compass that will take us on our journey of progress and development.

In conclusion, I feel that every experience taught me the importance of the values that we learn from interacting with our fellow human beings—not from encounters with computers or machines. As administrative systems become more efficient by deploying technology to create paperless offices and faceless grievance redressal systems, it may result in increased isolation, a loss of emotional intelligence, and even the loss of a sense of humanity. How do we efficiently balance what technology offers with our sense of being, without eroding either? This is a question I ponder over as I look ahead. I really do not seem to have any answers.

15

Fulfilment

Journey, Not Destination

V. ANANTHA NAGESWARAN

Working in and for the Government

It was 2 June 2023, around six in the evening, on a typically muggy day in Singapore. My daughter and I decided to go for a walk. I had gone there for a short stay because my son had landed there after his first year of college in the United States. It has now become difficult for all four of us to be under one roof. But that was something that an unseen pathogen had managed for nearly two years—in 2020 and 2021. We miss those days. Yes, can you believe it?

But this essay is not about the virtues of a virus. My daughter asked me whether I was feeling fulfilled in my job. I had not thought about it. I have been too busy to reflect, and not reflecting, in general, has its pluses and minuses.

I told her that I would break down fulfilment into four elements. First, the core content of the job—what one does, day in and day out. The second is the ecosystem, which comprises the values and the integrity of the people and the organisation that one is working for or is associated with. The third is material compensation, which has to, at the minimum, allow for a comfortable living. The fourth is the social or public impact.

The last one needs some clarification. There may be no direct effect caused by one's efforts or actions in public service. The timing of the outcome is uncertain, and it is best not to focus on it but on one's efforts. If one works with the public good in mind, that is good enough.

On these four criteria, my current job, as Chief Economic Advisor to the Government of India, scores well. But being fulfilled is also a function of simplicity. That is elusive.

Challenges, Frustrations, Stimulation, and Rewards

Many factors and many people—local and global—influence policy considerations and decisions. With the advent of social media, the temptation to judge, unhindered by the need for evidence, analysis, or a consideration of the counterfactuals, is irresistible to many. The world of public policy has become more 'wicked' and a great deal more complex than it was earlier.

Horst Rittel and Melvin Webber wrote a seminal paper in 1973 about planning (policymaking) being a 'wicked' problem, as opposed to being an 'easy' one. I am sure they would be looking for a stronger adjective today. Most situations are unique or unstructured and do not lend themselves to easy answers. However, the good thing is that this forces us to keep it simple, to focus on the essentials, and to think constantly about the factors that one can influence. One needs the wisdom to know what one can and cannot influence. Otherwise, it will not be easy to keep one's wits about oneself.

After about three-quarters of a century of relative peace and tranquillity, the world is in a state of churn. Many assumptions and arrangements that guided world affairs—for better or for worse—are being questioned. We are in between two steady states. The feeling of unease is real. The effort-to-reward ratio or the effort-to-outcome ratio is very high in this milieu.

Therefore, the learnings from working in a public policy role in the current global context are unmatched, that too in a country that is easily the most complex in the world. 'The frustrating thing about India,' Cambridge economist Joan Robinson is reported to have told her student Amartya Sen, 'is that whatever you can rightly say about India, the opposite is also true.' It is easy to lose count of the number of variables at play in any given situation. It is hard to imagine that any technology or artificial intelligence will equip us to deal with the challenges that come up, both regularly and unexpectedly.

An important challenge about policymaking in a large and diverse country such as India is finding the right balance between the 'Urgent' and the 'Important'. It is not easy, but it has to be found. Learning to manage both will serve one well in both personal and professional affairs. The government workplace is a good training ground for that.

It All Began in the Public Sector

My career began with the public sector and is probably ending with it too. In between, there were international private-sector employers in Switzerland and Singapore. It is hard to compare the learnings from the two different experiences. But since it is a matter of personal judgement, I would venture to say that the public sector taught me more, especially the importance of interpersonal sensitivities.

G. L. Srinivasan, my first boss in Madras Refineries Limited (now Chennai Petroleum Corporation) during 1985–1986, taught me how to break down complex tasks into simpler deliverables with milestones by encouraging me to question him. Corporate planning, mission and vision statements, and long-term planning had all then been introduced into the public sector by Prime Minister Rajiv Gandhi. The resistance among senior executives to commit themselves to a plan and be held accountable for it at the end of the year had to be overcome carefully, especially considering the vast gap between their ages, experience, and wisdom, and my own.

Srinivasan reminded me that their resistance was not because they were indifferent to the targets, but because they cared about them. Think about it. For a young 22-year-old executive, that was an important insight. It taught me to respect their resistance, not be dismayed by it, and to work better at persuading them that, with their competence and experience, they had nothing to fear from committing themselves on paper.

My next boss, V. Swaminathan, whetted my appetite for public policy by giving me the role of Officer on Special Duty (OSD; Executive Assistant, as it was called then) to the General Manager (Finance) in 1986 and then to the Director (Finance) once the post was upgraded. My exposure to issues at the industry level in the petroleum sector and the nuances of interaction between a public-sector enterprise and its administrative ministry was due to the opportunities he afforded me.

One of the meetings of the oil industry finance executives in 1985 was inaugurated by Balachandran, a joint secretary in the Ministry of Petroleum and Natural Gas, and his fluent English and calm delivery left a lasting impression on me. One of his sentences, which has stayed evergreen in my memory even after thirty-eight years, is—'The logic of inevitability is not a matter of presumption.'

Swaminathan's efficiency, innovative working capital management, and ability to accept the trade-offs and challenge of making decisions with imperfect information and not being stuck in a 'paralysis by analysis' mode were invaluable for a young employee. It was truly an apprenticeship. The potential for learning by observing goes out of the window when we work from home. Besides, humans are social animals. We need human connections. Lockdowns and 'work from home' are wrong ways to build immunity.

I was living in Chennai, and the refinery at Manali was about 25–30 kilometres away. So the commute both ways in the chartered buses took about 2.5 hours every day. I calculated that if I stayed in my job until retirement, I would spend 2.5 years of my life sitting on the bus. So, I wanted to leave.

Swaminathan graciously offered to give me a ride into the city whenever he came to the refinery and was leaving around the close of day. That saved some time. More than that, the conversations with him on the ride home were life-changers. He guided and goaded me into applying for a Ph.D. programme in the US, to venture out and seek new experiences. The current seat, therefore, is owing to a seed he sowed then.

To round off my recollection of my first job with a lasting memory, a senior colleague in corporate planning, ten years older than me, gave me a piece of advice that I have repeated faithfully to scores of youngsters—'Be smart enough to recognise cleverness, but be good enough not to practise it.'

Witness to Financial Crises

After my doctoral studies in the US in 1994, I was lucky to find a job in Switzerland with the then Union Bank of Switzerland (UBS now). The stints in the private sector—with three Swiss banks—continued into Singapore till 2011.

Just as the advice given by my senior colleague in Madras Refineries has stayed etched in my mind, the advice given by my first boss, Pierre Baer, at Credit Suisse in Singapore on the day of my first meeting with him in 1999 is also fresh in my memory. Two of us, Fidelis Goetz and I, went to meet him as we were both new to Singapore, having moved from Switzerland. As we were preparing to leave his cabin, he said, 'Gentlemen, whatever you do, don't take yourselves too seriously.' He lived up to it himself. He had a great temperament.

Interpersonal conflicts were rife in a competitive wealth management institution. Baer used behavioural experts to open communication between different teams and executives, persuading them that conflicts should be celebrated, not suppressed. In a culture where open rudeness was an exception but sniping behind someone's back was not, this was a bold move, and it paid dividends before his tenure was cut short due to some inexplicable reason.

My two-year stint as a hedge fund manager between 2004 and 2006—an entrepreneurial adventure that did not succeed—was invaluable in many ways. It made me more grounded and helped me better understand financial markets. Investing is decision-making at every moment, whereas writing investment strategy reports with forecasts and estimates is not. Investing is a very spiritual activity.

Think about it. We need to accept the primacy of someone above us (Mr Market), whether we like it or not. We have to accept that only the effort is in our control (analysis, planning, and decision-making), not the outcome. We have to learn to accept our failures and draw a line under it. In other words, we have to close many chapters if we are to write new ones. More importantly, we learn that successes and failures may result from factors beyond our control. Luck plays a vital role. An exaggerated sense of self-importance is injurious to sustained investment performance. Does this not apply to life too?

Also, a philosophical lesson was that the notion of being independent, which many associate with being an entrepreneur, is as illusory as the feeling of being subservient when in employment. There is a dependence on others in all circumstances. So it is our state of mind, our ecosystem, our colleagues, their values, and our luck that determine what works for us. There are no general lessons here.

I returned to employment at Bank Julius Baer in Singapore in 2006, after the misadventure of managing a hedge fund. The world economy was booming, and there was exuberance everywhere. As someone not employed in investment banking or broking, I could see the world differently. A report by a New York-based home building sector analyst of Credit Suisse, published in early 2008, was an eye-opener on the excesses building up in the US residential real-estate mortgage market. Even if one ignored or did not know about securitisation, there was mispricing across several asset classes. It was not that difficult to spot. I warned my colleagues at the headquarters that something did not feel right. They listened politely, but no one wanted to stop dancing when the music was still on. People close their eyes to things when their livelihoods depend on not seeing them. One of the important lessons of the 2008 financial crisis was that forecasting or market predictions are about what is likely to happen, not about what we would like to see happen. Clients trust us to tell them the former, not the latter. I doubt if, to this day, many have absorbed that lesson.

I was in Switzerland when the Asian crisis of 1997–1998 erupted, and I was in Singapore when the global financial crisis of

2008 occurred. In that sense, I did not witness them first-hand. But the policy responses to both crises left indelible impressions on me. The World Bank and the IMF sparred on the response to the Asian crisis. The public fight between Joseph Stiglitz and Kenneth Rogoff was ugly, but held important lessons. The IMF's conditionalities had been earlier questioned in an article titled 'Refocusing the IMF' by Martin Feldstein in *Foreign Affairs* in March–April 1998. That paved the way for creating the independent evaluation office at the fund.

How do these matter? The interaction of these global developments with the financial markets, with which I was more intimately connected, was to shape my courses and their content when I began teaching in 2006 at the Great Lakes Institute of Management in Chennai. After leaving the corporate world in 2011, teaching became even more significant. Even a vicarious participation in the crises was good enough to shape my thoughts. The feedback from students was that they valued the unconventional perspectives that my courses acquainted them with.

Meaning of it All

It was in 2007 that the Hindustan Times Group started the daily, *Mint*. After writing for *BusinessLine* and then *The Financial Express*, I switched to *Mint* in 2007 as a regular columnist. It was an association that lasted fifteen years before I joined the government full time in January 2022.

In the initial years, the run-up to the financial crisis of 2008, the crisis itself, and the policy responses to it provided enough fodder to write about. The persistently loose and accommodative monetary policies in much of the developed world well into the second decade and their many consequences were the subjects of many a column.

The column was also a witness to the transformation of India over the years. The global financial crisis of 2008, caused in large part by the dominance of financial-sector interests with an inherent inability to police themselves, gave me the confidence to write a book on the subject with my good friend Gulzar Natarajan. The book, *The Rise of Finance: Causes, Consequences and Cures*, was published in 2019 by Cambridge University Press and launched by Finance Minister Nirmala Sitharaman. I would not have been able to write it had I not had a ringside view of financialisaton for nearly two decades.

I quit the world of finance, capital markets, and investment advice in 2011. I was relatively young at forty-eight years at that time. It was not a time to quit. But I did because one of the core elements of job fulfilment–the enjoyment of the job–had gone away with the 'print money; make profits' paradigm that set in after the financial crisis of 2008. Investing in financial markets became more of a brain-dead activity.

I have no regrets. As the reader can see, I learnt some important life lessons from my elders and colleagues. Global and regional crises were the other teachers. The opportunity to work in Europe and Asia was a privilege. The opportunity to groom many youngsters in investment analysis when I was working in Singapore was a blessing. From the time I began working in 1994, my bosses, colleagues, and the youngsters I mentored remain friends to this day. It is satisfying. The more I think about it, the more I feel that fulfilment can never be a full stop. It should not be. It is always a pursuit and shall remain so.

The workplace is constantly evolving. As the partnership between capital and labour became unequal in the last few decades, technology emerged, not as a workplace productivity enhancement intervention but as a replacement for labour. The more technology displaces labour, the less demand there will be for products that capital generates with such technology. Workplace and labour market stability undergird social stability as well. Therefore, the joys of the workplace encompass everything–from the personal to the social.

16

Human Connections, Human Learnings

K. Srinath Reddy

There is no professional life which provides more extensive human contact and a greater diversity of emotive learning experiences than that of a doctor who interacts with thousands of patients, their families, and friends. I lived the greater part of my professional life as a clinician who tried to live up to the dictum that a physician must endeavour to 'cure some, relieve most, but comfort all'. I then transitioned to the field of public health, which deals with the dimensions and determinants of health at the population level. While technology was an aid and ally in both phases of my professional life, my work was more influenced and guided by the human interactions I had, from parents, to patients and colleagues at work, to co-members on committees and expert panels.

Did I decide to become a doctor because my mother was a doctor? No, that was not what guided me to the profession. Of course, I admired her work. As an obstetrician and gynaecologist working as an unpaid honorary consultant in government hospitals and running a private clinic at home, she cared for so many patients. They included VIPs of both kinds—very important persons and very impoverished persons—and middle-class persons. She provided all three groups the same quality of competent and compassionate care. I admired her work, especially because she provided relief to many sick and socially outcast women with leaky fistulas between the urinary bladder and vagina. She also provided any poor patient who knocked on her clinic door with a free consultation, and often also money for transport back home.

No, it was my father who persuaded me to take up medicine. As a lawyer, politician, self-educated social scientist and economist, he was a voracious reader of books. They opened the world to me too. When I wanted to take up humanities in college and aspired to be a social scientist, he advised me that as a doctor I could be useful to society throughout my life. He also said I could be a self-directed learner in humanities, whereas professions such as medicine needed structured formal education. I bowed to that logic and became a cardiologist who loved his profession. I later sublimated my desire to delve into the social sciences when I trained as an epidemiologist and took up a public health career after a long stint as a cardiologist at the All India Institute of Medical Sciences (AIIMS) in New Delhi. I joined as a Junior Resident in 1974 and was Head of the Department of Cardiology when I left in 2006.

Medicine has become increasingly technology intensive over the last six decades, with a huge surge in the scale, scope, and success of new devices and digital technology applications. Of course, there is also the increasing cost and complexity that comes with using them. Yet, human interactions cannot be overshadowed or replaced by technology. A doctor must possess the attributes of care, concern, compassion, courtesy, and cogent communication for dealing with any patient. Even an unconscious or comatose patient and her/his family members must receive such attention. No technology can replace that. These are the values I learnt from my teachers and colleagues, and which I, in turn, have tried to transfer to my students.

There are many values one learns from patients—fortitude, courage, trust, gratitude, and solidarity with others seeking care for their ailments. While there are many lessons I have imbibed from my patients, one particular instance is indelible in my memory. A poor elderly patient was hospitalised at the AIIMS with a cardiac valve lesion and a paralytic stroke that had resulted from a blood clot that had travelled to his brain. One morning, I found his son cleaning the faeces his father had passed on the bed, thereby soiling himself. I asked him why he had not called the ward boy to do it. The son replied, 'Sir, when I was a baby, my father must have cleaned me so many times. Let me do this service now. I have no problem.' Which technology could have touched my heart and mind as that simple villager's words did?

In a hospital environment, medical decisions on the care of hospitalised patients are usually made collectively after the treating team evaluates the patient, interprets the results of tests, and deliberates on the probable diagnosis and preferred methods of treatment. If needed, other specialists are consulted. Even when patients are seen individually in the rush of an outpatient clinic, the opinion and advice of a colleague or senior can always be sought when a difficult problem is encountered. Often, human help is far more useful than reaching out for algorithmic flowcharts on a digital device.

Practical skills are also developed with the help of others at work. Experienced nurses gave me my first lessons in starting an intravenous drip and even taught me how to diagnose a cardiac rhythm abnormality on a fast-moving ECG trace on a beeping monitor in the intensive cardiac care unit. My seniors taught me how to insert and steer a thin flexible catheter tube from a vein or artery in the groin or arm into the chambers and blood vessels of the heart. No robot could have taught me that so patiently and expertly. Nor can robots replace a full surgical team that must care for a person before, during, and after surgery.

The patient too is a partner in guiding a treatment to its goals. It is easier to achieve a good adherence to treatment when the doctor and patient set goals together. Tele-consultations make communication easier, but the content, clarity, and quality of the advice given are dependent on the human agents involved.

In my later public health avatar, I connected with communities and experts across countries on varied subjects—from sustainable development to universal health coverage, and food systems for nutrition security to climate change. Whether my work involved measuring blood pressure in community surveys or sitting with other international experts to prepare World Health Organization (WHO) guidelines on the treatment of hypertension, a close connect with people most often required direct contact, not a technology-mediated digital connection. Not only are facts verified and concepts clarified in close and candid conversations, but consensus is also easier to achieve when people speak face to face. My office colleagues patiently helped me navigate a long learning curve to become comfortable with the regular use of digital communication devices. In other words, they demystified many applications which had initially left me apprehensive.

Even while working in the community, I learnt a lot from the community health workers and members of the community. Their perspectives informed my understanding of their health challenges and their experiential wisdom enriched the solutions that we designed for their identified problems. Even programmes for health promotion required collective community acceptance and action. We used technology to increase awareness and create the motivation for a change in behaviour (for abandoning tobacco or alcohol, adopting healthier diets, and increasing physical activity) in community and worksite settings. However, the key catalysts for change were the conversations among neighbours in community networks or peer persuasion among workers. The learning my colleagues and I gained was that a consultative engagement is far more effective than a top-down approach.

Even when we became relatively isolated for long periods during the Covid-19 pandemic, seeing each other on the screen and hearing each other's voices brought a cordiality to our interactions that impersonal emails could not. This is true of an office environment as well. In the early years of my career, co-workers would converse with each other and discuss matters that needed a sharing of information or opinion, or to resolve a problem before it became a conflict. In recent years, a spate of impersonal and increasingly aggressive emails has become the way to escalate things to an embittered relationship when a chat over coffee could have clarified misconceptions and resolved a difference of opinion. Walking across to talk for a few minutes can often avoid a war that lasts several months.

Can technology make work fully automated, directed by devices and orchestrated by algorithms? I doubt it. The cognitive component of analytic decision-making will certainly acquire greater efficiency, but the emotive component of executing those decisions will still require an empathetic work environment. That will hold true for many years in medicine, public health, and probably most other professions. I am sure ChatGPT will say the same thing, albeit in much faster time than I took to write this piece. But can it reflect the reverence that I have in my heart for Y. V. Reddy, who invited me to write this personalised perspective?

Part IV

Banking

17

Forty Years at RBI
A Journey of Challenges and Joys

USHA THORAT

I served the Reserve Bank of India (RBI) for almost four decades. Nineteen of those years were before 1991 and nineteen were after 1991, totalling thirty-eight years. Only after nearly two decades of service in the RBI was I considered sufficiently senior to be given fairly responsible positions. This coincided with the crisis of 1991 and the major monetary and financial-sector reforms that followed. While there were several global experiences of liberalisation and models of development, including the 'Washington consensus', Indian policymakers had to craft something that suited the Indian political milieu and institutions. For example, although advocated globally, total privatisation of the banking system was not really an option. The 1990s were uncharted territory for the RBI, and personally for me it was both a challenge and a joy working in such an environment.

All this was in the future when I joined the RBI in 1972, as part of the first batch of direct recruits in Grade B. I joined the RBI soon after my postgraduation from the Delhi School of Economics, followed by a one-year stint as a lecturer in Lady Shri Ram College for Women, Delhi. I shunned further academics as I wanted to practice in real life what I had learnt in textbooks. At the back of my mind was a vague idea of doing research at a later stage, based on what real life was like.

Economics was not exactly my first choice. Nevertheless, five years of studying economics convinced me that this discipline had practical applications in evolving policies that could change the lives of the people of this country. Hence, a career with the RBI. Undoubtedly, the administrative services were a close, if not better, choice, but it so happened that the RBI's offer letter arrived even before it was time to start preparations for the Indian Administrative Service (IAS) exams.

After the initial training and probationary period of two years, I was posted in the Department of Banking Operations and Development in 1974. Here, I had to wade through piles of reports on what was euphemistically called 'centre wise inspection'. These inspections entailed an RBI officer evaluating whether nationalised banks were moving towards their objectives in terms of branch coverage, lending to priority sectors, and so on. The reports were unbelievably repetitive, boring, and dry. Unable and unwilling to suffer any longer, I approached Executive Director K. S. Krishnaswamy, who happened to be an uncle of a friend from the Delhi School of Economics. I told him I regretted joining the RBI and if this was the kind of work I was required to do, it would really be a waste of all my studies. The presumption of youth!

Thanks to his intervention, I was posted to the Credit Planning Cell, a department under him where credit was literally being rationed among different sectors according to national priority—a very exciting function in a controlled economic context. The joys of working in a challenging environment helped me forget my initial regret.

The Credit Planning Cell was a motley crew of people drawn from different, so-called specialised departments—economics, statistics, and banking. The collegial working culture of the department made it very different from the rest of the RBI. Even staff at a very junior level was allowed to express their views independently and fearlessly. Also, working with persons such as R. K. Hazari, K. S. Krishnaswamy, A. Raman, and R. K. Seshadri made this a stimulating phase in my career.

One incident stands out in my mind. I sent a fax to the Finance Secretary, Punjab, communicating a sanction of Rs 50 crore for public food procurement operations. I became very nervous when I realised I had made a mistake in the figure. I went to A. Raman, who was Adviser in Charge of the Credit Planning Cell. He responded very calmly, 'It's okay—just ring him up and advise the correct figure. Follow it up with a fax correcting the earlier one.' I also rang up the State Bank of India (SBI) and said there had been a mistake. I was struck by the fact that I was not pulled up by Raman. It taught me two good lessons—always double check figures before sending out faxes and letters, and always be conscious of how we handle subordinates.

My next posting was in the Banking Policy Division of the Department of Banking Operations and Development in 1978. It dealt with all policy matters relating to public-sector banks, foreign banks, and private-sector banks. The reports of the Kamath Committee, the James Raj Committee, the Gunvant Desai committee, and a few other committees also came out at the same time—all of which had to be examined and their recommendations analysed for implementation. The Tambe Committee on the 20-point programme followed, and we also studied the reports of the parliamentary committees on banking. All this added to the excitement of working in a place that was shaping national policy.

An opportunity to work in the Northeast presented itself in 1982. My posting in the Rural Planning and Credit Department gave me a chance to travel to all the seven Northeastern states, and expand my knowledge of banking policy and collaterals—the forms of landholding and community coherence in the Northeast that could serve as social collateral were concepts that were new to me. In later years, as a Deputy Governor looking at financial inclusion in the Northeast, I could draw on this rich experience. The lesson for organisations is to move younger managers around to give them a variety of exposure.

Elections were announced in Assam in February 1984. The administration was trying its best to maintain an appearance of normality by keeping banks open, while the people wanted to boycott the election and demonstrate that things were not under control. Bank staff was caught in between. The government wanted them to help maintain normality while even commandeering their services for election duty was difficult, given the hostility of the public.

RBI officers, including my husband, were rounded up and lodged in the bank's premises for nine days to make sure the currency chests were well supplied. Eight senior officers of the RBI had to thus spend their days and nights together in the office. Although relatively junior among the officers there, my husband took charge as a natural leader in this crisis and became the person coordinating the effort and talking to the RBI top brass, the state government, and SBI officials. The entire episode was tense while it lasted, but it provided a great subject for conversation for years thereafter.

We moved to Chennai in 1984, where I was posted to the Exchange Control Department. Today's generation may not understand the rigour of exchange control in those days. A popular joke was that even if one managed to elope and go overseas without letting one's parents know, the RBI would know! The RBI granted permits for allocation of 'scarce' foreign exchange for purposes ranging from personal travel and medical education, to investments overseas.

Our bright inspection team unearthed the practice of Indian banks providing guarantees for loans to non-residents at their overseas branches against a lien marked on US dollar deposits (called Foreign Currency Non-Resident Account, or FCNRA) accepted in India. These loans were then used to create more FCNR deposits, taking advantage of the higher interest paid on such deposits in India, compared to the interest on the loans. This practice resulted in increasing India's external liabilities without any productive benefit. Our team did not receive any specific commendation or appreciation. But it was a heady experience all the same–the knowledge that we had uncovered and stopped a practice detrimental to the country.

Some fun memories in the Chennai office are around the group lunches a whole lot of us ladies had at our friend Shubha's desk. She had suffered a bad accident when she was just eighteen years old, and was disabled. We all marvelled at her mobility and hectic pace of activities–movies, shopping, and eating out, amid counselling many others to be positive and cheerful. I think such experiences are missing in today's hectic pace of work (both remotely and physically), but they eased the pressures of work and personal life and somehow prevented us from being overwhelmed by them.

Back in Bombay in 1990, I was posted to the Industrial Rehabilitation Cell, or Sick Units Cell as it was called. I was dealing with Calico Mills, a Board for Industrial and Financial Reconstruction (BIFR) case, when I had to meet Governor S. Venkitramanan who wanted some information on the company. Soon after meeting him, I was abruptly told that I was to be moved to the Department of External Investments and Operations.

I went to Deputy Governor Janakiraman and told him that I could not take up such a high-pressure job as I had to look after my in-laws and needed to visit Kolhapur frequently at short notice. He said that I could go as often as I liked, but did not really have a choice. That said, a humane management earns the loyalty and commitment of working women—one remembers N. Vaghul and K. V. Kamath who, by following such an approach, spawned many women leaders.

As mentioned earlier, the 1990s were uncharted territory for the RBI and I had a chance to work in areas where the most definitive reforms were being carried out. The dual exchange rate system was introduced with partially fixed rates, later moving towards a managed float, schemes with exchange rate guarantees were wound down, and the bilateral payment arrangements with Russia and other East European countries were dismantled. India's currency became convertible on the current account. Global and national events began affecting the foreign exchange markets, and we had to learn to be nimble and follow all news—political, economic, and financial.

We learnt to deal with the sudden strengthening of the US dollar in October 1995 and the turbulence in the Indian markets at that time, and with large and lumpy capital flows (inflows and outflows). We also learnt to understand the link between the spot and forward markets, exchange market intervention and the impact on liquidity, and the use of monetary measures, intervention, and administrative controls (capital controls). Not to mention the tool of 'open mouth operations', as Y. V. Reddy named any public communication on exchange rates.

There was a buzz and an excitement in the workspace. We were a part of the team handling the impact of global events such as the Latin American debt crisis, the historic change in US dollar interest rates in December 1993, the savings and loans crisis in the US, the reversal of the US dollar exchange rate in September 1995, and the Asian financial crisis in 1996–1997, just after the release of the Tarapore Committee report on capital account convertibility. Dealing with the unknown without any precedent implied taking risks and always measuring the upside and the downside.

A big lesson from this period is how the RBI's senior management responded to fast-tracking the learning curve—by bringing in experts from around the world, sending us to various international conferences and training programmes, and setting up committees headed by well-known persons. These groups studied the global experience and best practices, drew lessons for India, and worked out a non-disruptive road map to achieve the goals. This lesson is relevant to all times.

Around the time that we were dealing with the impact of the global sanctions on India, following Pokhran in 1974, I was moved to the Internal Debt Management Cell, which managed the debt of state and Central governments and the open market operations of the RBI. Here, too, very exciting reforms were taking place to deepen and widen the government securities markets so that the RBI could perform its role as a debt manager and monetary authority in liberalising markets.

Annual interactions with state governments began at Y. V. Reddy's initiative and gave a completely new dimension to our understanding of Centre-state fiscal relationships. The role of contingent liabilities and government guarantees in threatening financial stability were matters we got into in detail. My involvement in working on the fiscal responsibility bills for the Centre and states, setting up the government securities dealing system, the Negotiated Dealing System (NDS), and the Clearing Corporation of India for better transparency and safety in trading and settlements were significant milestones in market development, and provided me great satisfaction.

The period 1992–2010 provided a very rich opportunity to work closely with icons such as C. Rangarajan, S. S. Tarapore, Bimal Jalan, Y. V. Reddy, Rakesh Mohan, D. Subbarao, and also people such as Montek Singh Ahluwalia and Shankar Acharya in the government. This period saw quite a few stress situations that were specific or systemic, such as the fallout of the Harshad Mehta stock market scam, the market volatility of October 1995, the Asian crisis of 1997–1998, the sanctions post Pokhran, the Madhavpura Mercantile Cooperative Bank crisis of 2001, the failure of the Global Trust Bank in 2004, and the global financial crisis of 2008.

These situations called for quick coordinated responses, early recognition of problems, and close working with the government and with other regulators, especially the SEBI and the stock exchanges. A readiness to consult experts with humility, and putting in place crisis management institutional systems and practices were essential. Capacity building of the staff was most important, and this was something the leaders in the RBI actively encouraged by delegating responsibility and providing a clear guidance on the broad objectives. Each of us felt valued, however junior, and this made the work joyful, challenging, and fulfilling. There were many juniors, such as Rabi Shankar and Dimple Bhandia, who worked with me and have now become very senior in the RBI. I hope they received some mentoring from me, as I did from my seniors.

In 2003, Y. V. Reddy took over as Governor after his stint with the International Monetary Fund (IMF). He gave me charge of Banking Regulation as Executive Director. One lesson I can never forget is when I had taken two of my juniors to him and he explained to us how we should apply 'fit and proper' criteria for bank directors. He asked us to think of bank depositors as our daughters for whom we were seeking suitable grooms. He asked us what criteria we would apply if we wanted to be comfortable enough with the boy and his family to be able to trust them to look after our daughters through all situations.

How would we enquire about them? Clearly, we would find out the financial situation of both the boy and the family, make discreet but thorough enquiries about them from reliable sources—both official and through relations and friends—concerning their reputation, integrity, and track record. I have never forgotten this lesson, which was so apt and so suitable, whether we apply it as regulators to depositors or for investor protection.

Another trying situation arose during my stint as Executive Director when rumours of the financial position of ICICI Bank set off large cash withdrawals in branches of the bank in Gujarat and the suburbs of Mumbai. The news spread like wildfire and demands from the ICICI for cash from the RBI spread throughout the country. A control room was set up in my cabin, from where we monitored the all-India position on a real-time basis using telephones (there was no core banking at that time), coordinating with the RBI offices and N. S. Kannan of the ICICI treasury.

We had to ensure that cash was not withdrawn by the bank beyond the balances it had with the RBI. This called for working out the bank's balances manually on a real-time basis. The IMF–RBI meetings were on in Washington, D.C. at that time, and all the top brass was away. We had to issue a press release to calm the panic and G. P. Muniappan was the only Deputy Governor available. I took the draft to him, but he was quite reluctant to give orders on it till we convinced him that there was no other option. The TV channels were repeating the story over and over, and it was necessary for the RBI to act to stabilise the situation. It is to the credit of the RBI leadership that they had built the capacity and confidence of the bank's officers to a level that could handle different types of crisis situations.

The top management of the RBI encouraged even the most junior officers to express her/his opinion. Y. V. Reddy always said that we need biodiversity for a healthy ecosystem. I like to believe that this is something I encouraged my juniors to do—give their opinion, no matter how outlandish. When I moved from the Department of External Investments and Operations to the Internal Debt Management Cell in 1998, unlike in my previous posting, I found no one would express an opinion. Every morning, we would meet for 10–15 minutes to review the markets, and I would ask each person to say something. It took me three months to get them to feel comfortable with saying what they thought.

Crisis management skills reached new heights in 2008 when Lehman Brothers happened. Our banks were relatively insulated and excessively leveraged products had been discouraged, but the Indian economy and financial sector were not immune to the crisis. D. Subbarao had just come in as Governor, and his close relationship with the Central government proved very helpful in working out strategies to deal with the crisis.

Deputy Governor Shyamala Gopinath, my colleague, had to go to the US for her daughter's delivery (she had just admirably handled the Lehman impact on the Indian system), and Deputy Governor Vittaldas Leeladhar was due to retire in December. Fortunately, Rakesh Mohan was still with the RBI as a Deputy Governor. Anticipating that there could be a crisis, Governor Reddy had made us undertake several drills with different scenarios in January 2008, all of which came in handy in October–November 2008.

What I recall vividly is how Shyamala and I would communicate each day. At the end of the day, I would send her an email on the day's developments and summarise the suggestions and measures proposed. When I opened my mailbox the next morning, her reply to all my queries would be there, plus other valuable suggestions. The seamless way in which we worked together characterised our relationship at all times, and it is for me one of my happiest memories of the RBI. This was also true of working with others such as Anand Sinha, G. Padmanabhan, Prashant Saran, G. Mahalingam, and so many others. All of which leads to a single conclusion—the joy of working derives from the interpersonal relationships we have with those whom we work and the deep respect we have for each other.

In summary, here are some lessons that were learnt.

- Policy formulation should draw the most from global best practices, but be context-specific.
- Leaders should actively encourage their teams by delegating responsibility and providing clear guidance on the broad objectives.

- Officers must be proactive in grasping challenges and providing solutions.
- Interactions with stakeholders at all levels, and within the organisation, with the younger staff, are critical for learning and teaching.
- Humane management pays, especially when it comes to women, who always have to play multiple roles.
- Enjoy your work, and avoid a 'take-take' approach.

18

An Unexpected Journey in Banking

SHYAMALA GOPINATH

My career path was an accidental one. It was not that I planned to be a career central banker. Far from it. In the early 1970s, being part of a large family of seven, with me being the eldest, securing a job was important. With my father's modest job and a homemaker mother, for me it was for economic reasons. For my mother, it was for my financial independence.

Given an option, I would have studied to become a chartered accountant, having done my degree in commerce. I did land a job soon after, but my mother insisted that I complete a postgraduate degree, which I did in Mysuru (1968–1970). I had applied to both the Bank of Baroda and the Reserve Bank of India (RBI) and in the interim taught for a while in Bengaluru. Soon after, I joined as an officer at the Bank of Baroda in Bengaluru in 1971. Eight months later, I was one of half-a-dozen candidates who were selected in the first batch of Grade B officers and posted to the RBI in Mumbai. Moving was not an easy choice, though, considering that public-sector banks were expanding aggressively after nationalisation in 1969–1970. There was the prospect of overseas postings and better career opportunities in a commercial bank compared to what was then perceived as a slow career progression in the RBI.

The more difficult decision at that time in the early 1970s was for a young single girl to relocate from her hometown of Bengaluru to Mumbai. But my father was very clear that I should join the RBI. Such was the reputation of the RBI even then.

I realised early on that with little knowledge about the practical aspects of central banking and regulation, it was better to be humble and learn on the job from my junior colleagues who had more experience. During my probation period, I worked in the Exchange Control Department, approving 'P forms' for persons travelling abroad. The 1970s were marked by stringent foreign exchange controls and, as luck would have it, my first posting as a Grade B officer was in the Exchange Control Department, as it was then called in 1974.

A new law, the Foreign Exchange Regulation Act, 1973, had just been enacted and this department had to scrutinise applications received from foreign companies, branches of foreign companies, foreign nationals, and non-resident individuals doing business in India and decide if they could continue with their existing operations. It was a radical measure, and the RBI was mandated with implementing it. Coincidentally, my thesis during my M.Com. was on foreign investment in India and this helped me settle down faster.

The guidelines mainly required foreign companies to Indianise their operations by converting branches and subsidiaries or by diluting their holdings if they were incorporated in India. There were some exceptions, such as for banking, shipping, and airline companies. The rest were allowed to continue with either majority equity up to 74 per cent or up to 40 per cent, depending on the nature of their business.

Since foreign companies had to dilute their equity either by issuing fresh capital or by divestment, the preferred option was through the stock exchange. This resulted in many companies listing their equity shares in India. The price at which shares could be issued or divested was decided by the Controller of Capital Issues. This was the time when Coca-Cola and IBM decided to leave India, unhappy with the new foreign investment rules.

A big learning early on centred around dealing with change without disruption, and mentorship. I learnt from S. S. Thakur, who then headed the department, of the importance of implementing a new law in a non-discriminatory and fair manner. During that stint, I had to communicate with large companies when they visited us in connection with their applications. What I proudly recall now is that the RBI as an institution had a reputation for integrity even in those days of the licence raj and controls, even though it may have been accused of being bureaucratic.

In my career, there were many occasions when I had to handle problems or even crises. The first one was dealing with the impact of India's balance of payments crisis in 1990 on the overseas operations of Indian banks. The balance of payments crisis severely affected the overseas operations of Indian banks, especially those lenders who depended on short-term inter-bank borrowings. Some banks had borrowed in the inter-bank market to fund NRIs for opening foreign currency non-resident deposit accounts in India. There was also the issue of non-performing assets.

Handling these problems involved frequent consultations with my counterpart, Usha Thorat, in the Department of External Investments and Operations. India experienced the vulnerability of short-term debt when funding was cut short. The Indian Oil Corporation, through the SBI, had availed itself of the banker's acceptance facility to pay for oil imports, which used to get rolled over due to foreign exchange problems. Indian Oil had enough rupee resources, which it deployed in the market. To resolve this issue, the then Joint Secretary in the Finance Ministry, Y. V. Reddy, organised a meeting between officials of the IOC, SBI, and RBI.

This was my first meeting with Y. V. Reddy, who was later to become the Governor of the RBI. It was decided that Indian Oil should crystallise its foreign exchange liability in rupees at the prevailing exchange rate and settle its dues with the SBI. The RBI and SBI would work out a scheme to deal with the foreign exchange risk exposure that the SBI had to take till such time as these liabilities could be repaid. This involved once again the Department of External Operations and Investment and my colleague Thorat, who had to structure that scheme. During that period of crisis management, what counted were teamwork and the ability to come up with practical solutions without creating a moral hazard. This lesson proved valuable later, too. The other key policy learning during the 1990–1991 crisis was to closely monitor short-term debt and have the ability to use policy on external commercial borrowings as a macro-prudential tool.

Fortuitous Opportunity

Around that time in 1990–1991, discussions were underway on applying trade laws to the services sector because of the competitive advantage that developed countries had. This included financial services, which was a part of the Uruguay Round negotiations. The services sector was being discussed as a separate stream, called the General Agreement on Trade in Services (GATS), in the early 1990s. The services negotiations were unique as they included not only cross-border transactions but also commercial presence in the host country. The RBI assisted the government in negotiations on financial services.

Since these discussions involved market access to foreign banks, the International Banking Section was called in. My senior, Gopal Rao, attended the first meeting in Geneva, and I got involved after I took over from him. This was a completely new area and involved several meetings because, by their very nature, trade negotiations that lead to binding commitments take a very long time. The discussions centred on the liberalisation of cross-border transactions and commercial presence in financial services.

Since the focus was on banking and insurance, the late S. V. Mony, Chairman of General Insurance Corporation, Mohan Kumar, who was the senior negotiator for India from its mission in Geneva, and I used to participate in bilateral discussions with developed countries. We would brief India's Ambassador to GATT, B. K. Zutshi. I used to sometimes meet other negotiators and these discussions offered a much wider perspective. Since India was not ready to offer anything in insurance even on a conditional basis, I had to at times face the negotiators from other countries alone because we could only commit on services such as banking and some non-banking services. But invariably, the delegations would raise the issue of insurance. It was during this time that I learnt the art of not being stressed by pressure.

Soon after, we had the Asian financial crisis in 1997. The discussions in the GATS were then limited to seeking access for a presence in India and allied capital flows rather than free flows of capital. When the final commitments had to be submitted in 1997, there was very little time and I had to call Executive Director Vimala Visvanathan at dawn for her approval. She in turn spoke to the Governor, who then spoke to the Finance Secretary. My association with the GATS negotiations ended in 1997.

The post-liberalisation years were a period of hectic action. The RBI had to implement new global rules on capital, prudential norms accounting, and the treatment of bad loans. It also had to deal with high inflation, move towards a market-oriented system of borrowings by the government, and handle the fallout of the 1992 securities scam.

Although there was no formal mentoring as such in the RBI, I did get excellent exposure and guidance, which, looking back, I do consider as mentoring that prepared me to meet the challenges ahead. When I was General Manager, Department of Banking Operations and Development, Deputy Governor Reddy was in charge of Monetary Policy, Economic Analysis and Policy. He used to attend the Bank for International Settlements (BIS) meetings and would send the agenda that related to non-banking financial companies and other banking topics for my views. I also used to review the agenda papers of the SBI for Deputy Governor S. S. Tarapore.

Managing Reserves and Exchange Rate during Crises

When I was first posted as the chief of the Department of External Investment and Operations in 1998, I was apprehensive because I had to fill large shoes. More worryingly, we were in the middle of the Asian financial crisis. I got an opportunity to work with Deputy Governor Reddy and Governor Bimal Jalan. We introduced certain administrative measures to deal with the volatility in the markets, besides intervening in the foreign exchange market. Much later, when I was in the IMF, those administrative measures were acknowledged as one of the tools to manage extreme volatility as a transient measure. For Indian policymakers, it was a rewarding experience, with the designing of new forms of bonds—the Indian Millennium and Resurgent India bonds—to raise foreign funds.

The lesson then was to constantly innovate and learn from the mistakes of the past. The exchange risk was shared, and the RBI created provisions for the likely deficit on the exchange guarantee. Thanks to Governor Jalan, I also got an opportunity to assist the brilliant late M. Narasimham on some aspects of the terms of reference when he chaired the second committee on banking-sector reforms in 1998.

As my career graph rose, I was confronted with the dilemma many working women face—managing work and home. That was settled in an unconventional manner when my husband decided to quit his full-time job and opt for a consultancy career that gave him flexible working hours. So, he helped to take care of the children. Our salaries were modest in those days, although that has changed significantly over the last two decades.

What has helped is the institutional support provided by RBI, which has enabled women to do well professionally at the bank. When I joined the RBI, there were many women at the clerical level, but few at the executive level. Today, you see a sizeable number of women at the senior level at the RBI.

Confidence Booster

A stint in the monetary and exchange affairs department of the IMF in Washington, D.C., between 2001 and 2003 was hugely rewarding for me. My vision was widened by the broader global perspective that I gained there, and from what I learnt about new monetary and fiscal tools. The financial assessments of a few countries while I was there broadened my experience as well. The IMF is a great institution to work at, and I benefitted immensely.

From Bank to Conglomerate

On my return after the two-year stint at the IMF, I was promoted as Executive Director. Governor Reddy had a luncheon meeting with each of the executive directors and sought our suggestions. He also wanted to know about our concerns. It was 2003, and I pointed out that we need to have a framework for regulating and supervising financial conglomerates. Y. V. Reddy immediately constituted a committee comprising all three regulators—the RBI, the SEBI, and the Insurance Regulatory and Development Authority (IRDA)—to come up with a framework. I was the committee's convenor and we drew up a framework for reporting interconnected exposures. That is where I met Vaibhav Chaturvedi, who was assisting the committee, and he became my executive assistant when I later became Deputy Governor.

The RBI was one of the few institutions that had explicitly identified financial stability as one of the objectives of regulatory policy. It used macro prudential measures much before they gained wider global acceptance and recognition in regulatory policy after the global financial crisis in 2007–2008. Even the approach for market development and regulation was nested under the overarching objective of financial stability. It has also used capital controls as one of the macro prudential measures. What I learnt then was that such action must often be pre-emptive, implemented when initial signs of vulnerabilities come to our notice. Waiting for full evidence invariably results in having to deal with a bigger problem later. Further, it is important to understand the effects of the measures we take on the system as a whole, rather than just on individual institutions.

Global Financial Crisis

A crisis at the global level obviously calls for plenty of communication and coordination among various departments and also for swift action. D. Subbarao had just taken over as Governor in September 2008, and matters moved at a brisk pace.

The highlight during this period was a spate of committee reports on the financial sector. One of the suggestions was to dismantle controls on cross-border capital flows, and go in for market-determined exchange rates and interest rates to create a seamless bond, currency, and derivatives nexus. The role models were the major developed markets of the world.

The RBI always recognised the role of the financial sector as an instrument to achieve broader real economy objectives while maintaining financial stability. As Governor Subbarao said in Mumbai in 2013, in the pre-crisis euphoria cooked up by financial alchemy, we forgot that the goal of all development was the growth of the real economy and that the financial sector was useful only to the extent that it helped deliver stronger and more secure long-term growth. For all of us who worked on the recommendations of these committees and the inter-departmental interactions this involved, it was a great learning experience as well as an opportunity to put forth our points of view.

Conclusion

I am often asked whether women face discrimination in the RBI. My response has always been that one joins the RBI on the basis of a competitive examination and that gender does not matter. As the RBI is a full service central bank, there are several ways in which one gets mentored, such as working in different departments and having peers who point one in the right direction. The institutional culture of the RBI, which has been built over a long time, makes a big difference. It encompasses the practice of documentation, taking varying views into account, both internal and external, and having a professional approach. All these are attributes that enhance the Indian central bank's credibility.

I owe my career to all the wonderful people with whom I was fortunate to work in the RBI. Five decades ago, when I joined the bank, it was well-known, but was not so much in the headlines as it is now. Looking back, I had a meaningful, satisfying, and an enjoyable career as a central banker. When you join an institution and are focused on your work, you begin loving your career, even if it was all unplanned.

19

Collaboration, Coexistence

Vittaldas Leeladhar

For generations, modern life and society have evolved around two institutions known as the home and the office. I have enjoyed every moment of fifty years of my working life in such an environment. Many real-life events and situations come to mind while pondering over the future of the workplace, or even its absence–the benefits, the values, and the charm that a workplace brings, leading me to wonder how it will all evolve if every activity turns virtual.

I share some of my experiences drawn from diverse situations, each of them reinforcing the undisputed strength of people with a common purpose coming together for a common good, the essence of which must be preserved and promoted as a driving force to complement technology.

Mentorship: An Invaluable Human Relationship

The *Oxford English Dictionary* defines 'mentor' as 'an experienced person who advises you over a period of time'. A mentor has a profound impact on honing one's capabilities in a positive direction. I was fortunate to have had a number of mentors, both at home and the workplace, at various stages of my life.

I lost my father when he was thirty-six and I was nine. My mother had never gone to school. I was brought up during the early days of my life by my aunt, who had no children. In between her duties of tending to the needs of a large family, she would spare time for me at a specified time each day. My aunt became my first mentor.

She would hold my hand and make me write on a slate for about fifteen minutes every day, so that my handwriting would become as beautiful as hers. Every day, she would make me go through the Tarzan cartoon and narrate to her what I understood. This was later upgraded to reading the main items in newspapers and explaining them to her.

My aunt would also explain the importance of etiquette to me and point out how I should conduct myself. This included saying 'thank you' and greeting others with a 'good morning'. My aunt would thus spend about an hour a day with me, always assuring me that I would become a 'big man' one day, a day for which she was preparing me.

At school, Johny Master taught English. He was always pleasant and started every class by cracking a joke that would make everyone laugh. One day, I plucked up the courage to ask him where he was getting jokes from every morning. That led to my introduction to *Reader's Digest*. Initially, he would discreetly check whether I was reading it by asking a few questions. He was very happy when he realised that he had been able to enthuse me into reading the *Readers' Digest*, so much so that I enjoyed reading every issue from cover to cover. From the age of nine to seventy-six now, I do not recall having missed a single edition of this magazine.

Gradually, Johny Master introduced me to the *Reader's Digest*'s condensed books, and then to other books. He thus made me a voracious reader, which has helped me in many ways in my life and career.

At Syndicate Bank, my first bank, my mentor was its chairman when I joined as an officer trainee at the age of twenty in April 1969. Somehow, he took a liking to me and instructed his secretary that I should be permitted to meet him at least once in a month. At the first such meeting, he asked me about a credit proposal I had appraised, about which I had raised nineteen queries. He told me that I should go the very next day to the place where the project was located, meet the entrepreneur, collect all the information that I wanted, and then report to him on returning.

On reaching that place, visiting the unit, and talking to the entrepreneur, I felt very ashamed to realise how hollow and irrelevant my queries had been. At the office, I recommended the approval of the credit proposal, listing out all my queries and explaining how many of them were not relevant to assessing the creditworthiness of the borrower. My meeting with the bank's chairman lasted just thirty seconds—he smiled and remarked that it was a good education in banking, adding that we would meet next month. How many officer trainees these days get such attention from their branch managers in today's work culture?

At the Reserve Bank of India (RBI), my mentor was none other than Y. V. Reddy. Initially, I was diffident about my ability to be effective in a central bank with its unique structure and processes. I expressed this to Governor Reddy the day he invited me to his office and told me that he would like me to join the RBI as a Deputy Governor. He, however, would not listen to any excuses and insisted that together, we would make a good team.

Very soon, I had the order appointing me as a Deputy Governor of the RBI and that was the beginning of yet another valuable experience of mentorship in my life. During a year of working together, while my portfolios changed, our meetings became almost a daily affair. During an informal discussion, Governor Reddy would, in a subtle way, enable me to better understand the context and background of each project. This saved me many hours of time and effort. Again, in a discreet way, he would advise me on things we could do to balance home and work life. In retrospect, I would say that the experience was educative and enriching in many ways. If I had gone by my initial instinct and turned down the opportunity, it would have been the loss of a lovely part of my life, memories of which rejuvenate me even today.

Mentoring is an important ingredient in the development of a person and it takes place when there is person-to-person contact. Mentoring at the workplace acts like an anchor, preventing people from drifting around in search of their goals, and guiding them towards a healthy work-life balance. The absence of a lively workplace drove many people to depression, as we saw during the work from home days in the period of the Covid lockdown.

Managing Technology Fallout

Human ingenuity and efforts will be called upon on a large scale to avert the disasters that an over-reliance on technology can bring about–something we all saw with the Y2K problem at the turn of the century. As the Chairman and Managing Director of Union Bank of India at the time, I had to deal with the possible fallout of this technology problem that was expected to make every computer system fail on the birthday of the twenty-first century.

Many of today's youngsters may not even be aware of this issue. The year 2000 (Y2K) problem referred to errors that computers could make over the formatting and storage of dates on and after the year 2000. Many programs represented the year with only the final two digits, thus making 2000 indistinguishable from 1900. This had the potential to bring down computer networks worldwide.

A large number of information technology (IT) experts came up with different solutions for the same problem. Each bank trained their staff to face the challenge in their own way. The day came and went without any disruption of data, thanks to the massive effort that had been made to plug all loopholes that could trip the system.

The Y2K problem, however, had many positive outcomes. There was an unprecedented outreach by seniors in banks, right from managing directors, executive directors, general managers, and other senior officials. They moved to major branches to personally oversee the readiness to face the problem and create awareness about how to handle any fallout in the event of a problem.

As technology in banking was then at a nascent stage, this outreach by the senior management of banks eventually led to a better understanding of the need to equip staff members and officers at the branch level with computer technology and operating skills, which ultimately transformed the banking experience.

It was also a huge success in terms of mass communication–IT experts and operating staff, who till then had operated in silos as experts and generalists, directly discussed issues, taking the first steps in initiating a dialogue between the IT backend and the front office. This paved the way for a meaningful adoption of technology with people-centric solutions.

Town Hall Experiment

The lateral movement of chairmen and managing directors from one bank to another is a phenomenon in public-sector banking, but it is a mixed bag. While the movement was invariably from a smaller bank to a larger one in recognition of your performance, you also at times inherited some legacy challenges that called for taking steps to bring about behavioural changes in the new organisation. In one such lateral movement, upon taking charge as the Chairman and Managing Director of Union Bank of India in Mumbai on 2 April 2000, I sensed that the officers of the bank were excessively cautious about taking risks, which was affecting the growth of business.

I found that the bank had in the recent past introduced a very risky product and assigned some aggressive sales targets for it to a large number of branches. Officers who sensed that the product did not quite meet the prescribed standards were cautious about promoting its sale, and found themselves on the receiving end when it came to promotions and transfers.

This had resulted in an atmosphere of fear, in which officers tended to avoid taking risks–not good news for any bank's growth. I had several rounds of discussions with our top executives to find out how this trend could be reversed. Finally, I zeroed in on the idea of holding town hall meetings at important centres in the country, which would be decided on the basis of branch density, the volume of business, and the number of officers and employees. At some metropolitan cities, more than one meeting would be held.

A one-month programme for holding town hall meetings across the country was drawn up in my second month at the bank. To gain maximum impact, we invited everyone, from the regional head of the centre to all staff members in the clerical cadre. I spoke at length, supported by a PowerPoint presentation on facts and figures, covering the rich heritage of the bank, its financial strength, its impressive track record of customer service, and its above average productivity. Against this backdrop, I unveiled a sound and stable business growth plan and urged everyone to do their best on this journey. The staff was quite inspired, realising that each one of them had an important role to play.

To me, this town hall experiment brought out a simple truth—there is no more effective way of inspiring the rank and file than having a genuine talk from the heart, more so in a people-intensive industry like banking.

Making a Smart Move

Another hazard of lateral movement in public-sector banking is that it invariably happens in April, at the beginning of the financial year. You are required to put your signature on the balance sheet of the preceding financial year, although you were not even a part of that organisation then. I took charge of the Union Bank of India in April, when the annual accounts were almost ready. The performance in that financial year was not very good.

In those days, newspaper reporters were the ones who covered banking results with a detailed analysis. I wanted to ward off the negative impact of the poor result and have at least one quarter to try and improve the performance. I decided to announce the result on a Saturday, so that they would be published in Sunday papers, as many people hardly read the newspapers on Sunday. The next quarter saw a turnaround in performance, and much of the credit for this goes to the enthusiasm built through the town hall meetings. And sure enough, we crowed about our results from the rooftop to let everyone know.

Put Your People in the Driver's Seat

Once the bank's quarterly results, which were outstanding, had been announced, there were some celebrations at the head office building by the staff union. On the way home, I asked my driver what the celebration was about. He promptly replied that the bank had made a record profit. I was ready with my next question to him—how much profit? With great pride, he said, 'One crore rupees, sir.' He hardly believed me when I corrected him and said the profit was Rs 100 crore for the quarter.

From the next quarter onwards, he would wait to surprise me with the correct profit figures announced by the bank. At the end of my four-and-a-half years with the bank, when I got my orders to take charge as a Deputy Governor at the RBI, my driver requested me to not call for a car from the central bank but to allow him the privilege of driving me to the RBI building.

On the way, he said that if I had continued for six more months and completed five years, the bank would have celebrated by making a net profit of Rs 1,000 crore, a target I had set for my team in my first communication after taking charge of the bank. My driver had not only learnt to measure and understand the progress of the bank in financial terms, but also showed an awareness of the organisation's aspirational goal.

Customer-centricity

Traditional wisdom has it that unless your people sit across the table from their customers, your organisation's customer satisfaction will be less than optimal. In our bank, it was an established practice for all senior executives at the head office to have lunch together in a common dining room, which had an ambience comparable to that of a five-star hotel and wholesome food. After taking charge of the bank, I began inviting an industrialist for lunch. After the meal, the guest was invited to interact with the bank's senior management team.

Our first guest was Anand Mahindra. I received him in the foyer of the head office building and led him to our dining room on the sixteenth floor, making sure he felt how much we valued his visit. Post-lunch, in the course of his interaction with the bank's team, the treasury head brought up certain transactions that the Mahindra Group preferred to conduct through a foreign bank. He convinced the guest to try one such transaction with our bank to gauge our capability to handle such business.

In an hour, our people were with the Deputy General Manager of the Mahindra Group handling the business, and in the next half-an-hour, a transaction was concluded. I rang up Mahindra to tell him that the transaction was completed and the savings his company had made compared to the charges they would have paid to a foreign bank.

Almost eight years after this incident, after I had moved to the RBI, I had an occasion to invite Mahindra to address the executives of the RBI. He began his address with a detailed account of his luncheon experience at the Union Bank of India and said that overnight, it had changed his perception about public-sector banks and the people managing them.

A focus on customers, or customer-centricity, will remain only on paper if there is a reluctance to sit down with customers and discuss the issues that concern them.

Experience in the Private Sector

Upon the conclusion of my stint as a Deputy Governor at the RBI in December 2008, I was invited to join the Tata Group. Here, too, before taking up the assignment, I wondered what it would be like to work in the private sector after a lifetime in the public sector.

I found that it was a rewarding experience to work for an organisation that has been described as having the best characteristics of both the public and the private sectors. A valuable lesson for anyone at any stage in her/his career would be to look for an organisation with values to which one can be aligned. With the numerous options available today, this should not be a very difficult task.

Coexistence and Collaboration

I wish to emphasise that I have embraced technology and transformation through various phases of its evolution at different organisations, from commercial banks to central banks. It was a proud moment on 2 September 2007 when the Union Bank of India rolled out its core banking solution across all branches in record time and announced a seamless experience for customers from any point. But what stood out at the end of the day was the tireless human effort that had reached out to branches from Kashmir to Kanyakumari, dodging inclement weather, escaping a militant ambush, and fixing the antenna on a post in a remote village in the Northeast to bring them all under core banking.

The core banking solution is in itself a technology advancement that has enabled the financial services sector in India to move forward at a fast clip. Yet, what remains etched in memory is the human effort that makes technology work for us. It can never be the other way round, and it should not be so.

Artificial intelligence (AI) and its many avatars have great potential to enrich human life through studying and solving many needs in critical areas—from medicine to farming to the environment. Yet, to push AI with the single objective of replacing humans by creating virtual workplaces for every conceivable activity will be self-defeating. Personal communication and interactions have been the bedrock of culture, at work and home, and this has been built over a long period of time.

The human handling of many issues should continue to play an important role. And computers and AI tools should complement the efforts of the human mind.

20

Joys and Sorrows of a Working Life

Kaushik Jayaram

I started working in the years BC (before computers), when everything was done with pen and paper, be it writing briefs, reports, shuffling files, transcribing data, or writing letters.

Early in my career, I worked on a research project on rural wealth in Andhra Pradesh. We visited many villages in the fertile, prosperous district of West Godavari, which was, in 1979, a poster child for the green revolution. We met several individuals, largely from the Kamma and Kapu communities, who were economically and politically very powerful. But they were invariably courteous and when they understood the purpose of the study, they responded patiently to intrusive questions about their families and their wealth. I encountered educated and well-read farmers, with shelves full of books in English and Telugu, including, in one case, the collected works of Marx and Lenin. In short, they were very different from what I had imagined them to be. This was an early lesson that stereotypes often do not hold.

My working life was split into two halves—for the first eighteen years, I worked for the Reserve Bank of India (RBI) and the next twenty years at the Bank for International Settlements (BIS) in Basel, Switzerland. I joined the RBI in 1981, along with a group of thirty young men and women, many of whom went on to have very successful careers in the bank or outside it. The bonds formed during our training were strong and most of us became friends for life.

My first posting was in the currency department in the New Delhi office. Within a few weeks, I discovered a serious case of theft from the currency vaults. It created a furore in the press and in Parliament. At first, I felt rather pleased that I had uncovered this, but, to my horror, I soon realised that I might be regarded as a suspect by the police. One day, as I walked down Parliament Street, a police jeep drew up next to me, and my heart sank. It turned out that the Station House Officer (SHO), a burly Sardarji, who had become a sort of friend lately, had merely stopped to offer me a lift. I said thanks, but no thanks. I did not want to be seen being carried away in a police jeep. Eventually, the person responsible for the theft was arrested and convicted.

In the mid-1980s, the RBI embarked on the computerisation of banking and clearing operations, an early investment in technology that continues to pay rich dividends to this day. I was one of those selected to be trained at IBM Australia in Sydney in 1986. Those of us who were selected to run these computers grew close to each other, and we worked as a team across four metropolitan cities—in Mumbai, Delhi, Chennai, and Kolkata.

I was sent to Calcutta (now Kolkata) in 1987 to help start computer operations there, amidst strong opposition from the local trade unions. My years there were personally very memorable. Our two children were born in Calcutta and we made many good friends there. Of course, it helped that my wife was a Bengali. Even to very aggressive trade unionists, I was a *jamai* (son-in-law), to be treated with respect.

In 1995, there was a big crisis when clearing operations in Mumbai came to a halt after the IBM mainframe computers crashed. Engineers from neither IBM nor the Computer Maintenance Corporation (CMC) could fix the problem. I was flown in from Calcutta to lead the recovery effort. With a small team of colleagues from Mumbai, we worked for more than forty-eight hours and resolved the problem. This was a moment of triumph for us, and our work was much appreciated by the RBI Governor and by the management. As a result, I was transferred to the headquarters in Mumbai, which was not at all to my liking at that time. I was happy in Kolkata and did not want any disruption to our family life.

I joined the newly formed Department of Information Technology in 1996 and we began working on plans to introduce electronic payments nationwide. This included ideas like real time gross settlement (RTGS) and inter-bank funds transfer. It was a huge team effort, and those who have followed us have done wonders. The work culture was also changing—the typing pool vanished and was replaced by personal computers. Then came mobile phones and the internet.

A lot of my career was determined by chance. I was sent on a deputation to the BIS in 1998 without my asking for it. I had mixed feelings about going because we were settling in Mumbai and had a comfortable sea-facing apartment to live in.

Joining the BIS was a culture shock in many ways. I was used to a very hierarchical work culture, where deference was finely graded by rank. But, at the same time, there was much warmth and the feeling of being a family, even if it was a bit paternalistic. At the BIS, I discovered that everyone was on first name terms. It was possible to express our views freely in meetings, and this was even encouraged. A major difference from India was a natural sense of equality among the people, regardless of their job, whether in the common dining room or in interactions outside work.

An initial two-year stint turned into twenty-two years. I worked at the BIS till I retired in 2020. I soon adapted to the work environment and to different ways of communicating. A very important lesson was the emphasis on writing clearly and succinctly, with no long introductions and tedious background information. Similarly, in meetings and seminars, it was essential to get to the main points very fast. Relationships were mostly professional, although there were some personal friendships.

Over the years, I worked in different areas and in different roles. I worked on payment systems, financial stability, macro prudential policy, and administration. I also worked with the BIS external committees and groups. I led teams of many nationalities and learnt that the ability to interact with people from different countries and backgrounds is very important. I believe that my early habit of reading, both fiction and non-fiction, including history, politics, and culture, helped me considerably.

Along with evolving technology, I witnessed changes in the work culture, which became more transactional, with less emphasis on personal relationships. I never felt comfortable with this, or with getting rid of people in the name of productivity. As my former boss used to say, different people have different ways of working, and we are all the better for this diversity. The pressure to perform in accordance with some standard metric of efficiency can stifle creativity and innovation.

I never actively sought career opportunities. I was content to work hard and sincerely at whatever job I had. Opportunities came by when my work was recognised and appreciated. Is there a lesson in this? I do not know. But I do believe in doing work without anticipating rewards. I also think one should not be afraid to take the initiative, even at the risk of failure. The late Sir Andrew Crockett, former general manager of the BIS, encouraged risk-taking without being reckless.

New ideas like remote working and flexible working hours were already on the table when I retired, just before the onset of the pandemic. I was glad I had retired because I was not sure if I could have worked well under those circumstances. My working life was based on the separation of office and home, with a lot of social interaction at work. But everyone tells me it was not very difficult to get used to the new normal.

This brings me to the question of work in the future. Recently, a BIS colleague told me how he and other colleagues had begun using artificial intelligence (AI) in the form of ChatGPT at work. He gave me an example of a talk a senior economist from the BIS had given at an Ivy League university. The organisers asked him if he could convert his talk into a short paper. My colleague helped him to produce an almost complete paper in no time at all by using ChatGPT to process a video of the talk and the slides used. This task would have otherwise taken at least three or four days.

To me, this story had both positive and negative implications. While this tool may raise productivity enormously, it could seriously erode an individual's ability to be creative, limit her/his reading and writing, and capacity to express ideas. We run the risk of reducing people to mechanical feeders of questions to machines.

I could, of course, be wrong. Our grandchildren might hopefully use these technologies for relief from the tedium of daily work and spend their time and energy doing better things.

From Soapstone to ChatGPT A Journey

B. Sambamurthy

My grandson and granddaughter were at times curious to know how I studied, worked, and lived without a mobile phone, iPad, the internet, and Google. They were amused when I told them that in primary school, I started with a slate made of some stone and we wrote on it with a stick of soapstone (called *balapam* in Telugu). They suspected that I belonged to the 'stone age' because of this. Their suspicion only deepened when I told them that writing by hand with pencil and pen had continued until 1984, when I turned thirty-six.

Even while studying to be a chartered accountant in the early 1970s, a mastery over numerical skills, including doing divisions and multiplications in the mind, was as important as knowing the principles of accounting and taxation. In the initial months of training, we honed our numerical skills by playing with telephone numbers in the directory. There were no calculators, much less computers, in those days.

My career in banking began at Canara Bank in 1974 and went through Syndicate Bank and Indian Bank to Corporation Bank, where it ended in 2008. Career 2.0, which involved serving on the boards of financial market infrastructure organisations, lasted fifteen years, till 2023. I therefore had a ringside view of the evolution of computerisation in the banking industry in India. It was at times exciting and at times challenging, not only from the technology perspective but also that of managing people, change, and skills.

Initially, I worked in the internal audit divisions of Canara Bank and Syndicate Bank. This was almost an extension of my C.A. education because the job involved, among other things, numerical operations like verifying interests manually and writing reports by hand.

I was posted for the first time as a branch manager of Syndicate Bank, Delhi Green Park Extension in 1984. The staff devoted more than half their time to doing back-office work such as reconciling accounts of the day manually, and it used to take months and, in some cases, years to reconcile these accounts. I have not seen drudgery worse than that. The time for customer service was limited till lunch time. The balances of thousands of accounts were then noted down, totalled, and tallied manually.

Major Breakthrough

The pen and pencil, good handwriting, and nimble numerical skills ruled at banks till the early 1980s. A major breakthrough happened in 1984. Deeply concerned with issues such as low productivity and the mounting arrears of accounting, including balancing and reconciliation, which resulted in poor customer service, an RBI committee headed by Deputy Governor C. Rangarajan recommended mechanisation (not computerisation). Trade unions stoutly opposed this move and even manhandled him. But he refused to yield. As with the introduction of any new technology, the usual reason was that it would result in job losses, which did not happen.

A Small Beginning

My Delhi branch was selected as a pilot branch for mechanisation in 1985 after I volunteered for it. After *gheraos* by unions, court cases, and plenty of negotiations, a beginning was made in computerising (sorry, mechanising) banking operations. It was very rudimentary hardware; for instance, these machines could process only at a very limited speed (8 bits, which is 1/125 of a megabyte [MB]). Today's computers in banks can process numbers 10,000 times faster. Hard disks were not permitted and there was no internal storage. Computers without internal storage were a unique Indian innovation! Floppy disks of 256 kb (1/4 of an MB) were the storage medium. Floppies were so delicate that they had to be transported in special waterproof boxes with great care, as exposure to hot weather, dust particles, or water could corrupt the data.

Three Phases

Computerisation of banks in India went through three distinct phases from the early 1980s to the 2000s. The first was the mechanisation of the back offices of branches, which saw a shift from ledgers to advanced ledger posting machines or ALPMs, and then their front offices. The second phase of total branch automation (TBA) was marked by computerisation of the entire branch, with branch-level servers and multiple terminals. The last phase was core banking solutions (CBS) for the entire bank itself. Banks were also active in developing in-house skills in programming, system administration, systems analysis, and development.

IT Services for Customers

This enabled banks to introduce new services like automated teller machines (ATMs) and internet banking. Customers could operate from any branch of the bank. They got good-looking passbooks, which were much better than the manually written but mostly indecipherable passbooks till then. Most importantly, customers were served for longer and transactions were processed faster. Employees were happy when they found that the drudgery of back-office work had been significantly reduced, and they began demanding increasing computerisation. With computers, air-conditioned offices also came as a bonus.

Data Analytics: Machine Learning

Having computerised routine operations, banks began focusing on how to deliver a better customer experience. Some banks have taken to using big data analytic tools to predict customer needs and offer services. Banks have also developed new business models and strategies to improve the number of products per customer and better the lifetime value (LTV) of customers.

Modernising Payment Systems

Alongside all this, the RBI was taking initiatives to automate, or computerise, the process of making remittances and payments. During the early 2000s, the RBI began making the payment system electronic. It introduced the real time gross settlement (RTGS) and the national electronic funds transfer (NEFT) system, which made payments in real time. Another major transformation was brought about in cheque clearing operations. With the introduction of the cheque truncation system (CTS), the practice of millions of cheques physically crisscrossing the length and breadth of the country was eliminated. It helped to clear cheques faster, increased liquidity, and reduced operational costs.

Institute for Development and Research in Banking Technology

To encourage and accelerate the adoption of electronic payment systems by the people at large, the RBI established the Institute for Development and Research in Banking Technology (IDRBT) in 1996 in Hyderabad. It operated the payment systems on behalf of the RBI, besides carrying out academic activities. All the banks were connected to a closed user network called INFINET, a kind of information superhighway connecting all banks and the RBI in 1999. This has revolutionised payment systems in the country.

A national ATM switch was established and launched in 2004, which connected all the ATMs of various banks on a single network. This enabled customers to go to any bank's ATM to draw or deposit money at any time. Thus, interoperability and public good policy came together in a way unique to India.

The IDRBT had been drawing up training programmes towards capacity building. It has also established labs or centres of excellence in the areas of big data analytics, mobile banking, and cyber security.

National Payments Corporation

To give a further impetus to digital payments, the RBI and the Indian Banks' Association created the National Payments Corporation of India during 2008–2009, which has become an umbrella entity for payment systems in the country. This is a one of its kind organisation in the world. It supervises a user-operated system and the RBI has no equity in it, but a seat on its director board under the law. The unified payment interface (UPI), with its current monthly run rate of 10 billion transactions, is its flagship product, which has become very popular not only in India but also internationally. It has now begun offering the service in some foreign countries as well. The National Payments Corporation helps in ushering in a cashless and paperless society, where banking does not need one's physical presence. Its operative words are innovation, creativity, and collaboration.

A Public Good

The RBI mandates that payment services shall be a public good and shall be interoperable across the banking industry. Even a mendicant has as much access to a digital payment system as a millionaire. Thanks to these initiatives, India today boasts of one of the most sophisticated payment systems, which even developed countries are seriously thinking of emulating. There was the National Financial Switch in 2004 (ATM Switch), the UPI in 2015, and the Bharat QR code in 2016. Interoperability ensured that the UPI could clock more than 100 billion transactions a month on a single platform. This is considered the single largest platform globally. Most of the advanced countries, and even China, follow a walled garden approach and these payment systems are not interoperable. Even the US Congress has expressed the desire for such a payment system.

Banks have provided apps and the Omnichannel, a business strategy that aims to provide users with a seamless and consistent experience across multiple digital and physical channels.

I was lucky to have a ringside view of the computerisation process because I was associated with both branch-level and bank-level computerisation. After retirement, the RBI gave me the responsibility of working with the IDRBT and I was also on the NPCI's board as the RBI's nominee. Things have changed, but in today's world, the difference lies in the speed of change. The form and process of every aspect of banking—and, for that matter, finance—has changed beyond recognition. But the function of banks as an intermediary, with all its attendant risks and rewards, is as relevant now as it once was. If anything, it has become more complex.

Bank in Mobile Phones

My neighbour's son, who is in his twenties, is in a well-paying software job and has a mortgage loan, a car loan, and a credit card. He is a digital native and his engagement is with financial technology and apps. He once asked me, 'Do we need banks?' To emphasise this, he waved his mobile phone and triumphantly declared that he did not need a bank. But he was blissfully unaware that there are institutions, regulators, and enterprises to deliver services to his mobile, safely, securely, and efficiently.

Listening to this story, my grandson, another digital native, quipped, 'Count your age from 1984.'

In summary, I would say that experience without lifelong learning is at a discount. As nineteenth-century Danish philosopher Soren Kierkegaard pointed out, 'Life can only be understood backwards, but it must be lived forwards.'

Behind the Scenes of Pathbreaking Journeys

R. B. Barman

My journey from a small village in lower Assam, near the foothills of Bhutan, to the Reserve Bank of India (RBI) in 1979 proved most eventful, both personally and professionally. My daughter was just a year old then. I was a lateral entrant as a Deputy Director to the RBI's then Department of Statistics in Mumbai after leaving the Indian Statistical Service.

In June 1982, when I was learning the basics of central banking, I was posted to Calcutta (now Kolkata). I was to set up the regional office of the department and start the survey unit, where I continued to work for six years. This period proved very fulfilling for my family because my in-laws lived in Kalyani, just about 50 kilometres away.

I also saw the vitality of the city of Calcutta and its people, and their intellectual pursuits, even under trying situations, while travelling in local trains and at public gatherings. This made me think I required a deeper understanding of the process of broad-based economic development and socioeconomic transformation. So, on returning to Mumbai, I went to the Indian Institute of Technology Bombay on study leave in January 1989 to do a Ph.D. in economics.

The intention was to prepare myself to be an analyst, and to be of use when it came to policymaking at the RBI. This was a time when India was grappling with internal and external imbalances. I obtained my Ph.D. in 1993, and with this graduated from a statistician to an econometrician.

At the time, I became an active member of The Indian Econometric Society (TIES), becoming its president in 2006. A memorable occasion was when we invited Indian-American mathematician and statistician C. R. Rao, a founder president of the society, as the chief guest for its annual conference at IIT Bombay in 2007. Governor Y. V. Reddy was not only kind enough to invite him to visit the RBI, hosting a special lunch in his honour, but also personally very courteous to him and his wife. This was our tribute to the world-renowned statistician, who in 2023 was awarded the International Prize in Statistics, considered equivalent to a Nobel Prize, by the International Statistical Institute.

I became an Adviser in the RBI's then Department of Statistical Analysis and Computer Services in June 1995, taking over the responsibility after just a month there. It was challenging in many ways, and it has to be said that Governor C. Rangarajan reposed huge trust in me.

A part of the department had been carved out for a new Department of Information Technology (DIT), and I was expected to foster a research environment in the statistical set-up that remained. On the analytical front, we began developing models for the forecast of rate variables and certain components of short-term liquidity. The main inspiration for this was Deputy Governor Reddy, who conducted monthly meetings with the heads of departments under him to discuss policy issues.

Liquidity forecasting was one of the important issues. The conventional econometric models were not very useful as we did not have the data necessary for such modelling. At that time, we learnt the use of machine learning techniques such as neural networks and genetic algorithms for modelling high frequency data. Another work of major significance was the CAMELS rating system, which enabled us to suggest an approach for scoring banks. In the process, the department was rejuvenated for focused research, both for policy and market operations.

The path-breaking journey on data warehousing, which meant integrating data from different sources in different formats into one comprehensive multidimensional database for extracting analytically useful information, for the RBI began in 1998. Deputy Governor

Reddy was the chairman of the committee directing and steering the whole initiative. A. Vasudevan, then an Executive Director, was vice-chairman, and I was a member secretary. The members included experts from the IIT Bombay, the National Informatics Centre, and the Indian Statistical Institute. We found that even the Federal Reserve of the US did not have an integrated system of managing data processing using multidimensional models at that time. Developing a model for our data warehousing was a major challenge because of the complexity it posed. What we did with the help of I-Flex, our vendor, was nothing short of pioneering.

At the time, not even 50 per cent of the data warehouses in advanced countries' banking systems were considered versatile enough, due to both software and hardware challenges. It was almost like we were fools, rushing in where angels feared to tread. However, we were fearless. I mainly banked on my young raw talent to deliver on this dream project, placed under A. K. Nag, Director. I am happy to note that by providing an early example of data warehousing for a large central bank, we were noticed by premier international organisations such as the International Monetary Fund (IMF) in Washington, D.C. and the Bank for International Settlements (BIS) in Basil. The Irving Fisher Committee on Central Bank Statistics, BIS, of which I became vice-chairman in 2007, published its first paper on data warehousing in 2003, jointly authored by A. K. Nag and myself.

Our most difficult challenge lay in getting users to take advantage of data warehousing. Many people had a vested interest in controlling access to data so that they could remain important. In 2002, when data warehousing became ready for use, Deputy Governor Rakesh Mohan convened a meeting of user departments to understand their opinion of the newly developed data warehouse. The feedback was hopelessly negative, and it was quite discouraging for us. Finally, it was decided to throw data warehousing open in the public domain for the world at large to find its usefulness.

This move proved to be an instantaneous success. We were soon getting about 6,000 hits every month from diverse sets of users, some from as far away as Japan and the United States. Rather than going to the original sources, users began relying on the RBI data warehouse as a main source for their data needs. In due course, this pioneering project gained importance and became an RBI enterprise using big data and state of the art tools.

Meanwhile, the department's name changed to the Department of Statistics and Information Management. In 2000, the RBI's Central Board appreciated the innovative work carried out by the department. It was a great moment of recognition for us. We had gained huge confidence by then and were nurturing young talent to break new ground. These officers are now in leadership positions in the RBI.

With big data tools, the RBI is now one of the best in the statistical data processing field and even the BIS consults our experts on the deployment of cutting-edge tools. The journey that began under the chairmanship of Deputy Governor Reddy in 1998 in difficult conditions is now well-recognised, both in India and abroad, as a major source of information on economic statistics in India.

In my entire career, the digitalisation of payments is the initiative that I most cherish. In the RBI, developments on the digitalisation of payments between 2001 and 2008 took place when I was Executive Director, in charge of the Department of Information Technology and the Department of Payments and Settlements Systems. My first major job was to roll out real time gross settlement (RTGS), which is a system that allows banks and financial institutions to electronically transfer money and securities between themselves in real time. K. R. Ganapathy, who was the Chief General Manager of the Department of Information Technology, led the team. RTGS was online on 24 March 2004, although public transactions began only three months later. Once the technology infrastructure was ready, the RBI introduced some other applications for money transfer, such as NEFT (national electronic funds transfer) and NECS (national electronic clearing service), gradually convincing people and the government to opt for faster payment systems.

The idea of an umbrella organisation for retail payments was set out in the RBI's Payments Systems Vision Document 2005–2008 in May 2005. The document's vision was to establish a safe, secure, and efficient payment system for India, and the National

Payments Corporation of India (NPCI) emerged as a result of this. The RBI had sent a team of four to visit Sweden to study their banking and payment systems in 2004. Ganesh Kumar, who later became an Executive Director, was a member of the team, along with me, D. B. Phatak of IIT Bombay, and Ashok Kini of the State Bank of India. The most important idea that I carried back from this trip was the way they were driving the payments system through bankers as a not-for-profit company.

We too insisted on making India's umbrella organisation a not-for-profit company, which would deliver digital payments as a public good, protecting consumers against market manipulation. There were not many takers for such a model. There was heavy pressure from industry to make it a for-profit concern on grounds of viability. However, the RBI stood its ground. Today, the Indian payment system has had a revolutionary impact on retail payments worldwide. Its grand success in the country vindicates our conviction that promoting the welfare of consumers is the way forward.

Governor Reddy's unstinting support was our greatest strength in pursuing this important initiative. In my view, one of his most important accomplishments was that he solidly backed the idea of protecting digital payments from market manipulation. It is no wonder that the Open Network for Digital Commerce (ONDC), established by the government to develop open e-commerce, has opted for this model to protect small retail traders from large organised traders. Health and education are two important sectors where such a model could have a major impact on the lives of common people.

Starting with the National Financial Switch (NFS), which was taken over from the RBI's Institute for Development and Research on Banking Technology (IDRBT) in Hyderabad in 2010, the NPCI has been very successful in developing sophisticated and innovative products for digital payments. A. P. Hota of the RBI took over as the chief executive officer of the NPCI to lay the foundation of the organisation. Dilip Asbe, the first chief technology officer of the NPCI, is now its managing director.

The products–immediate payment services (IMPS), RuPay debit and credit card, Bharat Bills Payment Services (BBPS), Aadhaar

Enabled Payment Services (AePS), FASTtag for toll tax, and, above all, the unified payment interface (UPI)—have revolutionised digital payments in India. This has been a success without parallel, and it is now used as a model by countries in all continents. Personally, I am happy to have continued as an adviser to the NPCI from its inception. However, it was the combined effort of many sharp minds and leading institutions, such as IIT Bombay, IIT Madras, and Infosys, to name a few, and the RBI and the government, that was behind this exemplary success.

Unlike earlier payment revolutions, from barter to metal to paper, digital payments leave a trail, which can be converted into very insightful information. When mapped with real, financial, and fiscal-sector data at a granular level using the Geographical Information System (GIS), this knowledge can transform all society, right from the village panchayat upwards. It can make all of us much better contributors to the cause of socioeconomic development. In this age of artificial intelligence (AI), we must build such a system for sustained development with a focus on inclusive growth.

Data warehousing taught me how to integrate data to understand the dynamics of economic growth in a distributional context. I believe our quest for inclusive growth requires a different paradigm. It must be a bottom-up approach to development through meticulous planning, execution, and evaluation at every level of governance. As the chairman of the National Statistical Commission (NSC) during 2016–2018, I set up five committees to initiate this process, and their reports are with the commission.

Looking ahead, we need to convert a huge volume of transactional data, captured through business and e-governance, and survey data into information, and then knowledge. These data, tagged with the GIS as part of the data model, is capable of shedding light on the lifestyles of people in each village panchayat, their interaction with the market players surrounding them, the financial and fiscal systems they deal with, and the effectiveness of governance. This must be measurable and be a part of statistics, as a matter of public good. This will create a knowledge economy which makes the best use of technology, and it should lead to the transformation of society and the polity.

I have been visiting my village home at Wada in Palghar district near Mumbai every month since 2013. The district is dominated by Adivasi people, most of whom are very poor. The main source of income for families is paddy cultivation, just one crop during the monsoon. Even after seventy-five years of independence, they have not been able to grow multiple crops for want of water and capital. But the Vaitarna river, which flows through Wada, carries a huge volume of water to the Arabian Sea every monsoon.

If credit had been available and if it had been used for raising productivity, the farmers could have improved their cultivation practices, and things would have been very different from what they are now. They could have dug ponds to conserve rainwater and could have used them for pisciculture and irrigation, earning two or three times what they earn now. This would have unleashed a much-needed structural transformation, with shifting manpower being able to find productive work elsewhere.

With more productive workers earning higher incomes everywhere, it would be possible to move over to a virtuous cycle. We could eliminate poverty, hunger, and malnutrition as the country pursues inclusive growth and sustained socioeconomic development. In my view, the actual potential for economic growth is much higher than is normally assumed. This will, I hope, take our country to its rightful place in the world.

Part V

Media

23

Myriad Brilliant Minds

LATHA VENKATESH

In my early years, I was groomed for a 'no-career plan'. 'I want you to be capable of earning if the need arises. But I don't want you to take a job if there is no need.' That was a mantra my father often repeated. He was firmly of the view that families are stable and children well brought up only when the lady of the house is educated, but concentrates on the home.

I was an unquestioning disciple of my father on many issues, including this one. This had its advantages—I could opt for subjects (at least ancillaries) such as history and literature, which cultivate the mind but do not necessarily get you the best of jobs. The downside, of course, was that I did not even try to build on my reasonable capability in STEM (science, technology, engineering, and mathematics) disciplines. Given this inherited axiom of homemaking as my first duty, I slipped into teaching political science in a college as my first job. It had the advantage of not being a 9-to-5 job and the sop of allowing me to read more for pleasure than to earn a living.

But as I slipped into academia, the joys of working unfolded. The first joy was the pleasure of being with erudite minds. Be it the staff common rooms at the SIES college in Mumbai, and later Kirti College, where I was a lecturer, or the Kalina Campus Reading Hall, which teemed with researchers, I was always in an environment where I was a student.

At the SIES, my former teachers became my colleagues. I owe my introduction to the classics—from Thomas Hobbes to John

Locke, to Arnold Toynbee, and from William Shakespeare, to T. S. Eliot, to Ernest Hemingway—to my teachers: Professors Francis Mechery and Derek Antao. Good ideas were made and unmade in my hearing ever so often. How about de-schooling society, Mechery asked one day, arguing that the school system had done more to kill education than promote it. 'MNCs [multinational corporations] have converted a need for drinking water into a thirst for Coca Cola in Third World countries' was another subject of discussion that comes to mind. Bashing MNCs and the International Monetary Fund (IMF) was a popular pastime at that time.

The Kirti College staff room introduced me to the treasures of vernacular literature. I occasionally overheard Professor Ramesh Tendulkar chat with M. P. Rege, who used to drop by, and also listened to Professor Yashwant Phadke, who was invited for lectures. To read good fiction and non-fiction in Marathi has remained an unfulfilled goal.

As I was completing my Ph.D. in political science to qualify for a lectureship in Mumbai University, all hell broke loose. The Mandal Commission and the pro-reservation climate of the early 1990s led the university to enforce 'reservation' with greater vigour. In the colleges, the rule was that all non-Scheduled Caste/Scheduled Tribe (SC/ST) candidates had to be appointed on a temporary basis till a 'reserved' candidate was found.

I had trained to be an academic, and this came as a disappointment, but I had to cope. I joined *The Economic Times* as a sub-editor, and eventually moved to reporting on commodity markets and company affairs. But the academic training would not leave me. I approached my beat like a Ph.D. student trying to read up everything possible about the subject I was dealing with. But those were pre-internet days and it was very difficult to get much written material on these markets. I had to depend on my sources to school me.

Those struggling days as a reporter taught me two lessons. The first lesson was that a journalist had to always be a student. The second was that my sources comprised a myriad brilliant minds and they were willing to teach me. The journalist only needs to choose her teachers with care. The education will not come free.

You have to convince your sources of your sincerity and often trade information gathered elsewhere.

As I migrated from commodity markets and corporates to equity markets and then fixed income and central bank reportage over the years, my teachers grew in stature, sophistication, and erudition. Money market dealers, equity brokers, bank and corporate treasury heads, and equity analysts helped me learn and understand breaking news in record time. Chairmen of banks, private conglomerates, and public-sector companies taught me the intricacies of their sectors over lunches or coffee.

Another interesting source of information was train travel. Travelling by Mumbai trains and BEST buses was my best source of insights into the Indian economy. Academia and newsrooms taught me much, but I learnt about the daily drudgery of hawkers and the travails of working women and men of all classes on the trains. Far from being daunting, they became a good reason to stay employed.

But my best teachers were from the Reserve Bank of India (RBI)–governors, deputy governors, and executive directors. Some educated me through chance remarks during or after a formal interview–a chance comment could suddenly, like a switch turned on, light up a whole era or ecosystem. But many patiently invested several hours to teach me complex issues such as money multipliers, fiscal multipliers, bank-created money, high-powered money, risk weights, provisioning, and the rather complicated business of reading a central bank balance sheet.

A few specific incidents come to mind. In 2007, a policymaker called some of us financial editors for an informal, non-reportable press briefing. He had just returned from some international meetings and told us he expected horrible things to happen in financial markets. 'Don't praise this stock market rally. Instead, tell people to be careful. Warn people that bad things can happen in markets,' he said. In a few months, we realised what a prescient warning that had been.

The US investment bank Bear Stearns went under. I called up the policymaker to ask if this was it. Is this why he had warned us? 'No,' he replied, 'Far bigger institutions will fail; I couldn't tell you all this on that day, and even now I can't say publicly that more institutions will fail.' I only wish I had disseminated those messages more effectively, but in the days to come, I was better prepared to understand the problem of undercapitalised banks, dangerous derivatives, and ninja loans that led to the Lehman blow-up and the global financial crisis.

Another instance of big learning was the demonetisation of November 2016. On the first day, I could not understand what editorial stance to take—the goal of destroying black money seemed laudable, but something told me the move was too ham-handed. The policy was announced at 8 PM and I needed to know enough to at least assume an editorial stance by the next morning. Two former policymakers came to my rescue.

The first, speaking to me at midnight, patiently explained the numbers of notes that had been demonetised (I did not realise that 85 per cent by value was gone) and the administrative problems he foresaw—down to getting enough ink to print new notes, pressures on the honesty of the banking system, the very few benefits of the move, and the likely hardships. Another veteran policymaker, whom I was begging for an on-air interview, candidly told me, 'I have friends in government whom I can't oppose publicly, but this is the worst economic policy in my memory.' Armed with their arguments, I could lace my market commentaries with solid fact-based analysis. That senior policymakers were ready to speak late into the night to bring me up to speed is one of the perks of my journalism career.

These are but two instances. I can recall dozens where I have been audience to almost a Harvard master class on central banking and public finance. Journalism perhaps is the only profession where you get paid to learn your entire life.

Besides one's sources in the corridors of power, colleagues in the newsroom are a source of much learning. While seniors gave me perspective, very often younger colleagues enriched me with trivia, details, or just startling questions. And there are always those seasoned colleagues—I would never give an edit for publication without sounding them out.

The other big takeaway of a life in journalism is the series of dilemmas one faces. It is a perennial dilemma whether to retain a source or a valued guest on the show or to tear into her/him when a murky issue suddenly surfaces. Judging when one's evidence is adequate and when one may be overstating gives rise to another dilemma. Then there are bigger dilemmas about how far your organisation will support your story and the extent to which you may expose the organisation to legal challenges or the powers that be. Does one quit the platform at the first sign of censorship, or bide one's time, push the envelope, and use the platform when possible for the larger good?

The new digital medium has brought new opportunities, but the old media entities still retain clout, which enables the journalist to reach out to the most powerful decision-makers. Yet, social media is seriously challenging traditional media. Newspapers and TV channels are no longer the only or even the first source of news or even views. The journalist may still provide context and credibility. Traditional media may still enable the lay reader to confirm if what s/he heard on social media is right. But the existential threat to media as we know it is real.

Let me conclude with a different kind of success I experienced in my career. As a young mother, staying in Navi Mumbai and working at the other end of town, I encountered myriad struggles to balance home and career. The key central banking beat was denied to me when I joined *The Economic Times* simply because I was a young mother, and, by definition, unlikely to be reliable. Later, as I rose to become executive editor at my news channel, a self-assigned responsibility was to handhold and advise young mothers to ensure they stayed the course during their difficult years. I was a fierce fighter for their rights.

A few years ago, a former colleague, a young mother whom I had helped, and who has since migrated abroad, sent me a WhatsApp message on Mother's Day that I reproduce here: 'Happy Mother's Day, Latha ma'am, thank you for helping me to keep going when I was a new mother and ensuring I never got off the career path. Thanks to you, I am still working today and able to balance my home life.'

I treasure the message as much as my Ramnath Goenka Award for journalism. If father is watching me from the high heavens, I hope I have convinced him to change his opinion on women and work.

24

An 'Academic-Journalist'

C. Rammanohar Reddy

I have been in journalism since the late 1980s. During these decades, the world of journalism has changed dramatically. The technology used has of course radically changed the face of journalism. The structure of the profession of journalism has changed, and even its purpose seems to have changed.

The very vocabulary too has changed. Why, nobody talks about 'journalism'; it is not even 'the press'. It is now the 'media', which carries with it a meaning that is both a lot more and a lot less than speaking truth to power. How do I see my own path over close to four decades amidst these transformations?

I entered journalism only when I was in my thirties, but I had grown up with 'news' and 'newspapers' at home. My father was with newspapers for close to three decades and he was also a political person. At home, there were always more newspapers and magazines from across the country than one could read in a day. And what was right, what was wrong, and what needed to be done in the country was often a part of the conversation.

I grew up, then, with an awareness of social and political issues. While I was never involved in student politics, I did hope to understand the world better and eventually contribute in some way to making it better. That took me to the study of economics, then to research in the discipline, but with an eye on the real world. I eventually hit on journalism as a profession through which I thought I could intervene in public debates and the making of policy.

I have been in journalism for close to four decades, but many may not see me as a 'journalist'. I have done little reporting from the field, most of my work having been in writing commentary, and editing. If there was a term called 'academic-journalist', then it would fit me perfectly, since I did move mid-career from academia to journalism.

Yet, on entering journalism, I worked in two dailies—for five years with *Deccan Herald* in Bangalore and then a decade-long stint with one of India's most widely read and respected dailies, *The Hindu*. So I can say with some confidence that I have seen the insides of the press.

It is only now as I write this piece, decades later, that I ask myself if I fulfilled my ambition of bringing clarity and depth to the analysis of economic issues—domestic and international—and to do so in an accessible language, at least in the two newspapers where I worked. I think I did. I cannot claim any consistency, and I was always aware that my 'left-liberal' perspective informed my analysis.

The changes wrought by economic liberalisation in 1991 forced me to think through issues more clearly. That was a challenge, but if I were to go by what readers (especially college students) occasionally wrote in, by what my editors told me, and by the citations of my articles elsewhere, I perhaps succeeded. But, yes, I wished I had done more; especially by strengthening my writing with reporting from the field.

Much of what I could do as an individual was on account of the support I received from my colleagues. Readers and viewers are not always aware of how much of a collaborative effort is involved in journalism. In print, for instance, it is the editor, sub-editor, and reporter who together make that news report complete. I was a lateral entrant into journalism, and I could learn my skills only with the guidance of some of my editors and many of my colleagues. The importance of collaboration became all the more critical in my subsequent assignments, where I was the head of organisations.

An aside: journalists are often asked about 'writer's block'. There isn't any, for the simple reason that journalists cannot afford to have a writer's block. I remember early in my first job, going up one day to my then boss, B. R. P. Bhaskar, and saying, 'I am sorry,

I am not able to write the editorial today' (it was on something as dull as a new law on benami holdings). Bhaskar just looked at me and quietly said, 'Well, then there will be a block of white space in tomorrow's newspaper.' I never suffered writer's block thereafter.

The big question journalists are always asked is, 'How much freedom do you have to say what you want to?' and 'How often have your reports/articles been stopped?' It goes without saying that the press sometimes holds back, and sometimes stops publication at the last minute. For a news organisation to deny that this does happen is to be economical with the truth. It does happen; and the more often it happens, the lower the reputation of the publication.

I was aware of such instances, but none of major significance—although one can say that in the early days of my career, I may not have been aware of all such decisions as they would have been outside my pay grade. My own experience is that more than political and commercial considerations, it was lazy decisions, individual preferences, and an unwillingness to recognise major stories—all hallmarks of a lack of professionalism—that were important for omissions and commissions.

At both the dailies, I, for one, was able to enjoy a measure of freedom not available to most journalists then or now. I could choose the topics I wrote on (although the topics for editorials were decided by a group or dictated by the news of the day). I also had the freedom to say what I wanted. This was, of course, constrained by the fact that I was working in organisations whose boundaries I was aware of—more in one than in the other. The fact that my writing was mainly commentary/analysis allowed me to exercise a greater sense of autonomy than many reporters would have had. But then, reporters could also do much more than what I did, constrained as I was by sitting at a desk and writing commentary on economic policy.

A somewhat deliberate decision I took was to never work in New Delhi. For journalism, as for many other professions, the capital was where you had to be. It exuded power, it carried an aura of importance, and, for journalists, Delhi was doubly important for that was where you could get access to the decision-makers in government and political parties. (You could also rub shoulders with the powerful, be a power broker yourself, and enjoy an illusory sense of self-importance.)

Being located in the centre of power also meant many other things—a loss of perspective, an unawareness of what the country (and not just the national capital) experienced, and, most importantly, a vulnerability to getting corrupted by being close to power. My own view was that right from the 1950s onwards, the New Delhi-centric nature of English-language journalism has been as much its weakness as its strength. I have no doubt lost considerably by way of experience by not working in the capital. But I may well have lost much more in other respects if I had not stayed away from the seat of power.

Until recently, you could not claim to have been a journalist if you had not worked in a newspaper, and I am glad I spent a considerably long time in two dailies. The most satisfying work, though, was my subsequent eleven-plus year stint as Editor of the *Economic and Political Weekly*, Mumbai. *EPW*, as it was and is known, is a unique publication, not just in India but perhaps in the world. Published by a trust and not a commercial entity, it has been since 1949 an important part of both the public policy world and academia. It was a matter of pride for young scholars to have published in *EPW*. And for students of the social sciences, it has always been an indispensable source of educational material.

It was therefore an honour to be asked in 2004 to become the Editor of *EPW*, at the time only the fourth editor in its storied history. It was also a challenge for I was stepping into the shoes of its legendary editor of thirty-five years, Krishna Raj. Readers and writers of *EPW* have always been fiercely protective of the publication because they saw it as 'theirs', and not owned by some commercial entity. There was therefore much concern about whether *EPW* would survive when I stepped into Krishna Raj's shoes on his death (many directly told me so); there was much concern that as an outsider, I was not the right person (many told me this as well). In the event, I think I not only proved the doubters wrong, but was also able to leave *EPW* in a far healthier condition than when I found it.

During my decade and a bit, we made *EPW* livelier. We brought in new authors, and we covered new areas. We widened both circulation and readership. We were successful in embracing the digital era. We also streamlined its operations so that writers and readers had fewer complaints. And perhaps one of the most important achievements, we improved its finances so that a small community of employees began to enjoy far better compensation levels than before, even if they remained well below what was needed in Mumbai.

Looking back, I do not think there was any grand strategy involved. My first priority was to safeguard this important national institution. I was able to convey this to my colleagues, who reciprocated by giving everything they had to the institution. For our writers, the message was that we would look at whatever they suggested and that we would take a decision quickly. We could publish only a small fraction of submissions, but that the writers could sense that we were reading all that they sent was, to begin with, adequate. Nothing is more damaging to a publication than when writers feel that their work is arbitrarily dismissed, and that only known and 'famous' authors are favoured. And for our readers, the signal was that we would keep looking for new themes, new topics, and fresh perspectives.

An editor's job is in many ways a lonely one if you want to do it properly. If you try and please everyone, the publication will go down the drain. You therefore sometimes need to be brutal in your decisions, which will win you no friends. What I learnt early in my stint at *EPW* is that if the wider community of readers, writers, and subscribers know you are open and receptive, you can be sure of support for the publication.

There is always another side to working in positions of responsibility, especially in small and fragile organisations, even if they enjoy an outsized influence. The cost is borne by your family. The honour that came with being asked to become Editor of *EPW* was so immense that I do not think I thought it through before taking it up, moving to another city, and being away from my family. To be honest, I am not sure if I would have taken the same decision if I could have foreseen how much of a hole it was going to create in my family life, whatever the prestige of the position. These days, it is called maintaining the right 'work-life balance'. I think we should be more aware of that balance and not put work above everything else. Work is important, so too the family.

The lessons I learnt in *EPW* I have tried to implement while editing *The India Forum*, a new and independent venture launched in 2019 by a group of academics, journalists, and civil society activists to offer critical commentary. Curious, open, and alive to the world around us, *The India Forum* has established a niche for itself in the age of fake news in a few years. There is still a long way to go and the challenges of putting it on a sound footing will be immense, especially since we are now in an environment hostile to independent and critical thinking.

I began by writing about the changes in journalism over the course of my working life, and it is that with which one must end. The changes in the media in the past 30–40 years are far greater than perhaps in the previous 30–40 years.

Within a decade of my entering journalism, we had the explosion in news and entertainment TV (from the mid-late 1990s onwards). Then, from the early 2000s, there has been the growth of digital media—text, audio, and video. We have web magazines, we have podcasts, and now an explosion in 'YouTubers'. Print, after enjoying spells of impressive growth until the early 2000s, has declined in importance. So it is no longer the 'press' that is the mainstay of news.

In India, the earlier pre-eminence of English language journalism—reaching only a minuscule proportion of the population—has had to yield to the Indian language press, especially Hindi.

Journalists now have far more tools at their hand than the notepad and tape-recorder of before. The phone, more powerful than the desktop of the 1980s, can be used to write a story, take photos, record interviews, and shoot short films. Technology has empowered journalists. (Although at times, employers push reporters to be all things at the same time and, in the process, push them to the edge.)

There is another change and that is in the longstanding tension between journalism as a business and journalism as public purpose; this has shifted vastly in favour of business. From the mid-1990s onwards, as first newspapers grew, then TV, and then digital media, the publishing institutions recognised the profit potential of news and entertainment. Chinese walls between advertising and news came down, publishers had their eyes more on the bottom line, and with that, journalism changed. Hence, we now have the 'media industry'; it is no longer journalism or the press.

This change was not unique to India; it was a transformation the world over. Journalism does need to make ends meet and it cannot ignore costs and revenue if it wants to survive. The damage, in my view, has been caused by the emergence of news as 'a product' like any other. We have forgotten that journalism has a higher purpose and that it is supposed be one of the pillars holding up democracy.

With profitability now the main criterion and news a consumer product that had to be sold, media organisations have become vulnerable to government pressures. One telephone call from someone powerful in the government, and editors will pull a story. Government influence also works through advertising, including of the 'achievements' of prime ministers/chief ministers that adorn the front pages of newspapers and are a major source of revenue. Media organisations are loathe to jeopardise this income, and governments know this and use this leverage when they want to.

Media organisations have also branched out into different fields, and owners are terrified of endangering their business interests. Editors have long since lost their pre-eminence in their organisations as they are asked to keep an eye on what both the government and the markets say. This is what we have seen since 2014–the media is by and large no longer willing to speak truth to power, concerned as they are only with profitability. This, incidentally, has also made them less able to fight 'fake news'.

Journalism in India until the 1990s was certainly not a golden age for the press. It did not always stand apart from the State and it did not always take up issues that mattered to the common people. But it could on occasion carry out investigative stories, expose corruption, question the arbitrary exercise of power, and highlight the neglect of livelihood concerns. Today, it would seem that journalism is more concerned about mouthing the agenda of the State than in holding it to account.

Into this dismal scene has entered the disruptive power of artificial intelligence (AI). It may not happen soon, but the power of AI could soon remove many jobs, especially on editing desks.

Journalists are increasingly buffeted on all sides—by the State, by over-cautious editors, by rapid changes in technology, by 'consumers' (a new name for readers/viewers/consumers, but appropriate for the 'media industry'), who are armed with degrees from the WhatsApp University.

Young people looking at journalism/the media as a profession could not be facing a more challenging time. Yet, things are not quite as dismal as they seem. 'Legacy' media, as it is called, has lost much of its legitimacy, and it has begun to lose its reach too. It is the new, small, agile, independent news media in the digital space that has become the real platform for journalism.

These digital organisations are the ones now carrying the baton for journalism. The power of technology and the dissembled nature of this technology make it possible for small organisations to churn out news as quickly as legacy media, without caring about the large overheads or being burdened by the business interests of the legacy media. They are imbued with a sense of idealism and often venture into areas where the establishment is frightened to go. They have their own challenges, mainly financial, but that does not hold them back. Think of all the independent YouTube news channels that are run by small teams attracting millions of viewers and giving the legacy institutions a run for their money.

As societies across the world increasingly turn regressive and as States turn repressive, the space for honest media is certainly getting squeezed. But journalism remains alive in the new and brave digital organisations. It may be a challenging time for journalism, but young people entering the field now would also find it a more adventurous time as they seek to renew the public purpose of journalism.

Past Pleasant, Present Imperfect

Tamal Bandyopadhyay

On my first day as a trainee journalist at the Old Lady of Bori Bunder, we were taken to the large main hall on the third floor that was the domain of *The Times of India* and *Nav Bharat Times* journalists. *The Economic Times* was in a different hall on the same floor. I could see many people typing away furiously and wondered why the office had so many typists. Later, I learnt that those 'typists' were actually reporters.

We were supposed to go through the grind of being posted in every department of the newspaper, but I remained through my one-year training period with *The Sunday Review*, the weekend supplement run by an independent team.

I was one of the two men in a women-dominated department. Fatma Zakaria was the boss. I shared a long table, typical of newspaper 'desks' in those days, with six women. The other man in the group had a separate desk.

My immediate boss, Savita Chandiramani, often invited me to her house on Little Gibbs Road at Malabar Hill. She would serve coke or gin and tonic and I would end up having dinner with her family once in a while.

Running on a very tight budget (trainee journalists used to get a stipend of Rs 1,015 after a Rs 35 deduction for the Employees' State Insurance scheme), eating two meals a day was always a challenge. At the office, we had free tea, breakfast (mostly upma) for 20 paise, lunch for 50 paise (more, if we cared for egg curry or omelette or curd). Evening tea/snacks would cost 20 paise.

I would reach the office early and leave late—enjoying my work and the cheap food. In the evenings, *moong bhajiya* for 20 paise was crispy and delicious. Satish, the canteen boy who used to hawk *moong bhajiya*, was very shy. He would come and whisper '*moong bhajiya*' softly into our ears as if he were talking to his girlfriend in a theatre. If we were busy with work, we could miss it.

There was warmth and camaraderie all around. Once, when the astrologer's weekly prediction, a hugely popular weekly feature in the *Review*, did not come on time, I was asked to step in, as the paper could not afford to drop it. I went through the past three months of predictions and wrote the copy. For a Sagittarian, overseas travel was likely while a Scorpio could expect a surprise on the relationship front; a Leo may face some health issues.

I also had a memorable encounter with cartoonist R. K. Laxman. Over most weekends, *The Sunday Review* would be full of his illustrations. Laxman would need the photographs of real persons to draw them. As a trainee, my job was to rush to the library and get the right photographs for him.

Once, Fatma asked me to pass on an article on aerobics to Laxman for illustration. He had a quick look at it and asked me to get a photo from the library. I could not follow exactly what he muttered, but heard him saying giant panda. I picked up a few photographs of giant pandas from the library and rushed to Laxman's cabin, still puzzled as to why he would need pictures of a giant panda for illustrating a piece on aerobics.

As I dropped the photographs on his table, the creator of the Common Man looked at me and burst into laughter. R. K. Laxman laughing? Something I could never imagine. He got up, caught me by the scruff of my neck and dragged me into Fatma's cabin. 'Look at what this Bengali boy has done! I asked for Jane Fonda; he has brought a giant panda!' His laughter continued.

The best part of those initial days was the warmth colleagues exuded. I never felt that I was new to the city and had no idea about journalism before joining *The Times of India*. The colleagues and bosses made life easy and excited me about the profession. I never missed home. That's the key takeaway from my initiation into the profession.

Even though I started my journalistic career in Mumbai, I had a brief stint in Kolkata (then Calcutta), working on the desk of *The Economic Times*, where I was introduced to the world of tea, jute, steel, and heavy engineering. West Bengal was known for the first three in the early 1990s, while the fourth one was a sunset sector. A student of English Literature, I struggled to understand the subjects, but the people around me made the office interesting.

The very first day at the *ET* office on S. N. Banerjee Road in central Calcutta, next to Lotus Cinema, I was introduced to its Resident Editor, Jayanta Sarkar, a typical Bengali *bhadrolok*. Chief Reporter Kunal Bose was not in his seat. One of his colleagues told me that 'Mr Bose was at a luncheon meeting with an industrialist at The Oberoi'.

A little later, Kunal-da, as everyone called him, walked in, chewing *saunf* (fennel seeds), looking happy and content. A short, dark gentleman, Kunal-da gave me a warm hug. 'You must try out Jaga's next door.' Kunal-da was referring to Jagannath Hotel, a sliver of an eating joint next to the office gate.

Wasn't he coming from The Oberoi? No. That was the standard response the reporters would give to anyone enquiring about him during lunchtime.

Most days, Kunal-da had his lunch at Jaga's, a pice hotel where you shared a table with others and where everything was individually priced, a sort of *a la carte* as opposed to a thali, where one could eat as much as one wanted at a fixed price. At a pice hotel, even an extra helping of rice was priced.

The kitchen of Jagannath Hotel, like many of its kind in Calcutta in those days, was run by a cook from Orissa (the state was not called Odisha then). 'Go and try out the *murighonto* (fish head curry) and mutton,' Kunal-da told me.

I became a regular at that place. I swear he was not exaggerating. Many story ideas were generated there.

There were quite a few interesting characters in *ET* in those days. With them around, work was fun. One of them was news editor A. P. C. Nair, a quiet man with an impeccable sense of humour.

At the news desk, the person in charge of the night shift, who puts the paper to 'bed', had to write a report in a ledger-sized diary before leaving for home, mentioning the time he released the issue and reasons for delays, if any. As the news editor, Nair was too senior to run the night shift, or, for that matter, any shift, unless there was an emergency.

But when there was a staff shortage, Nair would step in. On one such occasion, he released the edition well before midnight, which was an amazing feat, as the normal time was around 2 AM. A very happy resident editor scribbled in the logbook the next morning, 'Well done. Keep it up.'

Reacting to this, Nair wrote in the logbook, tongue in cheek, 'At my age, it's difficult to keep it up every night.'

Another such person was Mohan Padmanabhan or Mohan-da. As a second-generation Tamilian living on Lake Road, a den for his community in Job Charnock's city, he had every Bengali trait, including loving Rabindra Sangeet and eating brinjal fritters and a dry curry of pointed gourd (*potol*) with mustard for dinner on night shifts.

He had done a stint with *The Strait Times* in Singapore, from where he had picked up the Malaysian habit of adding the suffix 'lah'. Spicing up every sentence, he would say—'What're you up to lah?' 'How's the copy lah?'

Yet another interesting senior was Kamala Kanta Mohanty, a chief sub-editor who used to eat, drink, and sleep economics, besides chewing *paan*, a habit with many who hail from Odisha. Such was his passion for economics that he named his son Kenneth (after John Kenneth Galbraith, the Canadian-American economist). As a chief sub, he used to run the shifts at the desk.

After the night shift got over, an office car used to drop us home. As I was a bachelor and living alone, I used to get dropped last. One such night, we were passing through Free School Street, a red-light area that was on our route. As usual, Mohanty stopped the car outside a cigarette-paan shop.

A few minutes later, he rushed back to the car, panting. What happened? While he was buying his paan and a cigarette, a streetwalker in a skirt and blouse had greeted him with a 'Hi!'

'*Oi didi-ta aamake hi bollo. Aami ki korbo?*' ('That sister greeted me. How do I respond?'), he asked us innocently.

Typically, he used to cadge cigarettes from others and no one had seen him buying a packet. Still, no one bothered because we learnt a lot from him. He would explain complicated economic theories to us while smoking.

In those days, the night shift in a newspaper office was very critical as the bulk of the reporters' copy would land on the desk in the late evening. The morning shift was more of a time pass in which we processed foreign news and updated the reports held over from the previous night.

As there was no business television and internet, most reporters were laidback and even if an important press conference took place in the morning or over lunch, the copy would not reach the desk before 7 PM. Typically, the chief reporter would come to the desk, waving a neatly typed report and explaining its importance to the news editor or the chief sub-editor late in the evening.

At the S. N. Banerjee Road office of *ET*, the press was on the ground floor and the desk and other departments were on the first floor. Once a copy was edited, a chief sub would scribble instructions on it for the press. For instance, the heading of the lead story on Page 1 could be 60 points across four columns and the second lead 42 points across two columns. If the text did not fit, the person in charge of making headlines would send it back. A department of proofreaders sat next to the press.

The rooms were not air-conditioned and the sub-editors would merrily smoke while editing the stories on desk mats, lined with blotting paper. Depending on the copy flow, the speed of editing, and the mood of the chief sub, we would go down to the press after having our dinner. Some ordered food from nearby restaurants while some brought home-cooked food. After putting the edition to bed, four or five of us would take the car home. It would drop us at different locations, crisscrossing north and south Calcutta.

Once I shifted to *Business Standard* as a reporter, my boss worked out a brilliant plan to take care of my ignorance about banking issues. Often, he would fix an appointment with senior bankers in Calcutta for a knowledge session, with me in tow. He made them explain the meanings of new norms and their impact on bank balance sheets to both of us, and how they would change the ways the banks worked and the lives of customers.

He claimed to know all of this, but I was an obstinate colleague who would not listen to him! So he found a way of teaching me banking. That was the time when the sector was opening up and prudential norms were being introduced after economic liberalisation.

Banking was an esoteric subject in those days and there was hardly any reporter covering banks and financial institutions. I could not understand most of the reports on banking. There was an assistant editor who knew the subject well. On the day of the monetary policy (there were two policies a year in those days—busy season and slack season policy, in October and April, respectively), there would be a hushed silence and no one was allowed to talk as the assistant editor pondered over the policy and wrote the editorial comment.

The chief of bureau would fly down to Mumbai a day before the busy season policy to interview the Reserve Bank of India (RBI) governor. He would prepare for it days in advance, spending time in the library and talking to many on the telephone. There would be extensive discussions with all of us on possible questions before he would catch the flight to Mumbai. On the day after the policy, he would fax the interview from the Mumbai office. We would be eagerly waiting for it.

Since then, we have come a long way. The mode of news gathering and presentation has changed dramatically. The guiding principle in most media houses these days probably is 'fastest finger first'—breaking stories, fighting it out with social media.

We used to keep piles of paper clippings on our tables and in our drawers to check references. We do not need to do that now. There is probably no need to visit a library, which was an integral part of the newsroom, any more because we now have Google and other search engines.

Before the arrival of the internet and the computer, in the letterpress printing days, we used to spend the night in the office on the Union budget day to smell the first copy of the morning paper before leaving for home.

The Covid pandemic has also taught us to work from home. We do not need to commute to the office; we can work in our studies with our pets at our feet.

We use our time in a more meaningful way now. But what we miss are the heated discussions on the RBI's monetary policy and budget in the newsroom over endless cups of tea and coffee. The discussion was never restricted to the corridor; it continued standing near the water cooler or the coffee vending machine. It could happen anywhere and everywhere—from the newsroom, spilling over to the canteen, pubs, and restaurants outside the office, and even in the homes of colleagues.

What we miss now is working with colleagues around, their stories, and some shoulders to lean on when we need them—for sharing ideas, knowledge, and even our joys and griefs. And the fun.

I hear and see intense competition among colleagues now—for promotions and better pay hikes. The competition was there even in those days, but it never spilled over to spoil our relationships. The seniors always taught the juniors the tricks of the trade. Much to my discomfort, one of my bosses in Calcutta used to make fun of me for my lack of knowledge about Satyajit Ray films, but that was his way of provoking me to understand modern Bengali cinema. Going beyond the call of the profession, he was always eager to help me appreciate things—be it a bank's balance sheet or a Ray film.

In *Mint*, my boss Raju Narisetti often used to catch a morning flight from Delhi (where he was based) and spend the entire day in the Mumbai office. In an open office, my driver, a namesake of the editor, was often seen loitering around, looking for tea or water. Many times, I yelled at my driver, 'Raju, *idhar aao*' ('Raju, come here') and the boss yelled back, much to the amusement of all, 'I am editing a copy, Tamal. Give me some time.'

At the end of the day, over dinner, we would discuss news stories and much more—life beyond work, family.

In August 2007, I had a serious accident in Kolkata while driving down from the airport to a hospital where my mother was on her deathbed. As soon as he came to know of my accident, Raju made sure that I was admitted to a hospital where I could get the best treatment. Over the next fortnight, he circulated a bulletin in the newsroom every evening on the status of my health.

An offsite event, planned in advance, was postponed by a few months. When it finally took place at a hotel in Neemrana in Rajasthan, I was still on crutches. The meetings were held at a hall in a basement over two days. There was no lift to go down to the basement. My colleagues, including the editor, took turns to carry me on a chair to the venue for every session.

I also remember that once, Raju was very unhappy with my editing of a news copy. He thought I had introduced a critical error in the copy. He openly showed his displeasure in a mail meant for a group of senior colleagues. I knew I was right. So, I wrote back to Raju (only him, not the group) explaining the logic–why I had changed the copy. Within a few minutes, the editor referred my mail to the group, with his apology. An editor can do this only if s/he does not suffer from any insecurity. That is very important for an ideal newsroom.

Give me those days back.

Postscript

What does the future look like for journalists in the days of artificial intelligence (AI), machine learning, and working from home? Tracking developments and reading data to get news will continue, but the art of cracking stories will change.

Apart from the expertise to write well and knowledge of the subject, a reporter's ability to spot 'sources' and nurture them plays a critical role in cracking exclusive stories. For that, we need to be connected with people. If we do not move around among people, this is not possible. A mouse and a keypad can replace a fountain pen, but talking over a mobile phone cannot be a substitute for a meeting across the table over a cup of coffee.

Sources cannot be cultivated over a phone conversation. They need to be nurtured over years. Converting someone into your source for stories is like growing a plant that needs water, fertiliser, sunlight, and lots of care. It is like making love or playing the piano. We need to know which keys to press to get the right chord.

Different persons become the sources for journalists for different reasons. One may simply like you, feel good in your company, and reciprocate by giving you 'stories'. Another gets a kick out of pitching stories and cultivating journalists. Yet another could be disgruntled, frustrated, and wanting to settle a score with the boss by leaking stories; and another could just be a well-wisher of the company, who has a high moral ground and wants to clean the dirt swept under the carpet.

Even without any of these attributes, one could be your source if you know how to make the person happy. Many times, while interacting with people in banks and corporate circles, I wished I had studied psychology instead of English literature. We may not crack two out of ten prospective sources, but there are ways of cosying up to the rest. It's not easy, though.

In cricket, once a batsman is set, he can see the whizzing ball as clearly as a football and hit it out of the boundary. In such a scenario, many bowlers lose their nerve, but there are a few like Muttiah Muralitharan and Ravichandran Ashwin who will patiently wait for an opportunity. Or Abdul Qadir, who will bowl a googly, draw the batsman out of the crease, and get him stumped. Patience pays—both for the bowler and the reporter.

If you do not like the cricket analogy, consider fishing. You use bait to attract fish and wait forever, looking at the float.

Someone may be proud of his daughter who is studying microbiology at a US university. Even if that person is very reserved, one just needs to make him talk about his daughter and how diverse life is on earth, and he will become garrulous instantly.

Another person may be a cactus lover. All one needs to do is talk about the Ruby Ball cactus and Dinosaur Back Plant and share tips on growing exotic cactus varieties at home. Yet another person may be very fond of dogs and cats.

If we do not move around, spend time with people, the art of 'sourcing' stories may disappear in the new world. Equally important is understanding one's colleagues and the willingness to be with them when they need you. AI and machine learning cannot replace these.

Three Careers

NIRANJAN RAJADHYAKSHA

I have been lucky to have had three careers till now—as an economics teacher in a college, as a financial journalist, and as a director of research in a public policy consulting firm. The long journey has not led to the gradual accumulation of certitude, but rather the sense that we know too little about the complex world around us. Most of us start our working lives with more answers than questions. We end with more questions than answers. Does that mean we have failed in our careers? No. It just means that we have learnt to live with the fragility of our knowledge, to trust imperfect human judgement when the data is ambiguous, to truly listen to rather than just hear what others are saying, and to collaborate since little can be achieved alone.

I look back on the daily editorial meetings at the financial newspaper I worked in as an example of iterative learning. In the fast-moving world of news, where twenty-four hours is an eternity, even the best can only capture a narrow slice of a wider reality. The senior colleagues around the table every morning brought their own unique perspectives to every issue of the day. For example, any policy change would evoke different reactions from the editors on the government, the central bank, the bond markets, Indian companies, international companies, farmers, and consumers. What came out of such collaborative discussions—and occasional heated arguments—was far more balanced than any one of us could have pulled off in splendid isolation.

The advantage of working together does not emerge only from such structured meetings. So many ideas come at the lunch table, around the coffee machine, or during a post-work *adda* (informal conversation). That is when the outlier ideas bubble to the surface. That a-ha moment. And such learning does not come from office colleagues alone. Here are two episodes when what I heard flicked on a bulb in my mind.

The first episode was in early 1998. Tremors from the Asian financial crisis had hit Indian shores a few months earlier. The Russian default lay ahead. The Indian financial markets were on edge. A senior policymaker had called some of us for a friendly chat that we were forbidden from writing about. He explained the various options, and it was clear to us that many of them had not worked.

After the informal chat was over, I found myself next to the policymaker as we walked towards the lift. 'Sir, does this mean that you have run out of options?' I asked him. His answer was succinct, 'Remember, the sovereign never runs out of options.' A few days later, the Indian government and the Reserve Bank of India (RBI) announced a coordinated policy package to defend the rupee, with many unconventional moves. That one insight—that a sovereign never runs out of options—can never be learnt from textbooks.

The second episode was nearly ten years later. Another senior policymaker had called a few financial editors for an informal chat over tea, in the middle of 2008. The financial shocks that rattled the markets in August 2007 had seemingly dissipated. An irrational exuberance was back. He had just returned from a series of meetings with peers in other countries. He presciently told us why he was worried that a storm was coming, and how India needed to build buffers before the trouble began. It was a view that most people in government or the financial markets did not share at the time. The North Atlantic financial crisis began a few months later with the collapse of Lehman Brothers. It was a judgement call by someone who had a profound insight into the economy, something more than an empirical model can deliver.

Such interactions are only possible under conditions of deep trust, which itself emerges from repeated interactions that are hard to replicate sitting in front of a computer screen. The value of speaking to people who matter is never lost on me. It need not only be the people who take decisions, but also those who are directly affected by those decisions—the powerful as well as the powerless. It is learning by walking around.

For example, during an assignment from the government of one of our more prosperous states in 2021, my colleagues at the consulting firm I work for realised while talking to citizens that they were not taking the Covid-19 vaccines. Why? Because they believed vaccines to be curative rather than preventive, or to be taken after one gets infected, not before the virus enters the body. The state government altered its messaging to the public after that insight, and vaccination numbers began to go up. Speaking directly to citizens during a crime victimisation survey in four large cities or businesses during a national survey on the ease of doing business gave the research team results that were at odds with government numbers on these two issues.

None of this is meant to belittle the importance of quantitative data, or the models based on numbers. When I began my career more than thirty years ago, getting access to even the simplest data involved a lot of work—stock prices, company balance sheets, auction prices in the money market, or inflation trends. All this is now available at the click of a mouse or a swipe of a finger. Many years ago, I remember sitting for hours at the Unit Trust of India office to get the latest price data on one of the India funds it managed in New York, at a time when foreign investors were not allowed direct access to the Indian share market. It was a waste of time.

Technology has been liberating in that sense, as a tool to help you perform your job better. A lot depends on how you use it. Every wave of new technology brings forth the same questions—will it make us stupid; will it lead to mass unemployment; will it reconfigure society in malign ways? The reality has always been better than what the initial fears made us expect. It could be the same with artificial intelligence (AI), but who knows for sure? The future is never a perfect image of the past. The point is that much will depend on how governments, companies, and individuals decide to harness artificial intelligence.

A final word on how I have learnt in the classroom, not as a student but as a teacher. Facing a class of forty intelligent youngsters who are not afraid to ask questions has forced me to think harder. The simpler the question, the harder the explanation that needs to be given. Telling a student that something is correct because the teacher says so is not a very convincing strategy. So, I have learnt as I taught. I have realised the same applies in the office as well. Seniors may have perspective, thanks to experience, but junior colleagues are often brimming with fresh ideas. I have found it useful to give them a voice rather than shut them down.

27

A Journey Through A Changing India

Shaji Vikraman

I started my career in journalism with what was then India's top national English newspaper. This was at the fag end of the 1980s. It was a heady time to be in the profession, at the height of a brand of investigative journalism, with a legendary editor leading from the front.

Those were interesting times as I began work in Madras, which is now Chennai. A government that came to power with a record mandate in Delhi was fighting multiple battles; there was President's rule in Tamil Nadu; and a political flux before polls were held again. Besides, there was a conflict in the neighbourhood, with the Indian army moving to Sri Lanka to battle Tamil militants–the Liberation Tigers of Tamil Eelam or LTTE–there, and a high-profile takeover battle involving one of India's famous but controversial business groups and government controlled financial institutions. And a little later in 1991, the assassination of a former prime minister at Sriperumbudur, 40 kilometres from Madras, a tragic event to report on.

Those were the days of early liberalisation, with the government moving towards computerisation of railway ticketing and later banking. Modernisation of India's telecom sector was also underway then to ease the long waiting list for landline phones, which ran into lakhs. The city was full of STD (subscriber trunk dialling) booths, where people lined up after 11 PM to make calls back home at discounted rates.

In the newsroom, the manual typewriters used by reporters were being phased out with the introduction of the word processor. A hard-driving boss made sure the rookies were at work for long hours on diverse assignments. These ranged from reporting on the courts, police, political rallies, meetings, and government functions. The office was sprawling but the infrastructure was basic. Over a dozen reporters, ranging from the most senior to the trainees, jostled for a seat before the odd word processor in a narrow room. The boss believed that the young recruits could do without a weekly break and would mark them for early morning and late evening assignments.

Once they passed his stiff test, he would take the young lot along to meetings with top politicians, including chief ministers, officials, business leaders, and occasionally big names such as Muhammed Ali, the heavyweight boxer. It was only much later that I recognised how much I benefitted from his mentorship, work ethic, and generosity.

It was a sort of school of hard knocks, but with useful advice from him to not get intimidated. In that era, access to leaders and senior government officials was easier with none of the stifling security that we see today. Journalists did not have to walk on eggshells when engaging with political or business leaders or senior government officials.

Language can often be a barrier to an outsider, especially when working in a new state. But learning a new language, Tamil, helped open many new doors at work, not just in the state but in many other cities. And it led to enduring friendships. It also fostered a better understanding of a state where three chief ministers had a close link to the celluloid world, and where sometimes the distinction between the reel and the real got blurred.

It was remarkable to watch competitive politics at play, with rival parties launching social welfare schemes dubbed then as freebies. The joke then was on what would next be on the list of freebies for voters after television sets, laptops, and gold.

Years later, the delivery of public services, recognised elsewhere as *labharati*, has been cited as a driver for the success of some political parties. It was only in hindsight that I could get a sense of the unique growth model of the state with such a geographically diversified industrial and entrepreneurial base. That was thanks to the insights of many policymakers.

I recall an aide of the Governor of the state telling me how miffed his boss was with the chief minister, who would not give in easily. The Governor's aide then let slip that his boss had, in the monthly report to the President, written that 'everything in the state is on sale except the Bay of Bengal'. Those five years were my first introduction to the world of political entrepreneurs.

A couple of years into the job, as the economic liberalisation process kicked off, the coverage of the economic and financial sectors was broadened even in the mainstream media. It was obvious then that focusing more on economic or financial journalism, with far less emotions at the core of it, would be more rewarding professionally. As yet another new financial daily was launched, I cast my sights on Delhi. But an editor persuaded me that Bombay, now Mumbai, the financial capital, would be a better city to start off in. He was right.

Salaries in the Indian newspaper industry were mostly tied to wage boards formed by the government. Pay packets were in the low four digits, but all that was forgotten in an environment of adversarial journalism, the company of talented professionals, and plenty of humour. It is a reflection of that era–the 1980s–that one of India's top newspapers could publish a cartoon portraying the head of the prime minister on top of a missile with the caption, 'India's famous dud missile', without fear of any retribution.

Mumbai was an exciting place to be in the early 1990s. When I moved there, India's financial markets had just opened up with the entry of foreign portfolio investors and increased activity in the capital markets. There was the immediate fallout of the 1991-1992 securities scam and the emergence of a new regulator, the Securities and Exchange Board of India (SEBI).

It was a compelling opportunity to learn about a new world of global and local equity and debt offerings, equity and money markets, monetary policy and banking. That was also a period of institution building. The first set of newly licensed private banks started operations, which provided the trigger for a huge transformation in the industry. India's finance minister was in Mumbai to inaugurate the operations of HDFC Bank in Worli in 1995 as well as the National Stock Exchange with its automated trading. The National Securities Depository Ltd (NSDL), which digitised stock certificates, followed soon.

However competitive the Indian financial media was then, there was little breathless commentary on major policies. The Union budget too had not quite become a spectator sport then. Meeting the Reserve Bank of India (RBI) Governor or the SEBI chief was not as challenging as it is now. They were far more open, offering new perspectives, including to those still trying to find their feet in the profession.

I also learnt there that patience and the willingness to listen are great virtues. Like when a senior central banker once explained the role of India's central bank as not just setting interest rates or fighting inflation and regulating banks. The RBI, he said, was a bridge between the government, the markets, and society. Some of these central bankers were perhaps the wisest men I have met, with their original thinking and feet grounded in Indian realities, despite their global work exposure.

Working in Mumbai was also enriching in an organisational environment with a culture that placed a premium on integrity and ethical behaviour. That was reflected especially in the work and conduct of my boss. Few could be as generous as this chief to young men and women in the profession, encouraging us to tag along for meetings with regulatory chiefs, senior bankers, and corporate titans without ever seeking to take credit.

The mid-1990s was the era of coalition governments in Delhi, when I shifted base to the city. Union budgets were unveiled only after 5 PM then. It was a struggle to meet deadlines. Culturally, it marked a big change from Mumbai with its focus largely on the financial markets and a general disdain for policymakers and politicians. It was a heady feeling to be able to meet cabinet ministers and some of the most powerful people in the country in small groups or even on a one-on-one basis. But a wake-up call came soon.

One morning, at a meeting organised by an industry body, a handful of us financial journalists met the finance minister after he stepped out. A colleague had a question on the provisions of the newly introduced company law. The minister, after checking his name and recalling that he had reported on the new law, delivered his punchline. 'The trouble with you guys is that you write a lot, but read little.' He then proceeded to reel out the relevant sections of the Companies Act offhand.

As Hugh Cudlipp has written, 'Snubs from the great go with the job.' A consolation perhaps was that this iron glove treatment was not reserved for hacks alone. Several officials, including regulatory chiefs, have testified to this.

What this underlined was the need to be more professionally equipped to report on fiscal matters or other issues. And to persevere. This was made possible because of a few open-minded officials in the government. They would explain the fine print in the budget papers or the backdrop and rationale for many policy decisions to us.

Politicians have great stories to tell, as I often found out in North Block, which houses the finance ministry. One finance minister and his team were told by a prime minister, when they went to him for guidance before a budget, '*Aap sidhant se kariye*' ('Make the budget on principles').

In contrast, a finance minister who had a boss whose interest in economics was as limited as his attention span, recounted that in a meeting to discuss that year's Union budget, the head of the government barely understood the proposals. But the minister, having obtained the licence from the prime minister to swing hard, did precisely that. He introduced several reform measures in that year's budget.

Another finance minister, who often confessed that he knew little about economics, told his officials bluntly that he did not want any tax raid during his stint. His reasoning was that no civilised country did that. Little surprise, then, that a finance secretary told a small gathering, including academics and economists, later that he would rather be guided by political leaders on the political economy than technical experts.

The lesson from all these politicians was that making value judgements is often fraught with risk. It can be humbling. It is important to remember that however cynical politicians may seem, these political risk-takers can surprise you.

Some technocrats too were not far behind. After the 1998 nuclear tests in Pokhran, as economic sanctions were imposed, one of them had good advice for India's prime minister. The key to securing nuclear autonomy for the country was to ensure that its fiscal house (discipline) was in order as few international friends would help, he told the prime minister. The advice was then heeded, but had mixed results later.

Commentators and journalists fashionably quote Bill Clinton's poll campaign advisor saying, 'It's the economy, stupid', to say that good economics makes for good politics in India too. But the reality could be different.

One finance minister had approved a deep cut in interest rates on small savings that were controlled by the government. This in turn led to a lowering of interest rates, which was good for the broader economy. But that did not go down well with a good chunk of voters in his constituency, who were pensioners. They were hurt by the lower interest on their savings. The minister lost the polls that year.

I often recall how, during those years in Delhi, the launch of the ambitious Golden Quadrilateral project, which sought to link the country through a network of modern national highways (described poetically by Prime Minister A. B. Vajpayee as the country's *bhagyarekha* or destiny lines), and a new telecom policy, based on companies sharing revenues with the government, were dubbed as major scams.

Much later, a senior policymaker, while highlighting some of the reforms of the 1990s, drove home the point that what looks impossible at one time may be possible later. And that there is no Gresham's law when it comes to reforms. A lesson from all these was that it is always advisable professionally to step back a little, have more conversations, rather than risk shooting from the hip and appearing foolish later.

As a profession, journalism offers the promise of helping shape a better understanding of the political economy, of events, people, and the country, lifelong. That is through privileged access, engagements, and conversations with some of the best minds in varied fields. What marked them out also was the breadth of their knowledge and how well-rounded they were. To make the best of it, especially in the modern era with so much noise and clutter, it helps to invest in deep reading across the board.

Much has changed post-2004—the boom years for Indian industry, financial markets, and the media. Subsequent technological changes and flexible work norms have changed the contours of industry. The mobile phone can effectively be an office. There is, however, the thrill of having made the transition to digital writing from legacy practices.

One of my most significant memories (and there are many) is a meeting in early 2016. On a winter morning in Delhi, I met one of India's senior leaders who held some of the best and most powerful jobs in the country in both the pre- and post-liberalisation years. At his home in Delhi, he opened up on his long years in government, and the reason why the country sometimes falters. According to him, it was because 'we act in a crisis and then it is back to the status quo'. He outlined the challenges of governing a diverse and complex country. There was the wisdom of someone who understood the country deeply in that conversation.

Like some of India's top leaders, he too chose not to write a memoir. And for good reasons. 'The truth hurts and I don't want to hurt anyone.'

Some are comfortable making history, others can at best report on it.

Part VI

Academia

28

Building People, Building Institutions

MAN MOHAN SHARMA

I was born in May 1937 and was brought up in Jodhpur, Rajputana (now Rajasthan). In 1954, at the age of seventeen, I moved to Bombay (now Mumbai) to study chemical engineering. I had done well in my Intermediate of Science (ISc), with outstanding scores in chemistry, physics, and mathematics, and was in the top ten of Rajputana University.

There was an engineering college in Jodhpur, fairly close to our house, but it had only civil engineering, which I did not like. My family had limited resources and chemical engineering was a subject difficult for them to understand. In addition, this involved unaffordable expenses in Bombay. I was somehow able to persuade them due to my deep interest in chemistry and mathematics.

My father was able to convince our neighbour, who had an establishment in Bombay, to support my education, who in turn convinced a friend of his to bear an equal amount of Rs 40 a month, which could take care of my hostel and living expenses. Thus, the role of philanthropists made a deep impression on me, and later in life I supported meritorious students who had economic problems.

My move to Bombay was quite an experience because I was from a small desert city with limited water supply. The monsoon rains were a lifetime experience, along with travelling on trams.

My four years in the chemical engineering course at the University Department of Chemical Technology (UDCT) were thrilling and life in the hostel was enjoyable. The chemical industry was on an upswing in 1958, when I graduated, and jobs were available before graduation—a rare phenomenon in those days. However, I was keen to do research and pursue a career in research and technology.

The scholarship for the Master's course was just Rs 150 a month and even that did not come on time. There was no hostel accommodation for postgraduate students on the campus. I managed to get admission in the Ramakrishna Mission Hostel in Khar, which was affordable. This led to my becoming a devotee of Ramakrishna Paramhansa.

Towards the end of my Master's, I got an appointment as a temporary lecturer in the UDCT on a salary of Rs 415 a month. I had to move out of the hostel and become a paying guest near the Ramakrishna Mission.

I was unusually lucky to get a full scholarship, with travel grant, to carry out doctoral work in the Department of Chemical Engineering, University of Cambridge, under the formidable Professor P. V. Danckwerts, from 1961–1964. This was a turning point in my life and I managed to do exceptionally well.

I was lucky to hit upon an idea that had commercial potential and my guide had connections to the renowned Shell company, which arranged a preliminary patent in my name. I presented my case to Shell at The Hague in the Netherlands and they bought my idea with a decent compensation. This was the first time in the department that an idea had been patented and sold, and this brought me attention. On my return to Mumbai, most of this money was given to my family in Jodhpur as they were facing financial problems.

My alma mater, the UDCT, had not had a full Professor of Chemical Engineering since 1955. When I was about to leave Cambridge, it was suggested that I put in an application for this post. I thought I did not deserve it and was only qualified to become a Reader (now called an Associate Professor). But Bombay University had different ideas and I landed the job in September 1964, when I was just about twenty-seven years old. This was quite an achievement for me, and it was a very serious challenge to perform to the expectations of the UDCT.

Financial support for research in those days was negligible and, as mentioned, I was bent on pursuing research, notwithstanding the extremely remunerative jobs in industries, including in Bombay. I was determined to carry out research in areas that were highly idea-centric and we succeeded in doing so. Within three years, our first Ph.D. came out and we were globally known. I am referring to all this because I want to inspire graduating students to pursue teaching and research and consult with industry in the applied sciences. My clearly enunciated desire was to build people better than me.

I now have erstwhile associates who are Padma awardees, fellows of scientific academies, and the like, and I can bask in their glory. To my own surprise, I received a Padma Bhushan in 1987 and a Padma Vibhushan in 2001.

I was a bachelor when I was appointed as a professor in September 1964, and being very busy, I decided not to get married for at least eighteen months. This was very uncommon in Rajasthan, where most marriages took place before the age of twenty-one. I had an arranged marriage, although I had met and talked to Sudha in Jaipur before getting married. I told her that I was pursuing a career at the university, with a much lower salary than in industry. She played a big role in my life in a very quiet way and we have a daughter and a son, who are both doing very well in the US.

Working in a state university, I faced many problems, but my engineering education taught me to get things done and make things work. It was unthinkable that a person like me would become a Fellow of the Royal Society, London, and that too as its first engineer from India. As of now, there is only one other engineer from India who is a Fellow and that is R. A. Mashelkar, my own undergraduate and Ph.D. student. I had, in 1989–1990, become President of the Indian National Sciences Academy, the first chemical engineer to hold this position.

I have mentioned that we must interact with industries in applied sciences. We made sure that we essentially concentrated on teaching and research, and also consulted with industries for a decent compensation—in some cases, a one-third cut to the university was more than the salary of a faculty member. Thus, the UDCT became a role model in India.

Apart from consulting work, which made my financial position healthy and enabled me to support my family back in Jodhpur, I had the experience of being a member of the board of directors of several companies, both in the public and private sectors, and this gave me an inside view of the corporate world. In 1990, I withdrew from all boards because the Company Law Board held that all directors are liable for action if a company engages in undesirable activities. These days, many companies offer a decent compensation to independent directors, apart from sitting fees, as up to 2 per cent of the profit can be distributed to directors. However, this has had no impact on me, and I remain steadfast on not being on boards. Of course, even at eighty-seven years, I continue to consult with industries and make a decent living.

In September 1989, I was persuaded to become the Director of the UDCT and this involved considerable administrative work. I was not fond of administrative work and offers of high positions in Delhi had not lured me in the 1980s. I made sure that all the branches of chemical technology, besides chemical engineering, grew in a remarkable way. The output of doctorates increased in a very impressive way and the UDCT moved into a higher orbit. As a mark of respect for my penchant for a higher output for Ph.D.s, which in a way is an indicator of the progress of nations, industrialists and well-wishers have come forward and donated more than Rs 25 crore to create more doctoral fellowships in the UDCT.

It was unthinkable that a lad who came from Jodhpur as a student would become the Director and occupy the spacious flat above the Main Building, built in the British era. In an unusual gesture, Mumbai University bestowed an LLD on me and even named the UDCT Library after me. Later, the University gave me the title of Emeritus Professor of Eminence. I was also fortunate to obtain honorary doctorates from many universities and Indian Institutes of Technology.

Working in a state university with a large number of affiliated colleges is very difficult as university departments do not get adequate attention. In spite of this, the UDCT was given autonomy as a department under the University Grants Commission (UGC) and support from the state government. This was an unusual achievement that had no parallel in India.

I was a member of many committees of the Government of India, but I would like to specifically mention membership of the Scientific Advisory Committee to the Cabinet and Prime Minister and the chairmanship of the Scientific Advisory Committee of the Ministry of Petroleum, which in the early 1980s also included petrochemicals. I came in contact with economist Vijay Kelkar during this time. I was also Chairman of the UGC Empowered Committee to give impetus to more Ph.D.s from universities all over India.

There are a number of prestigious awards in my name from different organisations and this has further humbled me. Surprisingly, even the Institution of Chemical Engineers in the UK has an international award in my name. There are three festschrifts in my name in *Industrial Engineering Chemistry Research* and *Chemical Engineering Science*, both respected international journals.

I had a surprise call from the Reserve Bank of India (RBI) in 2006, saying that I was under consideration for the main board of the RBI. As I mentioned, I had decided to withdraw from all boards and to not accept any new appointments. I decided to phone Kelkar, and he assured me that the RBI board was not like a company board. I was then glad to accept the offer. This led to my most enjoyable experiences with Governor Y. V. Reddy, whom I hold in very high esteem for his truly outstanding leadership and wit.

I must say that I had very rewarding experiences in the RBI. This was all the more as Bombay-based directors used to meet almost every Wednesday for an hour, and this gave me insights into the working of the RBI and how economists thought and worked and how financial experts carried out their work. I made attempts to emphasise that rapid economic growth came through technology. The RBI did respond to my suggestions and comments and even produced a decent paper on the role of technology in ushering in rapid economic growth. I would love to see this strategy implemented with greater emphasis.

Governor Reddy was unusually good to me and even invited me to deliver the convocation address at the Indira Gandhi Institute in Goregaon, Mumbai. I frankly said that it was necessary for faculty members to publish in internationally renowned journals. We in the UDCT had assiduously followed this practice, besides delivering to industries.

RBI board meetings provided an opportunity to meet renowned bankers, economists, and chartered accountants, and I do cherish these interactions. The RBI has an enviable record of integrity, confidentiality, and fairness in dealing with public- and private-sector banks. I do recollect gold was purchased in secret moments, but the public had no idea about these purchases. Cooperative banks have a different charter, but there too the RBI has cleverly managed to bring them under its wing. It is truly remarkable that no public-sector bank in India has failed and the RBI can take a lot of credit for it.

The RBI had the practice of holding one board meeting in a state capital, and it was refreshing to see the importance given to the RBI by the state governments and the esteem in which it was held. For me, it was an unusual experience, and I considered it a very laudable practice. While on the RBI board, in one of the Wednesday meetings, I suggested that we monetise gold. Apparently, it did not get much attention then, but I am glad that it was acted on much later.

I have a view that meetings that last for several hours do not achieve the desired results. I am glad that RBI main board meetings used to be over before lunch.

I was pleasantly surprised when Governor Reddy, at the time of his retirement, expressed a desire to interact with academics and scientist entrepreneurs. I was thus able to talk to the Vice-Chancellor of the University of Hyderabad and A. V. Ramarao, who after retiring as the Director of the CSIR-Indian Institute of Chemical Technology in Hyderabad, began undertaking research as a business activity.

29

Defining Work with the Power of Quitting

M. S. Sriram

The relationship with 'work' is largely a definitional issue. A recent but seminal book by James Suzeman called *Work: A History of How We Spend our Time* (2021) defines work in a broad sense. There is a physical demarcation between what we call 'home' and 'office', both trying to put physical distance between what can be done at home and what can be done at the office. But I frankly think it is somewhat seamless. We spend a large part of our time thinking about work, serving a master who expects some output from our presence at the office, although we do think more freely about various things when we are at home.

In a study of the Ju Honasi tribes in Burkina Faso, Suzeman quotes Richard Lee assessing that they spend about fifteen hours a week in hunting and gathering food–basically 'earning' for their survival–and about twenty hours a week in organising–cooking and housekeeping–and the rest of the time for entertainment. This is quite different from what our iconic business leader Narayana Murthy called for–about seventy hours of work in a week.

On the other hand, John Maynard Keynes had indicated as far back as 1930 that with the available technology, it was sufficient for us to work for only fifteen hours a week. However, as we see, the workdays get more stretched as we find more technology to fix our drudgery. We are constantly spending our workdays working hard to find more technology to make our life easy!

My relationship with work therefore has always been dictated by (*a*) the necessity to survive, and (*b*) feel at peace with what I am doing. Sometimes the need for (*a*) leads to a compromise with (*b*), but those are temporary periods. Otherwise, the relationship has been a peaceful co-existence between (*a*) and (*b*). I am still trying to find out what drove my career choices and I cannot find a rational explanation for it. I was possibly influenced by personalities who exhibited a higher calling, or I was possibly well provided for by my family circumstances, which did not push me to desperate choices. The birth lottery gave me the privilege of choice that many of my peers may not have had.

I began work as the lowest paid graduate from the class of 1984 of the Institute of Rural Management Anand. I had two other offers, a better paid one in Anand next door to the Institute, and other one next door to my home, but I chose to go to Hyderabad and work largely in the Telangana area. The choice was mostly dictated by my experience during a summer internship in Co-operative Development Foundation (called Samakhya during those days) under the leadership of Mamidi Rama Reddy and Shashi Rajagopalan in 1984. They were idealistic and spread the ideas of people's institutions, particularly co-operatives.

Having come from the influence of Verghese Kurien, a towering figure in the dairy sector, and having spent two years in Anand, it was an easy choice for me. My relationship with money was mostly dictated by this choice. I would not go looking for it, but it was okay if it came by. I learnt to lead a life that fitted with my means, resorting to indulgence only when I could afford it.

The work involved travel, interaction with people, and much socialisation with the co-operatives, which I enjoyed. The work situation provided what a family would have provided—a diversity of thought, a connection with a large number of people, and a redefinition of the purpose of life. I did not feel like I had made a sacrifice and felt a great sense of pride in what I was doing.

Two years into doing this, there were differences—largely on the direction that the organisation was taking. These were genuine differences in belief systems—between ideological positions and practical compromises for a longer ideal. I quit the job in 1986, not because there was something better at the other end, but because continuing was difficult. Eventually, I shifted to doing a

Ph.D. programme, which offered me a stipend. I was an accidental academic, with nagging doubts on whether I should continue because it was not a conscious choice. However, an involuntary move had allowed me to enter the hallowed portals of an Indian Institute of Management. Therefore, when one talks of building a career, I look at the serendipity in my life and chuckle.

One thing I discovered in academic life was freedom. One could structure work, leisure, and engagement as one wanted, and indulge in other passions essentially because academics was unhurried. Yes, there are milestones and deadlines, but they are more fluid. I began enjoying this and moved from being a student to being a faculty member, from Bengaluru back to Anand and the Institute I loved most at that time in 1992. It stood for a purpose and I believed that I would be at peace working in a place that had shaped much of my ideological positions.

I got married in 1991 and had a family, enjoying the seamlessness between work and home. As academics, living on campuses, work travels home and vice versa. Six years into academics, among young students and their dilemmas and career choices, I found that there was a sense of fatigue.

Possibly the problem was that there was a change in leadership at my workplace and the new leadership was not inspiring enough. Many of my peers began leaving and my intellectual network was slowly dissipating. Now, as I reflect, I realise the importance of a peer group rather than a hierarchy in making life exciting.

So I decided to take a break and join a start-up in 1997. This was an old acquaintance (who later became a dear friend), Vijay Mahajan, who was setting up Basix, a company for promoting livelihoods. It was exciting to join a start-up and move back to my old *karma bhoomi* of Hyderabad. Both the location of Hyderabad and the fact that this was almost like an informal group trying to build something helped me to move from the laidback academic life to a more hectic corporate life.

It was good for about a year, but at the end of the year, the performance assessment left me deeply disappointed. Here I was thinking that I was not only working hard but also effectively, yet someone else in my peer group was getting a much better rating and increment. Suddenly, what did not matter all the while seemed to matter: money and recognition. I guess it was the hierarchical set-up.

While I continued for more time with the organisation, there was a distance between the boss and me; between expectations and delivery; and between my perception and his. It was at this stage that my old professor Sanjiv Phansalkar restored the balance in my perception about money, ego, status, and multiple other things.

I was sulking and was not really enjoying work because I felt that I had not got my due. The corporate structure and the hierarchy were getting to me. Phansalkar asked me just three questions—(*i*) are you satisfied with the absolute amount you are getting as a salary? (the answer was yes); (*ii*) are you happy with the role that has been assigned to you? (yes, again); (*iii*) do you think this problem would not be there in any other organisation? (no, all organisations would have it). The moment I answered these questions, it was clear that my dissatisfaction was imaginary, and I was at peace. This really redefined my relationship with money and it has stayed with me. While I made peace, the overall sense of differences—partly ideological, partly to do with the growth model—made it difficult for me to continue. I quit in 1999.

There have been four resignations in my life, and three of them were without a clear path in sight. On two occasions, I filled up the interregnum by being self-employed and doing a consulting job. This in itself defined my relationship with work and the workplace. The first separation from my employer was because of youthful idealism in a fight between my righteousness and his. The second separation was for an alternative in sight. The third separation was again due to differences in values and systems. But the fourth separation happened for purely personal reasons.

While I had a job in IIM Ahmedabad, my family had moved to Bengaluru to be with my father after my mother passed away in 2010. I was hoping that my father would shift to Ahmedabad, and I could continue in the job (which I was really happy with) till retirement. Unfortunately, my father asked, 'Why do you want to uproot me? What is the use of all your education and achievements if it cannot fetch you a job in Bengaluru? My roots, siblings, and community are in Bengaluru and I am sure I will be miserable in Ahmedabad.' I realised that it was not only my father but also my in-laws who were in Bengaluru, and it made sense for me to move back.

However, I did not foresee a happy association with IIM Bangalore, having spent a year on leave. I could not think of an alternative that could be location specific. At that stage, I decided to just quit. I was on my own for about two years before I made peace with a job at IIM Bangalore. Quitting IIM Ahmedabad at the peak of my career was a significant decision, but it was not driven by any rationality, only by a purely emotional connection. This possibly defines the ultimate relationship I have had with work in an institutional framework. Even after quitting IIM Ahmedabad, I could continue to work and earn as a consultant. I have had no regrets about this decision, having spent time with my father in his last years.

My engagement with performing in order to get a remuneration continues. Employment is an institutional construct. Work in itself is narrowly defined as a delivery for pecuniary benefits. Over the years, I have learnt that it is possible to do what one likes. When one does what one likes, there is passion and an attempt at excellence. That in itself gets rewarded–sometimes directly, and sometimes with serendipity.

There is no need to run the race of hierarchy because there is always someone ahead. There is no need to run the race of fortune, there is always someone way ahead. The power of having a satisfactory work life has emerged out of the courage to quit when it was needed, irrespective of consequences. The consequences have never been regrettable. My lessons vis-à-vis money and hierarchy were embedded in the three Phansalkar questions.

Let me end with how work relationships define friendships. When I quit Basix, my boss Vijay Mahajan, with whom I had deep differences, said, 'How does it matter, who pays you a salary? Ultimately, you will continue to work for me.' He was obviously not referring to himself personally, but to the cause that he was espousing. The cause was something that both of us believed in. We differed in the intervention methodology. When I reflect, I think I continue to work for the larger cause. So, what he said was so very true.

Summing Up

Rear View

Y. V. Reddy, Ravi Menon, and Shaji Vikraman

In our efforts to make sense of the present, it is instructive to look at the past. The answers are often to be found there. In a book about work, it is useful to understand the political, social, economic, and cultural contexts and the driving forces that shaped the world of work we see today. A key factor is government policy—how it was shaped and implemented. In other words, to understand our work and life, we need a rear-view perspective of the last seven decades since independence. It is a fascinating story.

Early Challenges

India is now the fifth largest economy in the world and well poised to be the third largest in less than six years. It is hard to imagine that just eight decades ago, India did not even exist as a nation-state. Indeed, many expressed grave doubts about how long the country would exist before descending into chaos. Observers saw four obstacles to a continued existence as a cohesive nation. These were social conflicts arising from caste, language, religion, and economic disparity. The place was seen as too complicated to continue as a nation. The new nation could boast of little homogeneity in terms of culture, religion, or language, and had a number below the poverty line equivalent to the populations of large European nations. Little wonder then, that in a broadcast on 17 May 1946, weeks before the country became independent, Viceroy and Governor General Lord Wavell called India the greatest and most momentous experiment in government in the history of the world.[1]

Another reason for the scepticism of observers was that India's leaders had chosen Parliamentary democracy or the Parliamentary form of government. They also opted to move straight into universal adult suffrage rather than—as had been the case in the West—at first reserve the right to vote to men of property, with the working class and women excluded till much later. Another major challenge was that of the 176 million people eligible to vote, 85 per cent were illiterate. Hence the innovation of identifying political parties with pictorial symbols. That was not all. In some instances, problems of physical accessibility had to be solved almost overnight. In one of the most remarkable achievements of modern times, India successfully conducted its first general election in 1952. The chief architect of this exercise that astounded the world was Sukumar Sen, an Indian Civil Service officer who was appointed as the first Chief Election Commissioner. It is interesting that in most places he chose ICS officers as election commissioners. So the 'steel frame', an object of much resentment on the part of freedom fighters, came together with the new leaders to make adult suffrage a reality.

The path was never going to be easy and the newly independent nation had to confront formidable challenges. The early years were indeed turbulent. Independence also saw the partition of the country, a huge loss of lives in communal riots, several armed conflicts and wars, crises on the food front, and much more.

A daunting challenge initially was the staggering task of bringing together more than 500 princely states and provinces (they are all now an integral part of modern India). Each princely state was a kingdom with absolute powers vested in the ruler. The future of the country was in a balance. The ruler of each state had to be convinced to accede to the Indian union. The process was complex and made doubly difficult by the fact that there was little time to complete the task. This was achieved mainly because of the efforts mounted by Deputy Prime Minister Sardar Vallabhbhai Patel and his secretary in the ministry of states, V. P. Menon. A few princely states such as

Kashmir, Travancore (now part of Kerala state), Junagadh (now part of Gujarat), and Hyderabad (headed by the Nizam) were holding out or refusing to sign the instrument of accession. It came about that the two, Sardar Patel and V. P. Menon, were able to coerce or convince all the rulers to sign. In essence, today's states were created after the Indian federation came into existence.

There was a reorganisation of states based on language. There was the fallout of the Partition, the huge loss of lives in communal riots, migration, the rehabilitation of millions of refugees, and the task of economic reconstruction. Given our multiple languages, diverse cultures, and other complexities, many foresaw early disintegration and a descent into chaos.

It must be borne in mind that India was born in the aftermath of World War II. The Indian leadership decided to pursue an independent policy and not align either with the democratic nations in the West or the bloc led by the Soviet Union because there was a Cold War between the two. In less than a decade-and-a-half, India was consumed by four wars—the first Kashmir war in 1948, the Indo-China war in 1962, the India-Pakistan war in 1965, and the Bangladesh liberation war in 1971. The decade of the 1960s and the early 1970s were not just marked by the two wars and a hostile neighbourhood. It also saw the death of two prime ministers in relatively quick succession and a weakening of the dominant party, the Congress, and the emergence of regional parties.

Hence, the economic, political, and philosophical approaches and policies adopted by the early founders must be viewed against the backdrop of these extraordinary challenges in the decades soon after independence.

Drafting a Constitution

Importantly, a Constitution had to be drafted for a new sovereign republic, one of the first countries to be free of colonial rule during that period. In the neighbourhood, there was China, Ceylon (which is now Sri Lanka), Burma (now Myanmar), Indonesia, Singapore,

Pakistan, and many African nations. India's founding leaders were well aware of the magnitude of the task, and this was reflected in the long debates in the Constituent Assembly in the run up to adopting the new Constitution.

The chairman of the drafting committee of the Constitution, B. R. Ambedkar, a scholar, intellectual giant, and later India's first law minister, echoed that in his final speech in the Constituent Assembly on 25 November 1949. Ambedkar said,

> However good a constitution may be, it is sure to turn out bad because those who are called to work it happen to be a bad lot. However bad a constitution may be, it may turn out to be good if those who are called to work it happen to be a good lot.

It should be remembered that Ambedkar was also a trained economist. His dissertation at the London School of Economics was on 'The Indian Rupee' (1922–1923). A key draftsman of the Constitution was Benegal Narising Rau, a civil servant and constitutional adviser to the Constituent Assembly, who was one of three brothers who were to make a mark in India's political and economic history. (The other two were Benegal Rama Rau, a senior civil servant and later Governor of the Reserve Bank of India, and Benegal Shiva Rao, a lawmaker and journalist.)

India's leaders settled on a federal structure, based on a report of the Union Constitution Committee, which held that it offered the soundest framework. This meant a strong Central government with a distribution of powers between a union government and state governments.[2] Prime Minister Jawaharlal Nehru explained the rationale for this in a letter to the president of the Constituent Assembly on 5 July 1947. With Partition being a settled fact by then, the unanimous view was that the country's interests would be jeopardised if there was a weak central authority. Nehru felt a weak centre would make it tough to ensure peace and coordinate vital matters of common concern, and to speak effectively for the whole country in the international arena. While framing the Constitution, references were made to those of the United Kingdom, the United States of America, Australia, and Canada.

Gandhi and Ambedkar— Two Different Approaches

They also debated whether decentralisation in the form of powers to village panchayats as suggested by Gandhi or a powerful Central government that would allocate funds was the better option. Ambedkar was fiercely opposed to Gandhi's idea.[3] According to him, the country's villages had been the ruination of India.[4] They stank of localism, and were dens of ignorance, narrow mindedness, and communalism, he argued. Initially, the provisions for democratic decentralisation were a part of the directive principles of state policy before the Constitution (73rd Amendment) Act of 1992 led to the technical empowerment of local self-governments.

Choosing Political and Economic Approaches

India's leaders also debated the best political and economic approaches for the newly formed nation at a time when World War II had just ended. The world was in the shadow of a Cold War, with the US and the USSR jostling for global influence. Prime Minister Jawaharlal Nehru worried—as did many other leaders—that with India's massive social inequalities and poor economic indicators (literacy close to 12 per cent and a share of global GDP around 3 per cent), economic power would end up being concentrated in the hands of a few. A strong State, it was felt, was best equipped to steer the economy with planned development or economic planning by the State.

It was not that this mixed economy model, or what later was ridiculed as a 'messed up' economy, was thought of overnight. As early as 1938, the Congress had backed central planning, with the national planning committee headed by Nehru endorsing it. A group of businessmen headed by J. R. D. Tata, which included economist John Matthai, then part of the Tata group, had formulated what is now known as the Bombay plan. This envisaged a greater role for the State and a medium-term plan for the country to build its industrial capacity. Interestingly, Prime Minister Manmohan Singh admitted to the influence the Bombay plan had on him early in his life, going on to say how some of its central propositions were still relevant decades later. In an interview in 1981, J. R. D. Tata said that the performance of the Indian economy from the mid-1950s till the mid-1960s reflected the soundness of the mixed economy concept. He said that many countries at that time had a similar approach to planning, with some variations. He said one could conclude that the mixed economy approach is conceptually correct.[5]

An Inclusive Approach

Nehru tried to adopt an inclusive approach in the hope of a consensus. The first Cabinet of independent India's new national government had four outsiders or people without any affiliation to the Congress party. R. K. Shanmukham Chetty, the first finance minister (1947–1948), was a leader of the Justice Party in what was the old Madras state. He was part of a business family in Coimbatore and had attended the Bretton Woods conference in 1944. John Matthai, an economist who had studied at the LSE and Oxford and was part of the senior management in the house of Tatas, had been the interim finance minister in the run up to 1947. C. H. Bhabha, a Parsi businessman, was appointed as commerce minister in 1947. Among the other standout inclusions was Syama Prasad Mookherjee a leader of the Hindu Mahasabha. A former vice-chancellor of Calcutta University, he later founded the Bharatiya Jana Sangh, which later transformed itself into the Bharatiya Janata Party (BJP). And there was Ambedkar, even though he had represented the opposition and lost the election. Matthai, Mookherjee, and Ambedkar differed sharply with Nehru on various issues. In a speech, which would appear surprising today, Nehru said of his political opponents that men of integrity and ability like them were needed.[6] He said he admired and respected some of them. They were welcome, but all seemed to be pulling in different directions for now. What is even more remarkable is that this was an election campaign speech.

The new country was industrially backward. Conscious of the need to build a strong industrial base, the focus was on heavy industry or capital goods such as steel and hydroelectric projects. The wartime controls that had been in force before 1947 on the production and distribution of goods continued—except on imports and exports. The first industrial policy, which was introduced in 1948, made it mandatory for every businessperson or industrialist to secure a licence for virtually everything, be it the manufacture of steel, cement, or automobiles. The government, which approved licences, also specified the number of units that could be produced, the price at which they could be sold, and where the production units would come up. Indeed, if a company produced more than what the government had approved, it invited action. Private companies were barred or restricted from entering many areas. Little changed even after the second industrial policy almost a decade later.

It was not just export pessimism. The government was also wary of foreign capital and investment, besides foreign aid, in the early years, mindful perhaps of the potential pressures it could have on foreign and economic policy in a bipolar world then. It is interesting that India was a founding member of two major institutions—the International Bank for Reconstruction and Development (IBRD), or the World Bank as it is known now, and the International Monetary Fund (IMF). China and Russia were to join much later. Indeed, India secured the right as early as 1944 to nominate its own representatives to the boards of these institutions. It would also surprise many to know that even though India signed up with the IBRD as early as 1950 for assistance, Japan's request for aid from it was rejected.[7] Japan and Germany, two economic powerhouses now, were then struggling after the war.

It may be inconceivable for today's generation to imagine life in the 1950s, 1960s, and 1970s when families had to wait, sometimes even up to a decade, to obtain a gas connection, a landline phone, or a two-wheeler. The simple act of buying steel and cement for building a home required complicated permissions and procedures. In the early days, the government's approval had to be sought even to launch a new product or for issuing shares or debentures. For most citizens, it was difficult to get access to even basic services.

They perceived government offices as wasteful, lethargic, and weighed down by controls.

In the first decade or two, as a new Indian civil service structure was put in place, there may have been the hangover of the colonial administration. In those years, the workplace was bound by hierarchy. Rules were rigid. It is no surprise that in such a State-controlled economy, the work culture in private companies also largely mirrored government offices. Prakash Tandon, the first Indian chairman of the Indian unit of Unilever (now known as Hindustan Unilever Ltd) has described the work culture of the early 1960s in his memoir.[8] Tandon writes that except during the fortnights of the Chinese and Pakistan wars in 1962 and 1965, respectively, offices opened at ten, officers strolled in up to half-past ten, the clerks slightly later, and then had cups of tea and coffee. In the evening, the exodus began soon after four. The workmen in industrial units emulated this, according to him.

But the fact remains that the leadership had then sought the best available advice from experts, both international and domestic, to address economic issues. As early as August 1948, Nehru wrote to the premiers (the equivalent of chief ministers now) of states on how the government had invited several economists from differing schools of thought from across the country to offer suggestions.[9] Economists K. T. Shah, C. N. Vakil, V. K. R. V. Rao, and D. R. Gadgil suggested the re-imposition of controls on essential commodities, lower public expenditure, graded taxation, and vigorous public borrowings.

India was then a major port of call for many internationally reputed economists, who were inspired by the country's leadership and their new democratic experiment in a nation free from colonial rule. India punched much above its economic weight then. Distinguished economist Milton Friedman of the University of Chicago came to India in 1955 on the invitation of the government. He noted that the explanation for India's slow growth did not lie in its religious or social attitudes or the quality of its people. Rather, it was the economic policy which the country had adopted, especially its use of extensive physical controls.[10]

Another famous visitor was J. K. Galbraith, Professor of Economics from Harvard University and later the US Ambassador to India (1961–1963), who played a critical role in ensuring military aid to the country during the war with China in 1962. Galbraith first came to India in 1957 on the invitation of Cambridge-educated Prasanta Chandra Mahalanobis, who headed the Indian Statistical Institute and was a member of the planning commission.[11] Mahalanobis and C. D. Deshmukh as finance minister were principally responsible for launching the National Statistical Organisation (NSO) and the sample surveys, which are integral to planning and economic policymaking now.

India also sought the advice of Nicholas Kaldor, professor at the London School of Economics, on revamping the taxation system in the 1950s.[12] Considering the high level of tax evasion in India, he suggested the introduction of capital gains tax, wealth tax, gift tax, and an expenditure tax, besides income tax at a lower rate. Ignoring the advice of his officials, Finance Minister T. T. Krishnamachari went ahead with these proposals in the 1957–1958 budget. These measures did not have the desired effect and became another obstacle to growth. It was only many decades later that India began dismantling its regressive taxation system, starting from the mid-1990s under a short-lived coalition government.

It was during this first decade that another disquieting feature was institutionalised in the Indian taxation system and corporate affairs. This was the concept of the Hindu undivided family or HUF—used mainly as a vehicle to control family units or wealth. The HUF was recognised as a legal entity after the codification of Hindu personal laws in 1956. This, and the fact that India has no inheritance tax—one of the few countries not to have such a law—has only perpetuated inequality. The Indian regulatory system has also fostered this. It is noteworthy that there is still little discussion or debate on inheritance tax or on taxing the rich.

The early emphasis was on industrialisation. In retrospect, there was a feeling that agriculture was not given enough importance in an economy dominated by the farm sector, which contributed more than half of the national income and supported the vast majority, a large number of whom were poor and illiterate. In the first two decades after independence, India had to import food grains to feed more than 300 million people. That had to do with a legacy issue dating back to World War II when Britain diverted food grains from India to feed its soldiers and people, leading to the great famine in Bengal, which killed an estimated three million people.

It is noteworthy that five years after independence, famine was still being discussed as an issue in the country. This was despite the fact that a majority of the elected legislators of the time hailed from rural areas. A few decades later, most of the legislators were based in urban areas and had little direct knowledge of the problems of agriculture. This may well explain the government's approach to this sector–relying on subsidies rather than groundbreaking reforms.

This food shortage meant spending a considerable amount of the country's limited foreign exchange reserves on importing food grains. Starting with a wheat loan from the US in 1949, the government began obtaining supplies of surplus wheat from there, even though it was considered to be of poor quality. This was under an agreement known as Public Law or PL-480. Despite public criticism, this 'ship to mouth' arrangement continued till about the second half of the 1960s. The country's dependence on foreign aid and imported food grains imposed constraints on policy independence and autonomy.

But within the first decade itself, the fissures started showing. Few now realise that in less than a decade, India had four finance ministers. Shanmukham Chetty had to quit in 1948, a year after presenting India's first union budget, because of a grave error of judgement in Nehru's words on a matter relating to direct taxes. His successor, John Matthai, wrote later that Chetty was more sinned against than sinning.[13] Matthai was himself the main figure in a disagreement with the prime minister. As it happened, planning in India began with dissonance with Matthai resigning after the 1950 budget, perhaps the only budget which a finance minister delivered extempore without a prepared text, as is the norm now. Matthai, who had serious differences with Nehru on many issues, opposed the formation of the planning commission, which he felt would virtually be a super cabinet.

C. D. Deshmukh, an ICS officer and the first Indian Governor of the Reserve Bank who then took over, left after five years in 1956 over the issue of the separation of Bombay from Maharashtra. T. T. Krishnamachari, the next finance minister, whose family had business interests in Madras and who was a close aide of Nehru, had to step down in 1958 after the LIC Mundra scandal, along with his principal finance secretary H. M. Patel, who later became India's finance minister in the late 1970s.

Looking back, it is fascinating to note that despite many differences, the leaders could persuade Matthai, who had quit the government, to head the taxation enquiry commission (1953–1954) to restructure India's tax system, and to head the State Bank of India as its first chairman in 1955 after the government took over Imperial Bank.

Two other ministers quit too. Ambedkar left in 1951 because of differences on the passing of the Hindu code bill and Syama Prasad Mookherjee quit in protest against the Nehru-Liaquat pact, or agreement on the protection of minorities, in 1950. Sardar Patel, the heavyweight in the government, passed away in 1950, adding to the enormous burden on the prime minister. Chakravarti Rajagopalachari, the first Indian Governor General who was India's home minister, also abandoned the Congress party in 1951, following differences.

Financing the ambitious Second Five-Year Plan (1956–1961) posed huge challenges to the government, given its need for overseas funds and reliance on foreign assistance. By then the euphoria generated by the grouping of some of the newly independent nations led by India, which included Indonesia, Egypt, Ghana, and Yugoslavia, had begun waning. That non-aligned movement received a renewed lease of life later in the 1980s.

A Suicide and a Separate State

Leaders of the Congress party and others such as Ambedkar were against the reorganisation of states on linguistic lines. They resisted such demands as long as they could. It took a suicide to make them concede. At that time, erstwhile Andhra Pradesh was part of the state of Madras (now Tamil Nadu) with C. Rajagopalachari as its chief minister.

As can be imagined, both Rajaji and Nehru were adamant that they would not have a state created on linguistic lines. They saw such a trend as the first step towards the disintegration of the country. Yet, despite Nehru's enormous popularity, the party won only 46 seats of the 146 it contested in the Madras Legislative Assembly election of 1952. Nehru repeatedly appealed to the people on the grounds that while the idea of linguistic provinces was not a bad one, the time was not opportune. This was in May 1952. Meanwhile, there was political turmoil when T. Prakasam, leader of the Kisan Mazdoor Praja Party, a former chief minister of Madras state but originally from Guntur in Andhra, staked a claim to form the government, spearheading the opposition. The Congress, though the single largest party, did not have a majority and was invited to form a government by Governor Sri Prakasa. Rajaji emerged from retirement to head that government.

Discontent simmered. In October, a man named Potti Sriramulu started a fast unto death for a separate state of Andhra. The public face of the agitation was Swami Sitaraman. In any event, Sriramulu refused to listen to reason and did not call off his fast. Rajaji and Nehru had discussions about tackling the issue but failed to arrive at a solution. Fifty-six days after his fast began, Sriramulu passed away. Government offices and trains were attacked and the loss was estimated to be in millions of rupees. The prime minister was left with no other option. Days after Sriramulu died, on 19 December 1952, Nehru reluctantly announced that a separate Andhra state would be formed. Prakasam became the first chief minister of the newly formed state.

A counterfactual could be that newly independent Indonesia in 1945 continued to write its modern Indonesian Bahasa in the Latin alphabet that had been brought to the region during the Dutch colonial reign. It is a moot point as to whether we could have avoided a lot of strife if we had popularised the Hindi language with a Latin, or Roman, script, thereby making it more acceptable.

Ambedkar was opposed to the demand for linguistic states. In a statement to the linguistic commission in 1948, he said that this could be accepted only if the Indian Constitution said that the official language of every province should be the same as the official language of the Central government. That was necessary, he felt, to ensure that the country's unity was not jeopardised. It is an issue that has been festering since then. The boundaries of many Indian states were redrawn after this in the 1950s and 1960s.

The other major dissonance in the first decade, which was to cast a long shadow on the future relationship between the RBI and the government, was the exit of the longest serving governor of India's central bank, Benegal Rama Rau, in 1957. A former ICS official, Rau had a conflict with Finance Minister T. T. Krishnamachari over a proposal in the finance bill to raise the stamp duty on bills issued by banks to secure funds. He felt that the move could have an impact on interest rates and opposed it.

The issue was discussed in the Cabinet and the prime minister backed his finance minister, leading to what many perceive as the beginning of the process of undermining the autonomy of the RBI. TTK went public to dub the RBI as a clerical minded department of the finance ministry. Nehru wrote to Rau, who had also been a former ambassador to Japan (1948–1949), that the 'whole approach [of the RBI] seems to be an agitational approach against the central government'. The prime minister made it clear that the RBI could not challenge the main objectives and policies of the government. 'It has to advise but it also has to keep in line with the government,' he wrote to Rau, signalling an assertion of political authority.[14]

By the end of the 1950s and early in the next decade, there was trouble on the external front. Sardar Patel turned out to be quite prescient in this case. In a letter to India's secretary general, the modern-day foreign secretary, Girija Shankar Bajpai on 4 November 1950, Patel identified the dangers posed by China.[15] India's home minister was clear that given the situation then, there was no way the country could be on friendly terms with China. Rather, it was time to think of preparing a defence against what he termed a determined, calculating, unscrupulous, ruthless, unprincipled, and prejudiced combination of powers whom China would spearhead.

During that decade, India was to be drawn into two wars—the first with China and the second with Pakistan. The war with China had a significant impact because India was forced to lean on the US to secure military aid.

What may have gone unnoticed during the first decade was the introduction of the mid-day meal scheme for children in elementary schools in the then Madras state headed by K. Kamaraj, a senior Congress leader.[16] It was the first of many such welfare schemes that have endured in the country, which have been equally praised and criticised.

By 1965, the government under Lal Bahadur Shastri and Agriculture Minister C. Subramanian unveiled a new agriculture policy with a focus on the adoption of scientific and modern methods of farming and a higher investment in agriculture. This was the first step towards ensuring a higher return for the farmer by increasing production. This was a recognition that India could not be held hostage for long to overseas assistance for food grains. By 1967–1968, the strategy on agriculture began paying off. India, which had launched a Grow More Food Campaign in the 1940s after the end of World War II, is now a massive producer of rice and wheat. It currently faces growing criticism about the environmentally debilitating effects of the boost to agriculture and the fiscal costs attached to the procurement of food grains.

Incidentally, Shastri, a true grassroots worker of the party whose sympathy was with the farmers, was not a consensus candidate but nominated by party leaders. Shastri's successor, Indira Gandhi, continued with the agricultural policy and despite two consecutive droughts in 1965 and 1966, it paid off. The success of what came to be known as the Green Revolution helped India to put an end to food aid by 1972. It was followed by the white revolution after the promotion of the National Dairy Development Board (NDDB), an umbrella organisation of milk cooperatives headed by Verghese Kurien.

The economic, political, and philosophical approaches and policies adopted by the founders of our republic must be viewed in the context of these extraordinary challenges in the decades soon after independence.

One critic of the mixed economy model was C. Rajagopalachari, the first Indian Governor General (1948–1950) and former chief minister of Madras state (1952–1954). Rajaji formed the right-leaning Swatantra Party in 1959 after differing with the Congress over its economic philosophy. He pointed out that planning in India had proceeded on the assumption that people did not know what was good for them and therefore must be told what to do. As early as 1959, Rajaji warned against a command economy, where the Central government made all major decisions.[17] So did B. R. Shenoy, a prominent economist and a rare contrarian in those days, and a few others.

Government the Supreme Arbiter

Over the next couple of decades, the government emerged as the arbiter of allocation of resources and investment. Leaders and policymakers distrusted market forces and controlled private involvement. Licences were required for investment, production, and imports, while the availability of foreign exchange and credit was limited. Even prices and interest rates were controlled by the government for a long time. The shortage of foreign exchange prompted the government to adopt a policy of import substitution, which meant manufacturing most goods locally. It only encouraged protection to Indian firms while making the country's exports non-competitive globally and creating a thriving black market for goods from abroad and also for foreign exchange. The import of technology was also highly restricted.

Yet it is to the credit of our leaders and officials that despite the need for foreign aid during this period, they did not succumb to pressures by multilateral institutions and the US to raise money from international capital markets. As we have seen later, countries that went down this road, especially from Latin America, faltered.

In the early phase of the country's growth, this economic model helped to gradually build the foundations of industrial growth and laid the base for high-quality institutions that would impart technical education and conduct research. These included the Indian Institutes of Technology (IITs) and many other central research institutions. (Although some have argued that this came at the cost of neglecting primary education and health and institution building at the state level.)

An attempt to make an economic course correction with the devaluation of the rupee in 1966 to obtain funds from the IMF and the World Bank did not work. Devaluation was not followed by liberalisation, but by only a slight easing of controls. The political scars of that devaluation were visible for long until the 1990s. The second half of the 1960s was also marked by an industrial recession. The political weakening of the Congress party by 1967 and its split in 1969 had a big impact on the future economic trajectory of the country.

In that decade, the government reviewed India's licensing system under a committee headed by R. K. Hazari, a professor at the University of Bombay and an honorary consultant in the planning commission. Hazari did identify the shortcomings of such controls and the cornering of licences by a few business groups. But again, the changes were very modest.

India continued with the strategy of import substitution, especially given the lack of adequate foreign exchange and foreign capital, and a foreign exchange crisis in 1956. Policymakers continued to be sceptical of export-driven growth. Manmohan Singh, then a scholar at Oxford University, believed otherwise, as his doctoral thesis, which was published by Clarendon as *India's Export Trends and the Prospects for Self-Sustained Growth* in 1964, showed. In this, he made out a case for policy support for exports and a review of the exchange rate.

While Deputy Prime Minister Morarji Desai, who was in charge of finance, batted for social control of banks, Prime Minister Indira Gandhi in a political move nationalised or took over fourteen private banks in 1969. The wisdom of that political decision has been debated for the last five decades, although it cannot be denied that it led to the spread of banks across the country besides encouraging savings and a greater flow of credit to many sectors, including agriculture. The RBI became a partner, if not an agent, of the union government in its developmental activities in the states after this move.

With bank nationalisation, the resources available to the government to design and implement development planning expanded and it gained command over the banking system. The immediate impact was that the RBI became subservient to the development goals set by the government and, by implication, to the government. A banking system controlled by the government was not considered foolish then because the role of the state was expanding even in the economies of advanced countries.

Nationalisation did not merely improve access to banks. Rather, the focus was on an expansion of credit, with the result that government deficits kept rising while public-sector banks financed them. Thus, there were constraints on lending. A positive fallout, if any, was the national integration of the middle class, with recruitment to banks being made on a countrywide scale, based on merit. Although nationalisation began well, by the 1980s it became an instrument of populism rather than development banking. So banking became more politicised than what anyone had earlier envisaged.

Another Challenging Decade

While the problems of the following decade were not so existential, the 1970s were difficult. It was marked by a war with Pakistan, the emergence of Bangladesh, and the burden of handling millions of refugees who had come in from East Pakistan, as it was known then. There were some who reckoned that what were Pakistan's problems had now become India's.

The economy was hit by weak monsoons and the oil shock of 1973, which resulted in hyperinflation at 35 per cent. In the aftermath of the 1971 war and frosty relations with the US, India decided to pull the plug on the US Agency for International Development (USAID). The anti-inflation package that was introduced then worked after a while, but squeezed both private firms and individuals with income tax rates as high as 97 per cent. Another blow was the reining in of bigger private firms and industrial groups when the Monopolies and Restrictive Trade Practices Act came into force in 1970. Following this, the Foreign Exchange Regulation Act of 1973 forced foreign multinationals to divest their shareholdings to locals. In retrospect, this divesting of shares to local investors helped build an investor base and gradually expand the Indian capital market. This period was marked by India's first nuclear explosion in 1974, high unemployment, labour unrest, and violence, which ultimately led to an internal emergency in 1975.

By the end of that decade, India continued to remain a closed economy with little or no competition and high tariffs. It was a period when other countries were denationalising and there was a resurgence of the market ideology. We neglected manufacturing and failed to take advantage of the emerging opportunities in the first wave of globalisation and missed out on its benefits, except services. On the geopolitical front, there were visible shifts with the US and China resuming ties after forty years and India signing a treaty with Russia.

It is interesting to note that even at that time, the economic gap between the two Asian giants was narrow. India's per capita GDP in 1972 was US$ 123 compared to China's US$ 132, although Pakistan was ahead at US$ 153. But on social indicators, the country still lagged—India's average life expectancy of 48.72 years was far behind China's 60.43 years.

The internal emergency declared in June 1975 lasted till January 1977 and a short-lived coalition signalled the end of a decade. By this time, the limitations of the early economic models were apparent. This was when many Asian countries began to transform their economies and the East Asian miracle began to be recognised. There was a new focus on the oil-producing countries of the Middle East who had formed a powerful grouping, the Organisation of the Petroleum Exporting Countries (OPEC). It was the start of the flow of remittances to India from the Middle East, which have since swelled considerably. However, India missed out when the oil-rich Middle Eastern countries began deploying their newly earned surplus in the West. Yet, it was only by the 1980s that there was a greater recognition in India of the severe shortcomings of the existing economic model. Of course, there are policymakers and leaders who reckon that the era of planning helped India avoid the pitfalls that many other countries did not.

The 1970s were a watershed from the perspective of relations between the federal government in New Delhi and the states. The Tamil Nadu Assembly passed a resolution seeking autonomy in 1974,[18] citing inherent defects in the Constitution. The attempt to build a strong centre on the foundations of weak states was like trying to build a strong building on a foundation of loose sand, Tamil Nadu Chief Minister M. Karunanidhi said while inaugurating the Forum for State Autonomy in Madras the same year. This is an issue that festers to this day.

It was in the 1970s that the idea of central banks focusing on price stability came into vogue. So too did notions of the independence of central banks, and this continued into the 1980s. India was, however, late in accepting this idea.

Need for Change Recognised. But...

In the 1980s and 1990s, China, under the leadership of Deng Xiaoping, embarked on a process of economic change—a move that fuelled an annual average growth of 10 per cent over the next two decades. The world took note of not only the East Asian miracle but also the rise of China. It was the period of Ronald Reagan and Margaret Thatcher and the rise of the public choice theory, which, in short, seeks to explain how public decisions are made in a political economy. That public systems could be influenced with politicisation was globally realised in the 1980s. But we in India did not work to rebalance the State. Instead, we went on expanding the State and the same thing happened with the banking system. However, by the mid-1980s, there was a realisation that the negatives of nationalising banks outweighed the positives. But efforts to change that did not happen until the Narasimham Committee recommendations were pursued during the reform period in the 1990s.

Up to the 1990s, during the era of planning, the RBI's role was subordinate to the government. Early signs of economic changes were visible in India, although they were very tentative. Growth rose in the 1980s, recording an average annual growth of 5.6 per cent[19] for four years, but it was on the back of high borrowings and borrowed time. At the time, warnings from the RBI, some government officials, and the Prime Minister's Economic Advisory Council of an imminent crisis were ignored. Perhaps the government was carried away by the fact that there was economic turmoil elsewhere, as in Latin America, where many countries battled financial problems.

This was despite a political recognition of the need for a change and for a review of the old strategy of self-reliance, controls, and a greater role for the private sector. Yet it was difficult to bring about technological changes because of the resistance of organised labour. The undivided state of Andhra Pradesh was one of the first to promote a company for the computerisation of office operations. The RBI and banks also had to combat nationwide protests against automation in a country, ironically, then led by a young, computer-savvy prime minister.

India was out of sync on making the transitional balance between the State and the market. Over the next two decades, it tried to make up for this imbalance.

Until the late 1980s and a little beyond, it was common to see the use of typewriters, fax machines, and telex messages in many offices. One can imagine the burden working was and the drudgery at the workplace, whether it was a public or a private office. And, of course, there was little efficiency, even as the world moved on, in an era of market-driven economies and a growing wave of globalisation.

By the end of this decade, the technocratic response was ready within the government in India, but the political will was missing. The 1980s were also a turbulent period politically. Successive governments had to tackle internal strife in Kashmir, the Northeastern states, and Punjab, all of which stoked fears of Balkanisation. The political leadership had to spend a considerable amount of time on firefighting and battling corruption charges. Indeed, the 1970s were a lost decade. Some economists have argued that the 1980s marked the beginning of an economic course correction.

The two short-lived coalition governments of the early 1990s were aware of the need for course correction, but did not have the numbers to initiate the necessary changes. V. P. Singh, a former finance minister who took over as prime minister in 1989, had commissioned a report to chart out reforms after having seen for himself the remarkable economic and social changes that had taken place in the Far East. However, he set off a major political and social firestorm by announcing affirmative action on the basis of a report by the Mandal Commission. Neither his government nor the next one headed by Chandra Shekhar (1990–1991) had the political backing to carry out the necessary changes. By that time, major geopolitical changes were underway with a war in the Middle East, the disintegration of the Soviet Union, and rapid globalisation.

Many policymakers in India were aware that a crisis was brewing well before it hit us in 1990–1991. That is evident in the number of expert committee reports[20] that were submitted during this period. However, we lacked the right political leadership. To put it in perspective, between 1990 and 1993, we had three prime ministers, three finance ministers, three RBI governors, three finance secretaries, and three chief economic advisers.

Unsung Heroes

Today, not many are aware of the critical role played by the interim government headed by Chandra Shekhar and President R. Venkataraman, and Finance Minister Yashwant Sinha in staving off the first major threat to our balance of payments. There was no option but to approach the IMF and the World Bank in 1990 to avoid a default on external payments. That this action was taken by a caretaker government makes it remarkable.

President Venkataraman gave the initiative his blessing in the belief that he was reflecting the will of the people. He did so knowing fully well that a caretaker government could not take such a decision on its own. It was fortuitous that India then had a president who, as finance minister in 1980–1981, had been involved in signing an IMF loan—soon after the second oil price hike but well before a balance of payments crisis.

It was also fortuitous that we had civil servants who were very familiar with the workings of the IMF and the World Bank and their negotiating style. We often tend to forget that personal relationships, working styles, and culture play important roles in successful negotiations between governments and institutions and, indeed, between governments.

The Turning Point—1991

It was only a year later, in 1991, that a government headed by P. V. Narasimha Rao, with technocrat-turned-politician Manmohan Singh as finance minister, was able to dismantle the economic model and its controls to open up the economy. What followed thereafter has been well-documented. The economic direction since then has not been reversed, despite multiple changes in governments. Inevitably, this has involved radical changes to existing laws and regulations. It is interesting that some of the contributors to this book have been a part of this historical process of change at the government level.

All these civil servants and technocrats had an exposure to multilateral institutions and their operating styles, and were comfortable negotiating with them. Other contributors have been observers and analysts, and all of them can testify to the impact of economic and financial-sector reforms over the last three decades. Although there was criticism then of economic reforms having been driven by multilateral institutions, the fact was that many of India's policymakers and some of the leaders knew what had to be done. In the 1980s, several expert committees had advocated major changes that, in many ways, were almost similar to what was carried out in the 1990s.

There were three unique features to our reform process:

The first was the removal of controls—this, it should be noted, was a marginal change, not fundamental.

We did not wait for legal change to implement reforms but took advantage of the fact that there is a wide area between what the law allows and what the law prohibits.

The last is the analytical framework. Although the changes were designed in India, we had the benefit of outside advice, which was, however, not blindly followed. It can be argued that the implementation of our reform process was one of the most successful experiences the IMF has had in this area.

All three of these attest to the unique ability of our country to handle a crisis when the political leadership and civil servants work together for a common cause.

Effects of Economic Liberalisation

Thirty years after the economic liberalisation process in 1991, we must remind ourselves that what are considered basic necessities today—be it phones, vehicles, or goods and services—were luxuries in our country at a time. We have seen a dramatic transformation in India's financial markets, too. The buying or selling of shares and the crediting of either funds or shares against such transactions now take just a day or two, compared to weeks almost three decades ago.

Similarly, fund transfers too are instant and across multiple platforms and not through what were conventional banking channels. Far gone are the days when customers had to wait for weeks to get money credited to their bank accounts. India's financial market infrastructure is now world class, promoting an efficiency that leads to productivity gains. And we now have a robust payments system and digital infrastructure with a central bank digital currency that has been recently introduced.

The dramatic changes since then are also reflected in the fading away of the old business groups and families, which dominated the Indian business landscape. Policy initiatives undertaken over the last few decades by our regulators and successive governments have helped fuel the growth of a vibrant digital economy and a strong private sector, which is dominant in many sectors. Similar moves over the last couple of decades have resulted in the building of a modern network of highways (the *bhagyarekha* or lines of destiny on the hand, as former Prime Minister A. B. Vajpayee described them), airports, and other infrastructure.

These reforms and rapid technological changes have, in turn, redefined work and the workplace. They have opened up a new world of opportunities, offering people more options. There has been a boom in the type and nature of jobs that have been generated. Self-employment and entrepreneurship have also become desired alternatives to working for someone else. We are now seeing the rise of start-ups and the evolution of a work culture in which many companies are far more mindful of the welfare of employees than earlier and of the need to be flexible. The old metrics of measuring work in terms of fixed hours and physical presence appear to be no longer relevant. As we saw during the Covid-19 pandemic, there was little difference between the workplaces here and the more advanced countries, although some felt there were disparities in productivity.

It is worth noting that while there were suggestions that the economic reform process should start first in the financial sector, policymakers in India were not convinced. They felt that the best way forward was to free the manufacturing, services, and agriculture sectors, with the financial sector complementing this. All this has led to a shift from government domination of the economy to a more market-oriented model, which has seen the private sector emerging stronger. However, although many controls were removed, the incentives for increasing productivity were missing.

Though there is much in terms of unfinished work, our success as a nation can be measured by our achievements, some of which have been listed earlier. Politically, we are free and democratic. In a postcolonial world, it is easy to ignore that many countries that gained independence soon after India have collapsed or have faced turmoil. With the exception of China, few countries have been able to sustain high growth over a long period of time.

Ishrat Husain, the former Governor of the State Bank of Pakistan, reckons that India's competitive federalism and administrative reorganisation of states, which lowered political tension and mistrust, infusing a sense of unity and common purpose, has proved beneficial to the economy. Encouragement of the private sector and private investment, political and macroeconomic stability, and predictability of policies despite political changes have also helped. This analysis was framed against the backdrop of the common legacy, and legal and bureaucratic structures of the two countries.[21] That apart, there was the wisdom of some of our leaders, too. Narasimha Rao's reported response soon after the 1991 reforms to criticism that his government had not pressed the pedal hard on liberalisation was that the collapse of the Soviet Union offered cautionary lessons on moving ahead too fast. Having been a foreign minister earlier and a keen observer of a changing global order, he should have known.

India started as a symmetric federation but now exhibits the characteristics of an asymmetric federation. A key challenge remains bridging the nation and the people. Milton Friedman had famously said that the goal for India should not only be high GDP growth but also the pride of having abolished poverty.[22] Sadly, that is still a long way off. It is ironic that India has produced some brilliant economists, who have measured poverty both here and abroad. Unfortunately, they have not been able to contribute substantially to tackling poverty.

An overview of the last seven-and-a-half decades shows that India as a nation is rich, but is unfortunately inhabited by the largest number of poor people in the world.

State and Market

Another view is that radical reform is possible only in times of crisis. On other occasions, we need to look at incremental reforms only. That is why we often hear about 'reforms by stealth' or gradualism.

It is in this historical context that one should view the relationship between the State and the market. The term 'market' is used to describe the composition of organisations, institutions, and other entities that coordinate and facilitate the production and consumption of goods and services through voluntary transactions.

It has been pointed out that the years immediately following 1947 were ones marked by idealism, when the country passionately believed in Nehru's dreams of a modern and just India. As it became increasingly evident that a State-controlled economy could not deliver, the spirit of the early years was forgotten and came in for criticism as well. Yet it must always be remembered that liberalisation and the years of growth that followed the changes of 1991 were largely facilitated by the fact that we were a free democracy. Also, that many countries, including some federations, have stumbled for decades after breaking free from colonial bondage.

Over a period of time, even supporters of the free-market theory have come to realise the importance of the State in the development of a country. The State can, at one end of the spectrum, do everything to allow citizens to flourish; at the other, it can become the biggest obstacle to their realising their potential and their dreams. In other words, the State is critical to progress. After all, free markets thrive on the back of a strong rule of law supported by tough regulators and an impartial, independent judiciary. As has been pointed out, dozens of countries instituted reforms at more or less the same time as India. Few have matched our country's growth. Being a functioning democracy does seem to make a difference. India's growth in the first decades following liberalisation was a process of rising from below, quite unlike the growth in China.

In the early decades, the dominant view was that the State was efficient and would work for the welfare of the people. The underlying assumption then was that the State represented the people and their values. Planning was a reflection of that. In that era, the presumption was that the market represented greed. Thus, in the eyes of many, the State was benevolent while the market was bad or evil. This view has undergone a change after the 1990s.

Markets and Regulation

The success of India's liberalisation process is often cited by free-market proponents to bolster their arguments. Minimum

State intervention is seen as the ideal situation. That is an oversimplification. The appropriate role of the government will depend on the type of political system, and it will also change depending on the era as well.

Left to themselves, private markets will undersupply some types of goods—typically public goods with benefits that can be enjoyed by all members of the community. In the US, the bastion of capitalism, it is the State that takes the initiative in investing in research and promoting innovations that have transformed the country. Some of the US' greatest successes were derived from government-supported research. These range from biotechnology to agriculture to the internet. Indeed, many products of Microsoft, Apple, and the rest are based on innovations that came from research initiated and funded by the government of the US.[23]

Markets are driven by self-interest and profit. So, it all comes down to incentives. Under what circumstances will markets provide the right incentives? Will private rewards be aligned with social returns? How can government align the two? These are the challenges of regulation.

That markets or the private sector will place profits before the public good was evident from the financial crisis of 2008, the details of which are too well-known to repeat here. This is not unique to the financial industry.

The biggest challenge for regulation is to ensure that there is still competition. The globalisation of finance empowers global capital and weakens labour. Therefore, there is a downward pressure on the share of wages all over the world, which heightens existing inequalities.

An example of how the market, the State, and regulations are ranged against the citizen will be useful here. Let us take financial markets. Whenever we, as common people, deal with a financial institution such as a bank or an insurance company, we provide a lot of information about ourselves. In the process, the banker or the insurance company knows a lot about us, but we have very little information about these institutions. When we buy health insurance, the insurance company knows a lot about our health condition, but we know very little about the financial health of the insurance company!

Regulation of the financial sector is, therefore, particularly challenging. Unfortunately, the world over, the financial sector has managed to influence the regulator. The regulators are 'captured' by the entities they are supposed to oversee, leading to a bias in favour of those entities' interests rather than the public's interest. This regulatory capture may well be perpetrated through opacity. Many feel this is the true problem of regulation. Global trends in financial-sector regulation may play out in terms of simultaneous re-regulation in some countries and deregulation in others.

As the economy opened up with a growing political acceptance of free markets, the controlling forces for citizens became the State, the market, and regulation. But as time went by and their roles evolved, what we now see is the State, the market, and regulation ranged against citizens. Our regulatory systems impose constraints. Overall, policy changes need much more improvement to mitigate the downside of technological innovations. On the whole, the more the technology, the better the service has to be for the people.

This brings us back to the foundations of inefficiency and the uneven treatment of citizens. The assumption in this uneven treatment is the inherent belief that the citizen is dishonest, without any logical basis. We need to change this mindset. For that, it is important to first define objectives, collect data, and all the relevant information before using policy instruments. If they intervene, the government or regulators should do so only after assessing the cost of such an exercise. What this means is that any policy intervention should ideally be after assessing whether it will benefit consumers, firms, and other stakeholders without causing any major disruption.

It is a tragedy of this country that this approach has not always been followed in policymaking and in the framing of rules and regulations. Sadly, the ability of the State to effectively design and implement public policies varies greatly across India. The Indian State is not failing, but it is often seen to be flailing, or unable to deliver. On the one hand, India can organise elections for close to 900 million voters, conduct a census for 1.2 billion people, and run a highly effective space programme. Yet, on the other hand, its record in providing basic public services, from health to education and water to sanitation, ranges from modest to dismal.

A very valid argument is that India is a hard soft State—hard on 90 per cent of the population and soft on 10 per cent of it. And the tyranny of the 10 per cent (organised labour, select industrial houses, and the rentier class) determines government policy and helps them corner the benefits of State action. There are other weaknesses too. For instance, India is the only country that still does not have an inheritance tax. That itself is a source of inequality, besides the Hindu Undivided Family. The Hindu Undivided Family or HUF is an entity that helps Hindu families to save on their tax liabilities, and boost income and wealth by collectively taking advantage of tax deductions and exemptions. An attempt was made in the late 1950s by the government to introduce a tax wealth, but that was given up later.

Empowered Citizens

One cannot deny that the benefits of competition and deregulation have led to a greater empowerment of the citizen. Today, it is far easier to finance your home, to buy consumer goods, or to travel abroad than it was just a few decades earlier. A new world has opened up thanks to our digital payments system, in which we have been a pioneer, and e-commerce. Viewing and treating financial and digital infrastructure as a public good has paid off.

As the country changed, so did the workplace. The 1960s saw some improvement in the workplace, with large, hierarchical workspaces and an average work week of forty hours. This stayed the same through the 1970s, which saw the advent of cubicles and amenities to reduce drudgery, such as photocopy machines. There was also some socialising at work, centred around water-cooler conversations, extended lunch hours, and smoke breaks. The next decade saw dramatic changes, with personal computers, cordless phones, and fax and answering machines, although this was also the advent of greater encroachment of the office onto personal space.

The 1990s saw a move to a more collaborative style at work, with a shift in practices that saw a decline in smoking at work, more gender diversity, a respect for minority rights, and so on. The next two decades have witnessed increased pressure on the workforce with the coming of faster methods of communication, which have reduced response times and demanded quicker reactions at the workplace. Markets and customers have also been empowered with better access to information and a greater awareness of their rights due to easy, instant access to the internet.

Even before Covid-19, working from home and working from different office locations had become the norm in many sectors. It is interesting that work and life in India in the new millennium—particularly during the Covid-19 lockdown—was not vastly different from work and life in more advanced countries, although productivity levels may not have been comparable.

This is a short overview of our economic and social past. It is hoped that younger readers will see the options available to them slightly differently. A young adult Indian citizen has the opportunity to enjoy a much better quality of life than the contemporaries of his father or grandfather. In a democratic India, only empowered and informed citizens can create an atmosphere in which the country can realise its full potential.

Looking Ahead

It is impossible to predict anything about the future with anything remotely approaching certainty. As the world changes, regulators in times to come will face challenges of a magnitude and complexity that we can only imagine.

All regulation should focus on three outcomes—(*i*) how to ensure that the regulated sector serves society and consumers better; (*ii*) how to integrate the sector's policies better with national policies; and (*iii*) how to ensure that the regulated sector functions as a means and not an end in itself. Even as we state these desired outcomes, we realise the challenge raised by the second one—having a regulator with a national writ trying to regulate an entity with a global reach.

Digital technology offers a good example. Most countries now realise that the advent of digital technology has enabled the concentration of power in the hands of a few powerful companies. The dangers are that these companies (*i*) control enormous economic wealth and social, and even political, power; (*ii*) pose a threat to data privacy of citizens; and (*iii*) tend to create a new set of haves and have-nots. Governments are examining various options to regulate these companies while ensuring that the rights of citizens are not affected. It will be inevitable that conflicts will arise between governments and these 'techno oligarchies', as US President Joe Biden had described them recently. Today, we see three different, overlapping regulatory methods of tackling this issue—the US market-driven model, the Chinese State-driven model, and the European rights-driven model. It will be interesting to see how these conflicts are resolved.

In this mix, terms such as techno democracies and techno autocracies have emerged, capturing the approaches at opposite ends of the spectrum. Muddying the waters is the fact that some countries defy categorisation—are they democracies, limited democracies, or autocracies? Which approach will prevail in the contest for global influence remains an open question, yet their contrasting strategies are increasingly clear.

What applies to the digital industry applies equally to other areas—industries, the financial sector, and climate change. And the traditional challenges facing a regulator are still relevant—the danger of regulatory capture, the regulated being a step ahead of the regulator, the tendency to frame policy in consultation with the regulated, the global presence of the regulated, and so on. This is not to mention the disruption brought about by innovation and competition.

India has always been a country of many paradoxes. One can only hope that her innate resilience and the unbreakable spirit of its people who preserved a way of life through centuries of foreign domination will see her through. These aspects must ensure a better world for its citizens to lead lives of improved quality—with or without work.

Notes

1. Viceroy Lord Wavell's broadcast to the nation, 17 May 1946.
2. Letter from the Chairman, Union Powers Committee, to the President, Constituent Assembly of India, Report of the Union Powers Committee, 5 July 1947.
3. Ashok Gopal, A *Part Apart: The Life and Thought of B. R. Ambedkar*, Bengaluru: Nayana Publishing, 2023, p. 458.
4. Speech, Constituent Assembly Debates, 4 November 1948.
5. Ramachandra Guha, *India After Gandhi*, New Delhi: Picador, 2007, p. 693.
6. Ramachandra Guha, 'Recalling Jawaharlal Nehru's Campaign in 1951-51', *Hindustan Times*, 18 May 2019. Available at https://www.hindustantimes.com/columns/recalling-jawaharlal-nehru-s-campaign-in-1951-52/story-YVTlmMas7zCxOfzyvEAdlI.html (accessed October 2024).
7. B. K. Nehru, *Nice Guys Finish Second: Memoirs*, New Delhi: Penguin, 1997, pp. 271, 272.
8. Prakash Tandon, *Punjabi Saga*, New Delhi: Viking, 1988, p. 538.
9. Letters from the Prime Minister to Premiers, 23 August 1948.
10. Milton Friedman, *Memorandum to India*, published as part of Foundations of India, *Political Economy: Towards an Agenda for the 1990s*, Subroto Roy and William E. James (eds), pp. 163–176. New Delhi: Sage Publications, 1992.
11. J. K. Galbraith, *Mahalanobis: A Life in Our Times*, New York: Random House, 1982, p. 338.
12. Nehru, *Nice Guys Finish Second*, 271–272.
13. John Matthai, 'Mr. Chetty: "More sinned Against", in *Four Years in Office, V. The Times of India*,' Bombay, 30 July 1951.
14. G. Balachandran, *History of the Reserve Bank of India, Vol. 2: 1951–1967*, New Delhi: Oxford University Press, 1997, pp. 1151, 1157, 1158.
15. Letter from Sardar Patel to Girija Shankar Bajpai, 4 November 1950, New Delhi: National Archives of India.

16. C. Subramaniam, *Hand of Destiny, Vol. 1: The Turning Point*, Bharatiya Vidya Bhavan, p. 259.

17. C. Rajagopalachari, 'Bureaucratic Plans Stifle Economic Enterprise', Supplement to *Capital*, 17 December 1959, p. 19.

18. State Autonomy Resolution 1974, Government of Tamil Nadu.

19. C. Rangarajan, *Forks in the Road: My Days at RBI and Beyond*, New Delhi: Penguin, p. 312.

20. Some of the committees include the P. C. Alexander Committee on Import-Export Policies and procedures; Abid Husssain Committee on Trade Policy Reforms; and 'M Document', 1990.

21. Ishrat Hussain, *Governing the Ungovernable: Institutional Reforms for Democratic Governance*, Oxford University Press, 2018.

22. 'There is a tendency not only in India but in most of the literature on economic development to regard the ratio of investment [in] national income as almost the only key to the rate of development to take it for granted that there is a rigid and mechanical ratio between the amount of investment and additions to output.' See Friedman, 'A Memorandum to the Government of India', 1955. Friedman had come as Consultant to the Ministry of Finance, Government of India.

23. Mariana Mazzucato, *The Entrepreneurial State*, New York: Anthem Press, 2013. A later edition published by Penguin Books, 2018.

Contributors

Shankar Acharya, economist, senior government adviser, author, banker, and columnist, served as the Chief Economic Adviser to the Government of India (1993–2001). An honorary Professor at the Indian Council for Research on International Economic Relations (ICRIER) and Chancellor of the Central University of Andhra Pradesh, his career has included senior roles at the World Bank, as Member, Twelfth Finance Commission, and Chairman (non-executive) of Kotak Bank (2006–2018). He has been a *Business Standard* columnist since 2003. Acharya is well-recognised for his contributions to India's economic policy and analysis and his role in shaping economic reforms.

Tamal Bandyopadhyay is an award-winning author and journalist. Better known for his weekly column 'Banker's Trust', for which he has won the Ramnath Goenka Award, Tamal is a Consulting Editor with *Business Standard*. He has written seven books, the latest being *Roller Coaster: An Affair with Banking*. His previous book *Pandemonium: The Great Indian Banking Tragedy* has won the Tata Literature Live Award for Business Book of the Year. Starting his career with *The Times of India*, Tamal has worked with *The Economic Times*, *Financial Express*, and *Mint*, besides *Business Standard*.

R. B. Barman, a former executive director at the Reserve Bank of India, holds a Master's degree in statistics and a Ph.D. in economics from the Indian Institute of Technology Bombay. His professional interests span business information technology and payment systems. Barman has served as the chairperson of the National Statistical Commission and as a technology advisor to the National Payments Corporation of India.

Sheela Bhide, Indian Administrative Service officer (1973 batch), worked as Secretary of Industries, Andhra Pradesh and Joint Secretary in the Ministry of Corporate Affairs. She headed the Sheela Bhide Committee on the Andhra Pradesh–Telangana bifurcation. She now chairs the Women Entrepreneurs International Trade and Technology Centre and advises the Indian Institute of Foundrymen, and the Association of Lady Entrepreneurs of India. She also serves as Independent Director on the boards of Rane Holdings Ltd, Gati-Kintetsu Private Ltd, Ahluwalia Contracts India Ltd, Star Paper Mills Ltd, and Suryoday Foundation. Bhide is known for her work in socioeconomic development and industrial growth.

P. Chidambaram, politician, lawyer, and author, served as India's Minister of Finance at various times between 1996 and 2014. A member of the Indian National Congress party, he also held positions such as Minister of Home Affairs, Minister of Corporate Affairs, Minister of State for Commerce. Chidambaram's expertise extends to constitutional law, administrative law, tax laws, and corporate law. He remains a prominent figure in Indian politics, recognised for his intellect and contributions to economic development, reforms, and fiscal management during challenging periods.

Nitin Desai is an economist, international civil servant, and Honorary Fellow of the London School of Economics and Political Science. He has held key roles, including Under-Secretary General for economic and social affairs at the United Nations (1992–2003) and chief economic adviser in India's ministry of finance (1988–1990). He organised the Rio Earth Summit (1992), the Copenhagen Social Development Summit (1995), the Monterrey Finance and Development Summit (2002), and the Johannesburg Sustainable Development Summit (2002). Desai's expertise includes poverty alleviation, environmental sustainability, and international development cooperation.

Shyamala Gopinath was a former chairperson of HDFC Bank (2015–2020) and a former deputy governor of the Reserve Bank of India (2004–2011). She was actively involved in managing the global financial crisis and India's balance of payments crisis in

1991. She chaired the Committee on National Small Savings Fund in 2011, which recommended a market-linked interest rate system for small savings schemes. As part of the Narasimhan committee, she contributed to banking-sector reforms. Gopinath received a Lifetime Achievement Award at the ET Prime Women Leadership Awards in 2023.

KAUSHIK JAYARAM worked as the head of administration in the monetary and economic department at the Bank for International Settlements (BIS) and prior to that at the Reserve Bank of India for seventeen years. He has more than thirty-eight years of experience in central banking, technology, and economics. His expertise lies in payments systems policy, macroprudential policy frameworks, financial stability, and measuring systemic risk. His work involved analysing macroprudential tools and international financial statistics to enhance financial stability.

K. V. KAMATH was a former managing director and CEO of ICICI Bank, and later its chairman. He now chairs the National Bank for Financing Infrastructure and Development (NaFID) and serves as non-executive chairman of Jio Financial Services. He has also worked at the Asian Development Bank and was the inaugural president of the New Development Bank by BRICS countries. He received the Padma Bhushan in 2008. Kamath is known for his leadership in the financial sector, especially for transforming ICICI from a development financial institution into a leading bank.

VITTALDAS LEELADHAR is a former deputy governor of the Reserve Bank of India and the former Chairman and Managing Director of Union Bank of India and of Vijaya Bank. He was a fellow of the Indian Institute of Bankers and a director on the boards of the National Bank for Agriculture & Rural Development and National Housing Bank. Leeladhar was also Director at Tata Mutual Fund and served on the Boards of companies in the Tata Group. He is known for his contributions to technology developments in the banking sector and regulation and supervision at a critical period.

YEZDI HIRJI MALEGAM, a chartered accountant, was the president of the Institute of Chartered Accountants of India (1979–1980) and chaired the National Advisory Committee on Accounting Standards. He served on the RBI board for over two decades (1994–2015) and has been chairman or member of committees in the financial sector for the government and SEBI, including the Financial Sector Legislative Reforms Commission. Malegam was also a member of several international accounting committees. Awarded the Padma Shri in 2012, his expertise in auditing, accounting standards, and corporate governance is widely recognised.

JAMAL MECKLAI, a currency markets expert, is Managing Director of Mecklai Financial Services Pvt. Ltd, a pioneer in market risk consulting in India. He has served on RBI committees, consulted for the World Gold Council and the Forwards Markets Commission, and advised regulators in Malaysia, Angola, and the Asian Development Bank. Mecklai also provides analysis on currency markets, macroeconomic trends, and financial policies.

RAVI MENON served as General Manager (Training) at the Union Bank of India. He has been a leadership training executive for various corporations and banks. He has published articles in *The Hindu*, *New Indian Express*, and *The Wire*.

JOYDEEP MUKHERJI, managing director at Standard & Poor's Ratings Services, specialises in sovereign ratings for the Americas. With Standard & Poor's since 1996, he has extensive experience in credit ratings across Asia and the Western Hemisphere. Previously, Mukherji worked in corporate and investment banking at CIBC Wood Gundy, Canada, served as an economic consultant to the Asian Development Bank, and was briefly a financial journalist at the *Globe and Mail*. He holds an economics BA from the University of Toronto and a public policy Master's from Princeton University's Woodrow Wilson School.

NARAYANA MURTHY, engineer, entrepreneur, and author, founded global technology and consulting corporation Infosys. He served as Infosys CEO from 1981–2002, and was Executive Chairman until 2011. Murthy's leadership transformed the country's IT sector through innovation and ethical governance. Beyond business, he advocates for education and social justice. Recognised with the Padma Vibhushan and other accolades, Murthy's legacy includes shaping global delivery models as well as setting industry standards for transparency and corporate ethics.

V. ANANTHA NAGESWARAN is an economist, policymaker, and author. He is the eighteenth Chief Economic Advisor to the Government of India. Nageswaran was Global Chief Investment Officer at Bank Julius Baer and worked for Credit Suisse in Switzerland and Singapore, and the Union Bank of Switzerland (now UBS). He has also served as the Dean of IFMR Graduate School of Business, Sri City, and taught economics at institutions like the Singapore Management University and Indian Institute of Management.

NIRANJAN RAJADHYAKSHA is an economist, journalist, researcher, and author. He is the executive director at Artha Global and writes for *Mint*. Previously, he was the research director and a senior fellow at the IDFC Institute and the executive editor of *Mint*. Niranjan did his Ph.D. from the Mumbai School of Economics and Public Policy. He focuses on macroeconomics, political economy, and economic history.

G. N. RAO is an ophthalmologist, and founder of LV Prasad Eye Institute (LVPEI), a globally recognised centre for ophthalmic care, treatment, research, education, and innovation. He also served as the President of Academia Ophthalmologica Internationalis (AOI) and Chair of the Board of the International Agency for the Prevention of Blindness. He has received numerous awards, including the Padma Shri, and has published over 300 papers in peer-reviewed journals. His contributions to eye health have been recognised globally. Rao's philanthropic efforts focus on education and community development.

K. SUJATHA RAO is a bureaucrat, public health expert, and author. An officer of the Indian Administrative Service, 1974 batch, she spent twenty years working in the health sector at the state and federal levels, including as secretary of the union ministry of health and family welfare. She was a Takemi Fellow at Harvard School of Public Health in 2001–2002 and a Gro Harlem Brundtland Senior Leadership Fellow there in 2012. Rao's contributions include shaping India's healthcare policies, focusing on maternal and child health, disease control, and healthcare accessibility.

C. RAMMANOHAR REDDY is an economist, journalist, and author. He is Editor-in-Chief at *The India Forum*. From 2004–2016, he served as Editor of *Economic and Political Weekly*, overseeing its expansion and digital transformation. He briefly taught at the Centre for Development Studies (CDS), Thiruvananthapuram, before transitioning to journalism in 1988. He earlier held editorial roles at *Deccan Herald* and *The Hindu*, focusing on economic policy. His expertise spans economic theory, development economics, and public policy analysis.

K. SRINATH REDDY, cardiologist, public health advocate, and author, served as President of the Public Health Foundation of India (PHFI) and headed Cardiology at the All-India Institute of Medical Science (AIIMS). Reddy was the First Bernard Lown Visiting Professor of Cardiovascular Health at Harvard (2009–2013) and an Adjunct Professor of Epidemiology (2014–2028). Reddy's leadership includes global roles like chairing the Healthcare Thematic Group of UN Sustainable Solutions Network and membership of several WHO Committees. He is recognised for promoting cardiovascular health, advancing chronic disease prevention, and advocating healthy living across all ages.

Y. V. REDDY, economist, bureaucrat, central banker, and author, was Governor of the Reserve Bank of India from 2003–2008 and chaired the Fourteenth Finance Commission of India. An officer of the Indian Administrative Service (IAS), 1964 batch, he also was an Executive Director, International Monetary Fund. His long academic career spans teaching and research, focusing on economic policy, central banking, and public finance. In 2010, he was awarded the Padma Vibhushan. Reddy is known for his commitment to pro-poor public policy and financial inclusion, for inducing market efficiencies, and for innovations in payment systems.

B. SAMBAMURTHY, chartered accountant and banker, was director and CEO of the Institute for Development and Research in Banking Technology, Hyderabad, and chairman of Corporation Bank. He held executive roles at Indian Bank, served as RBI Nominee for NPCI, and served on other boards as an Independent Director. He was secretary of the Association of Indian Banks in London and vice-chairman of the Foreign Exchange Dealers Association of India. Sambamurthy contributed over forty articles on banking, technology, and the economy to financial dailies. He is a pioneer in Indian financial inclusion.

MAN MOHAN SHARMA, a chemical engineer, made significant contributions to academia and industry and was a Professor and Director at the Institute of Chemical Technology (UDCT), Mumbai. Awarded the Padma Bhushan and Padma Vibhushan, Sharma was the first Indian engineer elected a Fellow of UK's Royal Society and was awarded a fellowship at the Royal Academy of Engineering, UK. He has served on the Reserve Bank of India board, holds numerous publications and patents, and has been a consultant to industries for over fifty-five years.

ARUN SHOURIE is a journalist, politician, and author. His diverse career includes roles as an economist at the World Bank, consultant to India's planning commission, editor at the *Indian Express* and *The Times of India*, Disinvestment Minister (2001–2004), and Minister of Communications and Information Technology (1998–2004). He has received honours such as the Ramon Magsaysay Award (1982) and Padma Bhushan (1990). With a keen interest in philosophy and ethics, Shourie is a vocal advocate for transparency and ethical governance.

N. K. SINGH, bureaucrat, economist, politician, and author, served as a Janata Dal (United) Rajya Sabha MP before joining the Bharatiya Janata Party. Singh is President, Institute of Economic Growth and Co-convener, G20 Independent Expert Group on MDB reforms. He chaired India's Fifteenth Finance Commission and the Fiscal Responsibility and Budget Management Review Committee. An Indian Administrative Service officer (1964 batch), he was Union Secretary (Revenue and Expenditure), member, Planning Commission, and Secretary to Prime Minister Atal Bihari Vajpayee. He has received several awards, including Japan's 'Order of the Rising Sun' and an Honorary Fellowship from LSE.

YASHWANT SINHA, former politician, bureaucrat, and author, served as India's Finance Minister (1990–1991, 1998–2002) and Minister of External Affairs (2002–2004). A 1960 batch IAS officer, he held key roles in commerce and industries ministries and as Joint Secretary in Surface Transport. A Principal Secretary to former Chief Minister of Bihar, Karpoori Thakur, Sinha was also BJP spokesperson and Janata Dal General Secretary. He was awarded France's Officier de la Légion d'Honneur. Known for his political boldness, his crisis management skills, and his role in steering economic reforms, Sinha has earned recognition for his wisdom and statesmanship.

M. S. SRIRAM, Professor, Centre for Public Policy, Indian Institute of Management Bangalore (and earlier worked at IIM Ahmedabad), chaired the Expert Committee on the Formation of Kerala Cooperative Bank and served on the RBI's External Advisory Committee for small finance banks, financial inclusion advisory Committee, and the Expert Committee on Primary urban cooperative banks. Sriram sits on the boards of AU Small Finance Bank, NDDB Dairy Services, Indian Dairy Machinery Company, Selco Solar Light Pvt. Ltd., and Centre for Budget and Policy Studies. He is author and a Trustee of Pratham Books, Sanket Trust (Ranga Shankara), and Dastkar Andhra.

USHA THORAT served as a Deputy Governor of the Reserve Bank of India from 2005–2010. She joined RBI in 1972. Post 1992, Thorat contributed to the development of financial markets, debt management, external-sector management, and regulatory reforms in India. She represented India on various global regulatory fora. As DG, she served on the boards of NABARD and SEBI and chaired the RBI currency note press and the Deposit Insurance and Credit Guarantee Corporation. She has been recognised for her role in promoting financial inclusion.

LATHA VENKATESH, journalist and news anchor, began her career in CNBC-TV18 as chief of the Mumbai News Bureau, where she is now consulting editor. As a business journalist, she has specialised in covering stocks, currency, debt, and commodities markets. Before joining CNBC-TV18, she worked in *Economic Times* and *Dow Jones Newswires* for five years each. Latha graduated in economics and politics and has a doctorate in political science. She is a keen watcher of the Reserve Bank of India and a commentator on banking-sector issues, money markets, and macroeconomic trends.

SHAJI VIKRAMAN is a journalist with more than three decades of experience and had served as the National Editor of *The Economic Times* and Resident Editor of *The Indian Express* in Mumbai. He also had a stint with the *Hindu Business Line* and has reported and written on fiscal and monetary policies and the financial markets while being based in New Delhi and Mumbai.

KAVI YAGA is a writer. Her travel memoir, *Walking in Clouds, a Journey to Mt. Kailash and Lake Manasarovar* was published by HarperCollins, India in 2018. She was awarded a 2023 Yaddo Fellowship and won second place for the 2021 Calvino Prize for Speculative Fiction. Her works appear in *One Story*, *Swamp Pink*, *The Hindu*, *Outlook Traveller*, *Out of Print*, *The Bombay Review*, and elsewhere. In previous avatars, Yaga worked as a software engineer in Chicago and was a development economist in Centre for Economic and Social Studies, Hyderabad.

Index